Praise for
The Leadership Pause

"If you're looking for easy leadership hacks, this isn't the book for you. But if you're committed to becoming a more effective leader and seeking greater satisfaction and fulfillment in your work and life, *The Leadership Pause* is a must-read. Drawing on science, philosophy, her work with clients, and personal experience, Chris Johnson makes a compelling case for the power of pause. As one of Chris's clients, I've personally experienced the power of pause, and I know that if more leaders practiced the pause, their work and their lives would be more productive, satisfying, and fulfilling."

—Dave Mooney, FORMER CEO, ALLIANT CREDIT UNION

"Chris Johnson calls on research, experiences, illustrative stories, and analogies to craft the premise of *The Leadership Pause*. I know firsthand the importance of resilience in being a successful leader in the VUCA world in which we live and work. Applying the practices learned from this compelling book, I've come to understand how positively harnessing stress can be the fuel that feeds my resilience and motivation. While I will always be a work in progress, I'm committed to applying the lessons learned from Chris's book to become a better leader."

—Elizabeth Nohe, PHD, BOARD ADVISOR, AWESOME LEADERS (AWESOMELEADERS.ORG), AND FORMER CHIEF SUPPLY CHAIN OFFICER, MORTON SALT

"If you are ready to shift from feeling overcommitted, overburdened, and unfulfilled—despite your many life accomplishments—to a place of embodied leadership and authentic expression, *The Leadership Pause* is for you. Chris Johnson, PsyD, challenges readers to redefine our relationship with stress and reevaluate how we might be more effective. Skillfully applying biology and neuroscience research with actionable practices, she guides leaders 'to wait for our souls to catch up with our bodies,' to truly embody new ways of being that empower us to bring our best selves to any leadership situation."

—Adrienne Palmer, FOUNDER, GLOBAL IMPACT ADVISORY, GLOBAL BOARD DIRECTOR, ENTREPRENEURS' ORGANIZATION

"Pausing is an indispensable requirement of leadership—a necessary precursor to wise and principled action. The whitewater of our daily lives tricks us into believing that pausing is not possible. But this book makes the seemingly impossible a practical reality: a deeply nourishing gift for each individual leader that offers ongoing dividends to the organizations and undertakings that they steward. Essential reading for anyone striving to build a better world."

—Amanda Blake, PHD, AUTHOR OF *YOUR BODY IS YOUR BRAIN*

"*The Leadership Pause* provides a clear, pragmatic guide to centering on what matters to you and how to embody that care to make a difference in the world. Chris Johnson brings a wealth of experience and competency to addressing the key elements of transformation that lead to exemplary leadership."

—Richard Strozzi-Heckler, PHD, FOUNDER OF STROZZI INSTITUTE AND AUTHOR OF *THE ART OF SOMATIC COACHING* AND *THE LEADERSHIP DOJO*

"Are you ready to step into the dojo of your life? If so, it's time to surrender and embrace 'the pause' that is waiting for us just beneath the surface of the present moment. Delivered with a fierce yet quiet power, *The Leadership Pause* is filled with timeless wisdom that has been beautifully curated and skillfully translated for leaders who are ready to commit to the path of mastery."

—Rand Stagen, CEO, STAGEN LEADERSHIP ACADEMY

"This book offers practices based around the simplicity and elegance of a 'pause.' These practices can create powerful, positive shifts to engage with outdated patterns to shift them to connect you with your creative, resourceful self. Scientifically based and well researched, Chris offers real world examples of how people shifted their experience from frustration to inspired action. It offers hope to those experiencing malaise by clarifying that they are not alone in their struggles to find balance, ease, and resilience. *The Leadership Pause* is a gift and a resource for anyone who wants to be healthy, happy, and succeed in the world."

—Wendy Palmer, AUTHOR OF *LEADERSHIP EMBODIMENT*
AND *DRAGONS AND POWER*

"I have savored my time reading *The Leadership Pause*. Chris captures the true essence of the chaos we've all been facing and feeling: the intensity of the constant whitewater, the rush of anxiety in reacting. Tuning in to the reality of today's VUCA world and what's required of us helped me stop resisting stress as 'bad' and instead take on the mindset that stress can build resilience. By integrating research in neuroscience, somatics, and mindfulness with powerful storytelling, Chris makes our job as leaders seemingly less complicated. The simplicity of the pause brings the word 'doable' to mind."

—Jean Pitzo, CEO, ACE METAL CRAFTS

"At first blush, *The Leadership Pause* by Chris Johnson is a warm, accessible survey of the key ideas in leadership development today. Chris draws from many traditions, including martial arts, neuroscience, leadership theory, and spiritual practice set against the stories of real leaders' journeys to improve. Far more importantly though, her book is a pragmatic guide to improving as a leader through simple daily practices. *The Leadership Pause* challenges us to get out of our heads and into our bodies, out of the theory and into our daily experiences of life. Chris makes a compelling case for pausing, as access to the presence so crucial to being effective leaders in today's world."

—Thea Durfee Polancic, MANAGING PARTNER OF
CLEARSPACE, LLC, AND FOUNDER, CHICAGO CHAPTER OF
CONSCIOUS CAPITALISM

"I could almost feel my heart rate calming down as I read Chris Johnson's *The Leadership Pause*. Chris guides you on a calming journey to clarity. Her stories paint a beautiful picture of a world where we are attuned to nature and ourselves—all through the art of the pause. To keep our sights on the bigger picture of our lives, we need to pause, focus our attention, and listen. Chris provides the reasons why and the tools to make it possible. In short, *The Leadership Pause* guides you on your most important journey—the one toward clarity."

—Jennifer J. Fondrevay, CHIEF HUMANITY OFFICER,
DAY1 READY, AND BESTSELLING AUTHOR OF *NOW
WHAT? A SURVIVOR'S GUIDE FOR THRIVING THROUGH
MERGERS & ACQUISITIONS*

"Pause long enough to read this book, because in doing so, you will step onto a pathway that will lead you to a more grounded and compassionate humanity. Whether leading others or leading your own life, you'll widen and deepen your abilities to sense yourself and others, to make shifts in your being that open you up to the *more* that is always available to us, if we develop the eyes and the heart to see. Chris, in her inimitable wisdom and humor—as psychologist, leadership coach, workshop leader, somatic practitioner, and aikido *sandan*—brings all of herself to the table in *The Leadership Pause* so that you can learn what it means to bring all of yourself along too."

— **Renée Gregorio**, POET, *ABYSS & BRIDGE*, AND AUTHOR
OF *THE WRITER WHO INHABITS YOUR BODY*

"*The Leadership Pause* reminds us that as leaders, partners, parents, or positively contributing members of society, we have a responsibility to be fully present at the exact moment our innate gifts are required. So often there is pressure to be all things to all people when—in the end—what is truly impactful is our willingness to be the best version of ourselves—one individual at a time. Chris Johnson has gifted everyone who is willing to embrace the concept of embodied learning and deep listening with a consequential guide to mindfulness, personal fulfillment, and powerful leadership."

—**Mark Vance**, VICE PRESIDENT STRATEGIC PARTNERSHIPS,
HUEMAN PEOPLE SOLUTIONS

The
Leadership
PAUSE

SHARPEN YOUR ATTENTION,
DEEPEN YOUR PRESENCE,
and NAVIGATE THE FUTURE

The
Leadership
PAUSE

•••

CHRIS L. JOHNSON, PsyD

BrainTrust
INK

BrainTrust Ink
Nashville, Tennessee
www.braintrustink.com

Distributed by Greenleaf Book Group

For ordering information or special discounts for bulk purchases, please contact Greenleaf Book Group at PO Box 91869, Austin, TX 78709, 512.891.6100.

Design and composition by Greenleaf Book Group
Cover design by Greenleaf Book Group
Cover Image: Flower Mandala, Cycle Ring Complete Drawing, used under license from Shutterstock.com

Grateful acknowledgment is made to the following sources for permission to reproduce copyrighted material:

The Permissions Company, LLC on behalf of Graywolf Press, Minneapolis, Minnesota, graywolfpress.org: William Stafford, "The Way It Is" from *Ask Me: 100 Essential Poems.* Copyright © 1977, 2004 by William Stafford and the Estate of William Stafford. **Chan Meditation Center:** From "Practice" by Master Sheng Yen. Copyright © by Master Sheng Yen. All rights reserved. https://chancenter.org/en/

Publisher's Cataloging-in-Publication data is available.

Print ISBN: 978-1-956072-04-4

eBook ISBN: 978-1-956072-05-1

Part of the Tree Neutral® program, which offsets the number of trees consumed in the production and printing of this book by taking proactive steps, such as planting trees in direct proportion to the number of trees used: www.treeneutral.com

Printed in the United States of America on acid-free paper

22 23 24 25 26 27 28   10 9 8 7 6 5 4 3 2 1

First Edition

Contents

Acknowledgments . . . . **xiii**

Introduction: **1**

The Leadership Pause: Sharpen Your Attention,
Deepen Your Presence, and Navigate the Future

1   Our Current Present: Whitewater **21**

2   Pause into the Moment: What Is Pause? **49**

3   Catch Yourself Being Yourself: Pressure **81**

4   Learning and Growing Embodied Trust **105**

5   The Power of Mindset **129**

6   Presence: Tap Your Power **143**

7   Pursue Your Energy **173**

8   Purpose: What Do You Love? **199**

9   Perspective: Let Go of What You Think You Know **227**

10   Step into the Stream: Purposeful Practice **255**

Recommended Reading **275**

Notes **279**

Index **289**

About the Author **303**

Acknowledgments

I have many to thank for supporting me in writing the book you have in your hands. My dad, Roger, taught me the importance of pausing and its relevance to leadership and enjoying life; I miss him every day. My mom, Patty K, always there with a listening ear, and my sister, Shawna Oertley, have shown great patience when weekends in the country were cut short—you are amongst my most faithful cheerleaders.

The sturdy burr oak tree at the edge of our road, the one I came to call my own, stands, even today, at the foundation of my love of nature's beauty and power. Over the past two years of writing, I sought solitude and spaciousness in the hills of southwestern Michigan, the vistas of northern Wisconsin, and in the fields and cliffs of central Illinois to align my intentions with the natural world and have been sustained in the process.

Little did I know at the time I began practicing aikido that Morihei Ueshiba, the founder of aikido, had a profound connection with nature. "Learn from holy books and wise people. **Everything—even mountains, rivers, plants, and trees—should be your teacher.**" In sync with the rhythm of the seasons, he crafted an art that reflects the natural flow and fierceness of nature—of which we are all a part. Out of deep listening, he forged a profound methodology to develop and embody the qualities and skills required for effective, conscious leadership. I am forever grateful for this practice.

It was at Tokushinkan Dojo, in practice with founder Dianne Costanzo and my fellow aikidoka, that I came to love sincere attacks, grueling practice sessions, and shared burgers on Monday nights. Thank you.

Jon Kabat Zinn and his commitment to extending mindfulness into medicine, healthcare, and society inspired me many years ago as has Tara Brach, Sylvia Boorstein, Jack Kornfield, Pema Chodron, Michael Carroll, and Rick Hanson. Our Chicago Sangha has provided a safe and strong container over the past twenty years to cultivate awareness, deepen our practice, and grow our commitment to greater listening in life and leadership.

Mark Silver, founder of The Heart of Business, helped me tease out the idea for this book during a retreat just about ten years ago when I was at a crossroads in my own leadership.

Richard Strozzi-Heckler introduced me to somatics and the powerful world of embodied leadership. Thanks to my fellow students at the Strozzi Institute for their interest in embodied learning and engaging in practices together to grow our leadership. A special thanks to Renee Gregorio, whose heartfelt poetry inspired me to embody my best self, and Mandy Blake, a fellow neuroscience nerd and founder of Embright, whose curiosity and thirst for pragmatic learning provoked me and many others to explore exactly what it means to be a conscious, embodied leader in today's world.

Wendy Palmer, founder of Leadership Embodiment, embodies powerful feminine wisdom, extends it into the world, and loves a good scotch—thanks for sharing.

Ginny Whitelaw, founder and CEO of the Institute for Zen Leadership, for her pragmatic focus on developing our selves in order to better serve the world by "doing the work that's yours to do." I am grateful to all in the IZL community as we moved to do just that!

To those who pioneered learning in the space of mind-body science, making it practically useful: Peter Levine, Christine Caldwell, Randolf Stone, Ida Rolf, Moshe Feldenkrais, Judith Herman, Bessel van der Kolk, Staci Haines, Dawna Markova, Daniel Goleman, Daniel Siegel, Lewis Mehl-Madrona, Norman Doidge, Richard Davidson, and James Flaherty.

Fernando Flores for his rigor in bringing a new interpretation to language, and to Pluralistic Networks where I have been stretched and challenged in my ontology—or way of being—by a whole host of intelligent and inquiring seekers, including and especially on weekly calls with Team #3.

Members of the Chicago Chapter of Conscious Capitalism with whom I have planned and played to bring conscious leadership—*Elevating Humanity through Business*—to our day-to-day lives. And to those leaders in the conscious business space from whom I've taken inspiration: Rajendra Sisodia, John Mackey, Bob Chapman, Kip Tindell, Danny Friedland, Rebecca Henderson, and more.

To all my clients over the years, including those leaders who've shared their stories here, I bow deeply to you. Your willingness to take yourselves on and work your own edges gives me hope for our future.

The competent team at Greenleaf Book Group encouraged me each step of the way, especially Elizabeth Brown, who more than once re-directed my writing gremlins, and Jared Dorsey, who "got me" with a beautiful cover design.

Alyssa Baker, my assistant, kept me on track, while my right-hand thought partner, Jill Tyler, partnered, prodded, and provided me with just the right provocation to keep going in the writing process.

To all who made what you hold in your hand possible, and others too many to name: Holly Nelson Johnson, Kathleen Occhipinti, Ginger Carr, Jan Weller, Chris Lau, Dianna Stencel, Tasha Capen, Richard Zackon, Anthony Morris, Romy Sala, Dana Buska, Alexander Kalamaros, Mary Ann Ireland, Sarah Cove, Paula Drayton, Tony Carew, Chauncey Bell, Thea Polancic, Lee Capps, Andy Swindler, Dominic Perri, Nancy Pautsch, Marc Blackman, Jean Pitzo, Eileen Hamra, Mark Vance, Swati Garg, Betsey Nohe, Paul Bailey, Nick Blawat, Rand Stagen, Ron Rojas, Andy Swindler, Ahmed Hedayat, Nancy Rizzuto, Nick Sarillo, Dave Mooney, Darek Teeters, Debra Niewald, Amy Felix-Reese, Mark Melson, Peter Parthenis, Scott Shute, Don Catherall, Skip Shelton, Beth Davis, LeeAnn Mallory, and Suzanne Roberts.

Finally, to Brian Fippinger, my partner in life—morning barista, first editor, and favorite improv guy—your unwavering belief in me, your shared commitment to cultivating conscious leaders, and your unending patience when I became "pointedly focused" has made all the difference.

The Leadership Pause: Sharpen Your Attention, Deepen Your Presence, and Navigate the Future

> Do you remember how life yearned out of childhood toward the "great thing"? I see that it is now yearning forth beyond the great thing toward a greater one.
>
> —RAINER MARIA RILKE, AUSTRIAN POET AND AUTHOR OF *LETTERS TO A YOUNG POET*

T he landscape of life these days is chaotic, complex, and confusing. Do you know how to navigate it all?

Given the current environmental, economic, and political realities, finding a way to navigate through it all is challenging yet essential. It requires a skill that begins by accurately discerning your position, strategizing a plan, and only then moving forward. Steering through life is challenging yet essential for life and leadership.

The key? A simple pause.

If you're reading this, you've already taken an interest in this notion that we all must learn, in ways unexplored as of yet, to navigate new realities. Gone is your father's or grandfather's nine-to-five job, the one he held for his entire working life. Gone are the days of a single-income family, at least for the bulk of the populace. Gone are the strong community ties that held those previous ways of living and working in place.

It's as if a tidal wave came through, disrupting the relatively calm waters of our daily lives—or at least the fantasy about how calm we thought they were.

Historically, people have needed to change as the environment changed. And they did adapt. As human beings we're amazing creatures of adaptation. That said, it is how we work with, navigate, explore, and respond to the emerging contingencies at hand that will allow us as a species to create a better future for us all.

Today's leaders and their teams were already increasingly shaped and whittled into form in the time-crunched reality of marketplace opportunities, workplace experiences, and personal life choices.

Then came COVID-19, the mother of all societal tidal waves. The virus and its widespread impact upended all we thought was normal and disrupted not only our daily lives but also our ways of thinking about how to live and lead.

From executives to entrepreneurs to employees, we're caught up on the hamster wheel of expectation and obligation—especially in the digital age.

Leadership is the ability to take responsibility for something that matters to you and to successfully engage others in bringing it to life. It could be leading your local library board, a conservation project in your community, or your own company, like my client Paul, whom you'll hear more about shortly. No matter whether you're a mid-level worker or an owner, whether your current endeavor involves a formal title or is informal, or whether you're simply leading your life and want it to be on purpose—this book offers you a path to developing your leadership.

Leading well—on point, with care, and in collaboration with others— requires a balance between reflection and action to be effective, powerful, and impactful.

Yet, we live in a workaday world today where the predominant, under-lying value—the one that reigns supreme—involves constantly pushing and outperforming ourselves regardless of our natural energy levels. Space for reflection has been crowded out.

I don't know about you, but I want to make my best contribution in this life I've been given. I want to lead it effectively each and every day. To do so requires *full presence*. Such presence is the gift of mindfulness. To be here in this moment, nonjudgmentally, is to awaken to life as it's unfolding, with openness and heart.

It's tricky, this opening to what's occurring all around us. The impact of the coronavirus revealed cracks and fault lines that we either didn't know existed or couldn't bear to see before. This knowing is painful. It can feel overwhelming and more than a little disconcerting when it comes to know-ing how to lead and effect positive change.

If you take a quick glance at the news, it's easy to see any number of ways the world needs effective, visionary, and conscious leadership. Consider the recent gaps that some emerging and established leaders are stepping in to fill.

Climate

In a 2019 study assessing temperatures across all land and ocean surfaces—from North America to Europe to Asia, down to Africa, and across to South America—scientists at the National Center for Environmental Information (NOAA) determined that the impact of greenhouse gases has resulted in earth's surface temperature increasing by 1.7°F (0.95°C) from the twentieth-century average. In fact, the past five hottest global temperature measurements on record have occurred since 2015.[1] Further, a landmark report from the United Nations' Intergovernmental Panel on Climate Change (IPCC), which compiled data from more than one hundred sci-entists in thirty-six countries, warns that leaders today may only have until 2030 to keep global warming at bay by keeping surface temperatures from increasing more than 2.7°F (1.5°C).[2]

None of this is "new" news, but it's important news. It's clear that global temperatures are on the rise and the earth is consistently getting hotter. A shift in the surface temperatures would explain the rise in sea levels, the decrease in arctic ice, and a rapid increase in weather-related catastrophes—storms, floods, and droughts—around the globe.

In the same year that NOAA published its study, sixteen-year-old climate activist Greta Thunberg catapulted into international view with the message that "grown-ups" weren't taking action to preserve the future for our youth. In a speech at the UN Climate Action Summit in New York, she voiced provocative words for leaders today: "How dare you pretend that this can be solved with just 'business as usual' and some technical solutions? With today's emissions levels, that remaining CO_2 budget will be entirely gone within less than eight-and-a-half years."

Income Inequality

In a study by the Organization for Economic Cooperation and Development (OECD) comparing income inequality across all the members of the Group of Seven (G7) nations—UK, Italy, Japan, Canada, Germany, France, and the United States—US income inequality ranked the highest.

The Gini coefficient is a commonly used measure—ranging from 0 to 1—to assess inequality across countries. Zero represents perfect equality, while 1 signals complete inequality. Gini scores range anywhere from 0.25 in some Eastern European countries to scores in the midrange—like those in the G7, with the US at .43 and France at .32—to highs of 0.5 or 0.6 in some countries in southern Africa.

In the US,

- 41.4% of Americans are classified as low-income or part of low-income families;[3]

- between 1989 and 2016, the wealth gap between America's richest and poorest families more than doubled;[4] and

- the top 1% earns forty times[5] more than the bottom 90%,[6] while the median net worth of US families has decreased by at least 20% in lower tiers of wealth, including what we know as the middle class.[7]

In August 2019, the Business Roundtable—nearly two hundred CEOs of the largest US companies—surprised and shocked the business world by releasing a revised Statement on the Purpose of a Corporation. With its new declaration, America's premier business leadership group in essence redefined the purpose of business.

Long-held corporate orthodoxy has focused primarily on maximizing *shareholder* value, driving short-term profits and greed. Yet the Business Roundtable's statement includes all *stakeholders*—employees, vendors, customers, the environment, and shareholders—and focuses on delivering value to all.

Racial Inequities

Systemic racism has contributed to the persistence of race-based gaps that manifest in a variety of different economic indicators relative to both income and wealth. These include overall household wealth, healthcare access, educational opportunities, quality employment and wages, and home ownership. Measures of household wealth within BIPOC families shine a light on one of the starkest divides between racial groups, with implications for economic success, health, and well-being. Data from the Federal Reserve reveals that little has changed in the past thirty years in terms of wealth in the US. Today, in contrast to their White peers, who hold 85.5% of wealth, Black households have 4.2% and Hispanics 3.1%—both groups having increased their wealth by less than 1% in the thirty years.[8] Less wealth, including real hard assets like a home or investments, reduces the amount one can earn. Additionally, there's increasing evidence that racial and ethnic minority groups were disproportionately affected by COVID-19.[9]

Meanwhile, in the aftermath of George Floyd's cruel death at the hands of police officers in 2020, millions of protesters across the world rallied for an end to violence and an increase in racial equity across industries.

Gun Violence

Data on gun violence reveals that in the nation's fifty largest cities—from Chicago to New York to Columbus to Austin—homicides increased 24% in the first half of 2020.[10] As the impact of the 2020 global pandemic worsened—with record rates of millions unemployed—people began buying more guns, according to the nonprofit research group Gun Violence Archive. Typically driven by restrictive policies in prior years, gun sales were up in 2020 as a result of "COVID-specific things: uncertainty about the future, fear of people from foreign countries, and fear of the economy tanking," according to Lacey Wallace, a professor of criminal justice at Penn State.

Meanwhile, the surviving students of the shooting at Marjory Stoneman Douglas High School on Valentine's Day 2018—among them Emma Gonzalez—have risen together to demand stricter gun control laws.

Reality

The world today desperately needs each of us who lead to be on our best game—showing up, focusing, taking that next right step, and resting up to meet the demands of the day.

You might have been tapped to lead a particular project team, or simply to head up that local PTO fundraiser. It's likely that you didn't expect to be addressing larger-scale issues, yet that's exactly what you're being called to do.

It can be easy to get caught up in the rapidly shifting pace of today's world. It's easy for our attention to split apart and scatter like so much confetti, each tiny piece a legitimate concern gently knocking on our door.

We're human beings, and we're easily distracted. We can become overwhelmed and resort to a variety of behaviors to soothe our freak-outs, which are often characterized by anger, withdrawal, or numbing. At times, we move to compensate by shifting into task mode to get stuff done, feeling good to be in action yet potentially losing sight of the bigger picture of our lives.

Instead, we must train ourselves to pause, focus our attention, and listen.

Attention

The single biggest competitive advantage in the workplace today is training your attention on what matters most, with an eye to the long game.

Future success will depend upon our collective ability to pause.

Let me say that again with a different emphasis. *Your future success will depend upon your ability to pause.*

Viktor Frankl, an Austrian psychiatrist and Holocaust survivor who embodied presence, influenced Stephen Covey, an American educator and businessman, so much so that it "changed my life." Covey went on to write *Seven Habits of Highly Effective People* based on the notion that "between stimulus and response, there is a space. In that space is our power to choose our response. In our response lies our growth and our freedom."[11]

Stepping into a pause turns the key and opens the door to freedom and the space of possibility for self-awareness, conversations, and significant decisions to unfold naturally.

When we don't pause, we tend to rush through life, missing ordinary moments that might actually be extraordinary. Meaningful interactions with our colleagues and loved ones—those conversations that connect us human to human—don't have the space to occur when we're juggling and struggling with so many balls in the air.

When we don't pause, we risk losing touch with ourselves and our deepest concerns. We risk not being attuned to our natural rhythms and not feeling ourselves at all.

When we don't pause, we become myopic. We fail to take in the world around us—our kids, our colleagues and community, and the larger, natural environment that sustains and supports us all.

Pausing and training our attention is vital to our lives on the planet, not to mention in our day-to-day work and family lives.

To pause is to reconnect, if only for a moment, with what I call our *Core Presence*—that essence of our life, the invisible life force that directs who we become, how we come to lead, and the life that we'll create in the process.

Benefits of Pause

The world we live in now is light years away from the world of my youth, and likely yours too. Smartphones and apps have us glued to screens, broadcast news outlets keep us informed around the clock about events around the world, and our daily shopping and banking tasks can be completed online without ever having to engage another human.

Amazing advances in technology appear, on the surface, to have freed up time for us to be involved in more important concerns like spending time with family and friends, gardening, fly fishing, or whatever else nourishes. Yet the ubiquitous and insidious nature of technology brings with it a cost in connection with others and with ourselves that zaps us of our energies.

Those who fail to learn to *pause* to renew their energies do so at their own peril. Stress research reveals that those who work around the clock and don't allow for renewal and restoration are prone to illness, disease, and even early death.

Benefits of mindfully pausing are numerous:

- Improved attention and focus
- Better sleep
- A sense of wonder
- Clarity and better decision-making
- Decreased stress and increased resilience
- Perspective-taking
- Improved ability to work under pressure
- Mental flexibility and agility
- Increased empathy and compassion
- A Spot of Grace

Dawna Markova—an author, psychologist, and great life teacher—speaks to this essential connection between pausing, life, and leadership by way of a story that I believe is relevant to our life situation today and to leadership in particular.[12]

My grandmother began to stroke my forehead very slowly, the signal that a story was on its way. Her stories always made a silken tent for the two of us to crawl into.

"Imagine, my darling, that back in the very beginning of everything, there was an immense crystal bowl floating in the dark velvet sky. Imagine it was glowing because it was made of light."

I held my breath until she continued.

"We don't know how the bowl got there or how long it stayed. But we do know that one day there was a cracking, crashing sound that was almost as big as the sky. The bowl shattered into a million, billion, trillion different seeds of light. They flew everywhere, piercing everything alive in the world. From that moment on, each living being has had, hidden [in] its heart, one of those tiny seeds of light."

She bent over, looking right into me with her Coca-Cola brown eyes. She whispered as if she were telling me great secrets.

"One such seed is inside of you, and one is inside of me. I call it a spot of grace. Every one of us, whether we know it or not, is supposed to find that special light. Then we are meant to grow it and shine it into the darkness of the world, helping others find their light. When everyone does, the bowl will be made whole again."

"How come nobody talks about their spot of grace, Grandma?"

She leaned over and placed her lips against my ear.

"Most people don't know about the bowl or that little seed of light because they don't have a grandma like you do. So when you grow up, your job will be to help them find it. Maybe you'll tell them this story. And when you do, your spot of grace will glow ever brighter."

Spot of grace, spirit, essence, soul, or Core Presence—whatever name you care to use, it's the essential core of who we are and reflects what we care about in this lifetime.

We're all part of a whole and we've broken apart. Shards of light and life fill each of us. Until we can listen well and share that light, we'll continue to be broken and unable to lead effectively.

Pausing becomes the portal to accessing your Core Presence, your light. The very light that will guide you on your leadership journey.

If you dare. (Because it is tricky.)

The Long Game

I'm writing this book about pause because I need to be reading it. We all do.

Because we care. I care. You care.

As a psychologist working with trauma, including workplace trauma, I have come to a keen understanding of the importance, a requirement actually, of pausing to drop in underneath our own storyline and listening to our own *still, small voice.* That still, small voice within each of us guides, directs, nudges, and downright hollers at us sometimes to get us to listen. We've learned to not listen and instead to override this voice. It's exactly this kind of deep listening, however, that's essential for anyone who leads anything of value: a corporate team, a community food drive, the PTA, young climate activists, or a family.

As a practitioner and teacher of mindfulness, I've both experienced and witnessed the subtle power of a pause to usher in the moment and reveal the appropriate response to the situation at hand. Mindfulness has any number of positive health and work benefits including increased resilience, greater focus, and improved empathy and discernment in action—all essentials to effective leadership.

As a businesswoman, I've witnessed and experienced the tendency to rush decisions and move into action too quickly or out of fear. Conversely, I've also observed the not-to-subtle impact of slowing down in a pause, allowing the space for essential conversations to open up so new ideas and powerful outcomes can emerge.

As a martial arts practitioner—specifically aikido, the art of peace—I've experienced how soft eyes allow greater focus, how seeing the space around a move opens up vast possibilities for the best action, and how the committed practice born of pause can reshape a way of being.

As an executive leadership coach raised on the neuroscience of experiential learning as an overlooked foundation for effective change, I hold that the starting place to nearly any positive action we want to embark upon begins with the pause.

And I'll tell you why.

In the absence of practicing pause, it's all too easy to get caught up in the bustle of the day—thinking I know what will happen and how it will unfold, and following the path of least resistance that's bound up in reactivity rather than response.

In the spirit of essayist Anaïs Nin, I see the world not as it is but as I am. And likely, so do you.

The Magic of the Pause

At the end of more than a few coaching sessions and consultations with leaders and their teams, I've heard similar exclamations—"This is like magic."

I understand the sentiment.

To pause can seem like magic because the very nature of pausing to attend, observe, and listen to that particular moment spotlights what we can't see when we're overly focused or frenzied. When we pause, we step out of the crazy busyness of life and intentionally shift our perspective. New worlds and new possibilities become visible and unfold for us without our trying to make anything happen.

To pause is to interrupt an automatic, typically out-of-awareness behavior—a thought, an action, or even an emotion—to allow for observation and reflection.

To choose to take on a practice of conscious pausing is to tap the brakes on those automatic mental ruts that keep our wheels spinning in place, distancing us from what's directly in front of us. Pause shows us the opening where we can drop in our *felt experience* of the unfolding moment.

Pausing clears the cobwebs. It enables us to tap into the wisdom of the ages and honor the flow of life.

To pause in this moment, on purpose and nonjudgmentally, is to practice mindfulness of presence. Mindfulness is a force multiplier, expanding and amplifying your impact as a leader.

If we hold the truth of that premise in mind—that mindfulness is a force multiplier—then pause is the linchpin around which the flywheel of attention moves.

Which is why I'm writing to you.

You and Your Leadership

You may be deep in the weeds of a leadership challenge. Or you might be mystified that you're somehow in a leadership spot you neither expected nor could foresee.

Nonetheless, you're a leader and you're leading now. Or you're aspiring to do so.

You may be beginning to glimpse your own genius and contribution to the world. Of course, you'll want to be fully present for those moments—to be at your best, all-in for the conversations, engaged in the meaningful project, and enacting your convictions fully.

To be that present involves catching ourselves being ourselves. This is where we purposefully take note of the shadow side of our personality, those embodied aspects of our identity that often run the show if we're unaware. Unless we pause, stop the world in that moment, and begin to take stock of "what is so"—what's actually real—in our current lives, we'll be at the mercy of old patterns, habits, and strategies on the larger stage of life as well as on our personal stage.

That said, being present is not necessarily easy. We must train for it, with intention, focus, and a persevering heart ... because it's what we're designed to do.

As leaders, we're learners. As learners we can open ourselves up and learn to see what we don't want to see. The pause involved in embodied learning accelerates our growth and our leadership because it allows us to feel ourselves more deeply, to step into another's shoes more readily, and to explore new ideas and paths that surface creativity for working with life's tricky challenges.

You may have picked up this book for one of a few good reasons:

- You're desperate—okay, maybe not desperate, but living with a mild uptick in agitated energy—for something different to happen in your leadership. Leading can be overwhelming. You're hoping for a pick-me-up.

- You're looking for a bit of advice, or at least a hot tip on how to focus your attention with everything swirling around you.

- You'd love to rein in your distractibility and become a little less stressed, a little more settled, and a little more resilient.

- You're eager to learn more about the impact of technology on your own leadership, since it's constantly pulling you in. You see the speed and the need for greater agility in the marketplace but aren't sure technology has an answer.

- You're perplexed about the degraded quality of conversations you hear. You participate in and observe the degradation all around you but you're not sure how to address it.

- You've gotten this far. Yet, there's more and you know it. You want some of it.

The Leadership Pause might be a book someone recommended. Or it could be the beginning of a whole new way of leading.

The idea for this book began just over ten years ago, from a state of personal pause. In attempts to both listen and reflect on what I was personally experiencing, it became crystal clear that *The Leadership Pause* is essential to anyone aspiring to lead and make a difference.

You may be looking for more clarity and the courage to take that next right action in a job transition, at the office, or in a tender family conversation. Maybe you're at a place in your experience as a leader in which, though you're taking all the right steps, you're not quite sure how it's all going to turn out. You might wonder if there's a shortcut somewhere to improve your odds of success. Yes, there is.

Finally, you may be among those who've been hearing similar *still, small voice* stirrings and feel compelled beyond explanation to explore them now.

Welcome.

The funny thing is, though, it's probably closer to the truth to say that you possibly already know a lot about what to do—you're just not pausing to direct your attention, your listening, and your action to doing it.

Such as how to work with your stress. Or how real listening impacts day-to-day conversations. Or the importance of getting exercise and rest in order to make clearheaded decisions.

If you're like me, when time and stress and overwork are ratcheted up, your focus gets caught up in action and a constant state of being busy.

Your light and your wisdom are likely extended outward and forward to others more than inward and to yourself. Or they're buried deeply beneath behaviors that have become invisible to you—behaviors that no longer serve you or those you lead or the world. You've become blind to your own blindness.

Throughout this book, I'll invite you to pause, reflect, and record your thoughts, feelings, and insights. I'll ask you to embrace and practice the exercises here. You'll learn more about the necessity of deliberate practice in a later chapter. For now, it's enough to know that you're embarking on this next leg of your leadership journey.

Promises of What's to Come

In the pages that follow, we'll be taking a look at the current state of our world, our amped-up mode of being busy all the time, and the cost of multi-tasking to our lives and our leadership.

You'll meet a variety of leaders, hear their stories, and track their learning. We'll examine the impact of speed on our capacity to lead. We'll also review essential qualities for twenty-first-century leaders that highlight the importance of the long-overlooked pause.

When we're freaked out, not present, and feeling the pressure of life at our doorstep, we don't function so well. We have phrases for this—"freaked-out," "stressed-out," "at my wits' end," "needing a drink," etc.

When we're attuned to the moment at hand—present to it regardless of what is unfolding and whether we like it or not—we're able to sync up with life's natural rhythms, glimpse our own genius, choose our actions, craft careers, and grow businesses, families, and communities. We can make our best contributions.

This is power.

When we're most relaxed and at ease—slightly challenged but not overly so—is when we can feel into our passion and explore the larger purpose of our lives. We can answer questions like the following: Why is each of us really here today? What's our gift and responsibility to others and to the planet?

We'll explore the notion of being in a flow state and what it means, how pause is integral to presence and creativity, and how it taps our best passion to fulfill our purpose.

Practice is a key commitment that builds out our lives. It is essential to living a life by design rather than by default. We can also begin to grow our capacity to pivot, knowing when a decision needs to be renegotiated and when we need to drop into a conversation more deeply.

As we cultivate purposeful practices foundational to creating a life of meaning, especially as leaders, we'll come full circle to the cultivation of your Core Presence—the inner reservoir of life that sustains you and allows you to thrive.

To that end, we'll explore various kinds of pauses, with detailed attention to what occurs within the body when we're stressed and when we learn to pause.

Now before you go thinking something like, *Sure, if it were that easy don't you think I'd have done this?* or *This is guff, new agey* or *I don't have time to pause; there's so much work to do!*—all very common reactions, by the way—consider giving yourself a chance to get started with the pause.

It's simple, and you won't know how good this will be for you until you start experiencing your felt sense rather than simply thinking about taking a pause.

Practicing pause is smart personal hygiene for everyone, and you'll see many ways to practice pause in the pages to follow. Committing to the path of *The Leadership Pause* is not for the faint of heart. It will require all of you.

The path is only for those who can answer the following questions in the affirmative:

- Are you ready to listen to your deeper longing?

- Are you ready to make your difference in the world?

- Are you willing to step onto the path of self-cultivation and powerful leadership?

- Are you ready to commit to developing your ability to handle life's complexities with greater skillfulness and ease?

In the end, what matters is that you reclaim the seeds of your light in the world to bring about "healing the bowl," mentioned in the previous story. May all of us together make it happen.

Coming full circle is a path and process that begins with a simple pause and dropping into this very moment that we're alive—what philosopher Martin Heidegger called *being-in-the-world*.

Is This Book for Me?

You're passionate about the difference you want to make. You feel it in your bones. However, you also feel the pressure of this endeavor all too keenly. Your body and your energy levels reflect the stress. Despite having many tools in your toolkit, you find they're no longer as effective as they once were.

Others have told you that you need to raise your game—step up, speak up, and step out. Yet you're fuzzy somehow, feeling dragged down and stressed out. Where to go? What to do?

You need a new thinking partner, a way-of-being partner to support you while you pause to reflect. Someone who observes what you care about and the patterns that keep you from getting where you want to go. You need clarity, focus, and the fresh perspective that comes from learning the practice of pausing.

The motivation to act on what matters can easily be cut short by a variety of factors, especially feelings of being overwhelmed and a return to old habits. You find yourself saying: "I know what to do but I don't do it. I've read books, talked to coaches and shrinks, and still I just don't do it! I'm so frustrated with myself." Sound familiar?

Given the intense stressors of our lives today—constant disruption, rising fear and anxiety, and increased noise and pressure, all resulting in a lack of clarity and focus—it's clear that conventional leadership practices are no longer adequate to prepare leaders of the future to address today's complex challenges.

While leaders have always faced uncertainty, today its global, interconnected reach and scale are unprecedented.

As businesses are being challenged to turn toward purpose and meaning and away from a sole focus on profit, we need attentive, skillful leaders at all levels of business to step up, step in, and step out to move beyond reactivity to the responsiveness required to create a new future.

Crafting an inspiring vision for the future and bringing people along with you is what an authentic, conscious leader does by:

✓ leveraging attention and focus to get a read on life's unfolding—a strategic view that allows you to direct energy to power right action;

✓ embedding purpose and increasing engagement in those you lead;

✓ learning from your coworkers' emotions—no longer being reactively ruled by them—to become responsive and clear in decision-making; and

✓ shaping and committing to resilient, caring, and diverse work cultures to create a just, equitable society.

What if there were a single practice that would significantly maximize your impact?

What if the answer is so simple, and the science and results so compelling, that the only reason not to put it into practice would be an attachment to worn-out methods of leading?

You'll find that simple practice in *The Leadership Pause*, where you'll learn shortcuts for the long haul toward developing conscious, embodied leadership.

Committing to and cultivating *The Leadership Pause* in your day-to-day life and leadership will sharpen your attention, deepen your presence, and supercharge your leadership to collaborate and coordinate effective action for the greatest impact.

This book shows you how. It answers three questions:

✓ What is it about pausing that makes the practice so essential to conscious leadership?

✓ How will implementing pausing mitigate your biggest struggles?

✓ What results might be possible if pausing to listen deeply informs your actions?

The Leadership Pause shows you the way to making your greatest contribution. And it does so in a way that builds your resilience and generates energy.

This way of leading will teach you practices to reduce your level of stress, declutter your thinking process, and widen your perspective to include all the possibilities available to you.

Each chapter of the book is organized around common concerns facing professionals and leaders. You will see them in the stories that follow and will have the opportunity to explore questions and new practices at the end of each chapter. This book is rooted in the latest in adult developmental theory, interpersonal neurobiology and the science of somatics, mindfulness practices, and the best practices of conscious business.

Who Is This Book Not For?

If you're on a path of leadership and have already learned all you need to learn to step up, speak out, and step out into your best, most brilliant self—go no further. The stories, pauses, and reflections here won't be of use to you.

Put the book down and find another one that works best for you where you are today.

Let Your Light Shine

Still here?

This book is for those who choose to lead consciously, on purpose, and powerfully to create a new future for all.

If you love learning and stories and developing your self in service of making your big difference in the world, these pages will hold opportunities for you to move forward on your path, knowing you're not alone on the journey. Let's get started.

CHAPTER 1

Our Current Present: Whitewater

Water is fluid, soft, and yielding. But water will wear away
rock, which is rigid and cannot yield. As a rule, whatever is
fluid, soft, and yielding will overcome whatever is rigid and
hard. This is another paradox: what is soft is strong.

—LAO TZU, CHINESE PHILOSOPHER (604–531 BCE)

I f you've ever felt like you were running faster and faster, never quite catching up, you know the toll the daily chase can take on your energies and
enthusiasm.

Today, most people report that they're experiencing the world around
them as rapidly changing. They're not wrong.

Life's growing complexities are wreaking havoc on our capacity to lead.

It's as true at the local level as it is at the highest levels in the land. We
see and feel the press all around us, and despite complexities taking different
forms, the forces at play are shared.

From executives to entrepreneurs to employees, we're caught up on the
hamster wheel of expectation. We're exhausted when we get home, exhausted

when we leave the next morning, and exhausted dealing with employees and colleagues. We're exhausted with our lives.

According to the American Psychological Association, the most common form of stress—63%—is from work.[1] A study by the Center for Creative Leadership reveals that "88% of leaders report that work is the primary source of stress in their lives and that having a leadership role increases the level of stress."[2] Two-thirds of those same leaders report that their stress is higher today than it was five years ago, and they don't experience support within their workplaces to address it.[3]

The conventional narrative is to work hard, do more with less, keep learning new skills, treat people with the same respect you'd like to receive, and—in the end—all will go well.

So we try harder and work longer. We become reactive out of fear that our efforts may be wasted. Yet the accelerated pace of change, increasing competition, and higher expectations, coupled with limited resources and a low tolerance for error, are now the cultural norms. Our attentions are scattered by an overload of information that results in feeling overwhelmed.

Worse, the stress can feel like it's your fault, or it reflects something lacking in you or your leadership. You may find yourself redoubling your efforts and beefing up your skills so you can reclaim a modicum of control over your day-to-day life. The trifecta of technology, busyness, and comfort seeking, however, only adds to an ever-growing vicious cycle that leaves us feeling overwhelmed. Nothing seems to work—at least not for long.

Technology and Interruptions

Information consumes the attention of its recipients. Hence,
a wealth of information creates a poverty of attention.

—HERBERT SIMON, COGNITIVE SCIENTIST,
NOBEL PRIZE IN ECONOMICS

Let's explore your day, starting with your morning.

Think back to this morning and review your morning routine. Between sips of coffee or OJ and getting yourself dressed, were you checking your email? Browsing LinkedIn or Facebook? Reacting to overnight texts from work? Buzzing out to catch the train while shooting off a last-minute email to a colleague before the morning meeting?

Sound typical? You're not alone.

We're assaulted each day with increasing amounts of information. The onslaught of incoming information is breathtaking in its magnitude. Yet we continue to browse our phones nonstop and multitask our way through the day.

The myriad of activities crammed into your morning and your constant switching between them are likely making you tired. And so is all that "information" you're taking in from all of those outside sources—news headlines, friends' Facebook posts, Twitter posts, and endless emails.

It's no wonder we're tired. In 2007 Apple introduced the iPhone, and by 2011, with the continuing rise of Big Data, Americans took in five times as much information every day as they did in 1986—the equivalent of reading 174 newspapers.[4] Our ability to process all that incoming stuff is estimated at 120 bits per second—the speed limit of the incoming information that we can consciously pay attention to at any one time.

Further, studies show that office workers are interrupted about seven times an hour, or 56 interruptions a day. These daily distractions come in a variety of forms: approximately 121 emails, 45 text messages, and 22 calls—80% of which are considered "trivial," according to time-management experts. It's safe to say we feel the constant push, pull, and tug of each buzz, beep, and ding. A study by Basex, a New York research firm, found that these office distractions ate up 2.1 hours a day for the average worker.[5] Put into financial terms, we've collectively lost an estimated $650 billion annually—in the United States alone—to a tsunami of trivia.

Gloria Mark, a professor in the department of informatics at the University of California, Irvine, says that when people are interrupted (whether by someone else or themselves), it typically takes twenty-three minutes and fifteen seconds to return to their work, with most people doing two inter-vening tasks before going back to their original project.

More than 70% of white-collar workers reportedly feel stressed about the amount of information they must process and act on while working, while 60% report feeling overwhelmed. Of even greater concern are the 45% of high-earning managers who are too tired to converse with their spouse or partner after a long day at the office, which ends up wreaking havoc on family and personal lives.[6]

What happens when we can't take in or process all this information, much of which is useless?

Our brains default to trying to do it all, all the time. In other words, overloaded with distractions, our brains default to multitasking—further shrinking our mental control.

Multitasking

The very term "multitasking" is a computer-derived term, a reference to running multiple applications simultaneously on your computer. But we're not machines. When we attempt to multitask—to do two tasks at one time, alternating between each task, often without finishing the first—we expend tremendous energy. Neuroscientists tell us that human multitasking drains the energy reserves of the brain.

In reality, when we attempt to multitask, we don't actually do more than one activity at once, the way a computer does. Instead, we quickly switch between them. Managing two mental tasks at once reduces the brainpower available for either task. It can be done, but at a cost to our energy levels and our capacity for sustained attention.

One way we can examine the effects of multitasking on behavior and the demands it puts on relevant brain networks is by analyzing "task-switch costs." A switch cost is a reduction in performance accuracy or speed that results from shifting between tasks.[7]

Individuals almost always take longer to complete a task, and do so with more errors, when switching between tasks than when focusing on one task, or single tasking. Moreover, prolonged digital multitasking can impede learning to read facial cues that promote social and emotional learning, which can paralyze the development of empathy.

Why? Because all that switching is exhausting. It uses up oxygenated glucose in the brain, draining the same fuel that's required to focus on a task, including reading and responding to others' emotional states. "That switching comes with a biological cost that ends up making us feel tired much more quickly than if we sustain attention on one thing," says Daniel Levitin, professor of behavioral neuroscience at McGill University.[8]

Our Brain Cells

Our neurons—living brain cells—have a metabolism too, requiring oxygen and glucose to survive. When our cells have been working hard attempting to deal with the onslaught of information or trying to do a number of complicated tasks at once, we experience fatigue. Every email you check and news update you scroll at lunchtime competes for your brain's resources with the truly important concerns in your life: what to do with your financial portfolio, how to deal with your contentious work team, remembering to renew your driver's license, or how best to work with your partner to handle your aging parent's living situation.

Not all attempts at multitasking are equally draining. If you're doing something on autopilot, like laundry or cleaning your golf bag, then it makes perfect sense to read a magazine in between loads or listen to a podcast at the same time. But attempting to do two challenging tasks at once will lead to a drain in your energy and productivity. We can't do two demanding tasks in parallel.

Gloria Mark—the UCI professor—believes that we've become conditioned to frequently check social media networks and email. She explains: "Whenever you check email, every so often you get a hit, some great email received. That happens on a random schedule. In psychology, that's called random reinforcement and that's enough to reinforce behavior."[9]

Random, intermittent behavior can be incredibly difficult to combat because it's so addictively reinforcing. Mark's research has found that, after being frequently interrupted, people often develop shorter attention spans and begin to self-interrupt, weakening their mental control and making them more susceptible to future distractions. This means that when you absentmindedly shift your attention away from what you're doing and put it somewhere else, you're doing it more out of habit than intentional choice. Examples would be clicking over to check out LinkedIn or Facebook, making that dentist appointment that you suddenly remember, or scrolling over to place an Amazon order right after you got pinged by your colleague at work.

All of this switching of tasks comes at a cost—loss of quality. "Multitasking is going to slow you down, increasing the chances of mistakes," says David E. Meyer, a cognitive scientist and director of the Brain, Cognition, and Action Laboratory at the University of Michigan.[10]

The insidious part is that we don't notice our own impairment. We tend to believe that our brain can do more than it is capable of or was designed to do. Overloading our attention shrinks our mental control, reducing the quality of our attention as we execute one task, and decreasing our ability to refocus on the next one.

Results of multitasking include a(n):

- diminished ability to focus on a single task for attention;

- greater number of mistakes;

- reduced capacity of memory;

- increase in waste and re-work; and

- reduction in intelligence, because attention is required to learn new skills.

The bottom line? Having less access to social media and email gives our brains a much-needed energy break. One way to do this is to chunk work into smaller bits, allowing for greater effectiveness.

Try the Tomato Timer

The Pomodoro Technique promotes working on a specified task for twenty-five minutes and becoming fully immersed in it until a timer goes off. (Some even use a tomato-shaped kitchen timer [pomodoro is tomato in Italian], no batteries or electronics required.) This is followed by a short break to physically get up and move before starting another round of Pomodoro intensity. Millions have used this process to get a grip on their time and tasks without feeling rushed.[11] I used this technique to write this book.

Another simple solution is to turn off notifications on all your devices. You'll notice an immediate positive gain, as you can now choose when you'd like to see that incoming email or take a call.

It's also useful to plan for distraction time versus feeling at the mercy of incoming noise. Put plainly, you want and need a break. The key is that the break must allow your mind to relax and wander—whether that means going for a walk, listening to music, playing with your dog, or even staring out the window.

Busyness

We live in a culture that celebrates activity. Endemic, perpetual busyness has risen in status and become a sort of twisted badge of honor. It seems we've begun to collapse our sense of who we are—our identity—into what we do for a living.

A coaching client told me, "I just don't feel productive unless I'm checking things off my list." Perhaps you feel this way too. Many of us feel the need to chronically demonstrate that our worthiness is reflected in how busy we are, how much we can juggle at any one time, and how exhausted we are at the end of the day. Busy as ever, we prove that we matter—maybe even that we're indispensable.

This state begs a question. Is one's worth simply defined by the number of tasks checked off, projects completed, or deals closed? What's the price we pay for being in the grip of such busyness?

One thing is for sure: we cease feeling ourselves. Quite literally, we become numb to our physical sensations and our emotions.

"'Crazy-busy' is a great armor, it's a great way for numbing," says University of Houston visiting professor of management and best-selling author Brené Brown. "What a lot of us do is that we stay so busy, and so out in front of our life, that the truth of how we're feeling and what we really need can't catch up with us."[12]

Staying busy can be a distraction from boredom or other unpleasant emotions. As a result, we can miss out on the extraordinariness of the present moment, with all its beauty and possibility. We rush past the tender or fun moments with loved ones and become blind to opportunities to make a bigger impact than we could possibly imagine. The price we pay is the intimacy of living fully.

Thomas Merton—comparative religion scholar, poet, and Vietnam War activist—sums it up best:

> The rush and pressure of modern life are a form, perhaps the most common form, of its innate violence. To allow oneself to be carried away by a multitude of conflicting concerns; to surrender to too many demands; to commit oneself to too many projects; to want to help in everything is to succumb to violence. It destroys the fruitfulness of work, because it kills the root of inner wisdom, which makes work fruitful.[13]

● ● ●

AWARE OF BUSYNESS

There's an old Zen saying—"You should sit in meditation for twenty minutes a day unless you are too busy; then you should sit for an hour." Wise words.

◯ When's the last time you thought or said, "I'm too busy"?

○ What were the circumstances at the time? What choices were you contemplating? Or did you slip into busyness automatically?

○ Reflecting on this now, how do you feel as a result? What did you choose to do?

• • •

Technology and Continuous Partial Attention

The moments of silence are gone. We run from them into
the rush of unimportant things, so filled is the quiet with the
painful whispers of all that goes unspoken.

—L. M. BROWNING, POET AND AUTHOR OF *SEASONS OF*
CONTEMPLATION: A BOOK OF MIDNIGHT MEDITATIONS

We've become habituated to drinking from a fire hose of frenetic busyness—and to the technology that perpetuates it. With the world continually at our fingertips, the internet and social media provide us with perpetual instant gratification and, conversely, a perpetual lack of delay of gratification.

Back in 1998, former Apple and Microsoft senior leader Linda Stone coined a term that describes this phenomenon: *continuous partial attention.* Our divided attention creates "an artificial sense of constant crisis"—a state of being "powered on" that disrupts our real-life interactions—and produces what Harvard professor of human–technology interaction Sherry Turkle has called the Goldilocks Effect, in which we keep one another not too close, not too far, but just right.[14]

Continuous partial attention is distinct from the press of multitasking, in which we're typically motivated to be *more* productive and efficient or to have more time to ourselves. When we're hovering with continuous partial attention, Stone says "it's motivated by a desire to be a live node on the network."[15] In other words, we seek connection with others, so we scan for opportunities to be busy, connected, and alive.

Despite the fact that technology has opened up vast worlds of innovation and possibility, Turkle claims the "impact has been to make us forget what we know about life. When it comes to certain things, we really need people. What has been most striking is how difficult it is for us to give each other full attention when we have our devices and how much we're losing out."[16]

Split Attention

We feel imprisoned by the way we live in time.
However fast things may actually be, it seems that people
always feel it is too fast. This says as much about us as
it does about the world around us.

—ROBERT POYNTON, ASSOCIATE FELLOW, OXFORD UNIVERSITY,
SAÏD BUSINESS SCHOOL STRATEGIC LEADERSHIP
PROGRAMME, AND AUTHOR OF *DO/PAUSE*

In our attempts to get a grip on the incoming waves of information, Tom Davenport of Accenture's Institute for Strategic Change, tells what it will take to be successful: *"Understanding and managing attention is now the single most important determinant of business success."*[17] With our minds wandering about 47% of the time and being on task only 53% of the time, we must ask ourselves: Is the internet hampering our ability to pay attention? To learn?

Philosopher Martin Heidegger warned back in the 1950s against a looming "tide of technological revolution" that might so "captivate, bewitch, dazzle and beguile man that calculative thinking may someday come to be . . .

the only way of thinking."[18] His concern was that technology's influence would come at the price of meditative thinking, a peculiar mode of reflection he saw as the essence of humanity. Further, "Modern Technology, like [the] ancient [Greek term] *techne* from which it springs—and like science and metaphysics which is essentially one with it—is a mode of revealing." Technology not only reveals us to ourselves but also seduces and shapes us. A diminished capacity to sustain attention, resulting in an erosion in our ability to reflect, will compromise our ability to lead, to govern, to care for the earth, or to create the future.

By being constantly on, overstimulated by everything and nothing at once, our dominant mode of attention is split, ensuring that we're never truly present to what's unfolding in the current moment. Nor are we acting with decisiveness, which only contributes to feelings of being overwhelmed and dissatisfied—leaving us with a mindset of playing chronic catch-up. *We are so accessible* that we're inaccessible. Our latest, greatest, and most powerful technologies have contributed to our feeling increasingly powerless and stuck in "an artificial sense of constant crisis." These crises catapult us someplace else. Out there, we're everywhere except where we actually are in the moment.

Opiate Comfort

In response to the heavy influx of constant distraction and the full-on realities of juggling all the details of our lives and commitments, we tend to do one of a few things:

1. *Do* it all, resulting in constant multitasking.

2. *Fight* with reality to make things happen, otherwise known as "powering through."

3. *Avoid* reality by shifting our attention to something else that captures us.

4. *Numb* ourselves with behaviors designed to comfort and self-soothe.

Originating from the Old English term *frofor*, the word comfort means a "state of enjoyment resulting from satisfaction of bodily wants and freedom from anxiety." It is also defined as "a source of alleviation or relief."

Of course, comfort is in and of itself not a bad thing. Yet when we immediately and habitually seek comfort, we can end up overriding and neglecting our body's natural rhythms. We can become disconnected from ourselves and what's important to us. It's only a short distance to becoming disconnected from others and numb to the situation at hand.

It's human to seek comfort to mitigate the intensity of stress and suffering. Over time, however, we can quite literally lose touch with the sensations that let us know who we are and how we feel at any given moment. When we can no longer feel ourselves, it's difficult to know and act on what would nourish ourselves to greater energy.

Though most of us aspire to Helen Keller's declaration that "life is either a daring adventure or nothing at all," an overemphasis on comfort-seeking can keep us from challenging ourselves and stretching to reach our potential. What we're often truly seeking in comfort is a reprieve from the intensities of our complex lives. Behaviors that keep us lulled into a state of benign awareness, in which we keep life's trying or tender experiences at bay, are called *comfort addictions*. Though not inherently bad, these kinds of comforts— having that extra martini or glass of wine after work, continuing to fill shopping bags though the thrill is long gone, spending long hours on the golf course or playing ball every weekend—can easily slide into habit. They can start to take precedence over the important stuff of one's life: kids' soccer games, extended family visits, getting finances in order, etc.

Without requisite self-reflection and skill development, comfort— masked as deserving self-care—can simply lead to maintaining our equilibrium, with nothing of substance changing.

The Broader Picture

What we read about in the daily news reveals jarring systemic shifts that are continually unfolding: the rapid acceleration of technological change with uncertain outcomes, an enhanced greenhouse effect that's raising global temperatures to devastating heights, a global economy in a frenzy with skyrocketing healthcare costs, and a gradual and consistent rise in economic inequality.

This confluence of shifts is what the Center for Creative Leadership (CCL) has dubbed "perpetual whitewater"—the constant churn of the high rushing waters of complexity that results in unmitigated stress and a feeling of being overwhelmed.[19] The U.S. Army War College, back in the late 1980s, christened the phenomenon VUCA—volatile, uncertain, complex, and ambiguous. The world is increasingly *volatile*, changing rapidly for a multiplicity of reasons beyond our individual control. *Uncertainty* is now the only certainty. Predicting future outcomes will be increasingly challenging. Unable to know the effects of the interactions between the multiple variables that leaders must consider, *complexities* expand to yield *ambiguous* and often competing interpretations.

CCL's work was supported by research at IBM, which conducted a study with over 1,500 CEOs to inquire about their experiences in this shifting landscape.[20] The number one concern of those CEOs was the growing complexity of their environments. More than half of those leaders expressed doubt about their own ability to lead and to ride the waves of change without succumbing to the undertow. They recognized that they were in over their heads, with insufficient resources to capably steer through the daily whitewater of what we, today, call our working lives.

Of course, any number of factors contribute to this current dynamic state: information overload, dissolution of traditional organizational boundaries, new and disruptive technologies in the workplace, multigenerational values, and expectations of numerous cohorts all expressed in the workplace at one time. All of these factors are tipping points, in which critical mass is reached and the environment we're living and leading in rapidly changes to a new state.[21] With the greater complexity comes a need for a deeper, sustained pause to be able to clarify, translate, and communicate the next right moves.[22]

Through Line of Fear

What's perhaps more important is that the turbulent change brings with it a through line of fear that's becoming more predominant.

We see fear and its aftereffects run across our screens, read about it in the media, and observe it in our workplaces. We see it in an increase in anxiety, fatigue, exhaustion—a grasping after something to do to keep busy and a longing for certainty where none is to be found. We see it in an increase of the fear of the unknown, fear of others, fear of being left out, and fear of missing out (which even has its own acronym—FOMO). This fear of uncertainty is palpable.

And it's fear that drives the vicious cycle of busyness and lack of attention to what's important. This costs us the deep salve of connection and replaces it with the opiate of comfort, which lulls us into a sleepy stupor, far from awareness.

Leadership Identity and Opportunity

So what are we to do? We have an opportunity before us to wake up to the current realities of this particular historical moment in time and the responsibility we share with one another as human inhabitants on the planet. It's time for us to review, rethink, and rechoose how to live and lead.

Despite all the tangible and tragic concerns of society, life's complexities are also opening up spaces of possibility to explore new ways to work together and collaborate.

From the CEO to the PTO, we're at a point where a shift in the leadership paradigm is desperately needed.

Rather than hunkering down in fear and avoiding dealing with these complexities, a more effective starting point is to *turn toward the fear*. This radical orientation of leading involves a new way of seeing and being in the world, a way that's inherently uncertain, risky, and potentially dangerous. It will require you to be present in the moment at hand to attend to what is real and right in front of you, rather than being surprised and reactive when whatever occurs is different from what you've come to expect in your mind.

Shelly, one of my clients in the financial services space, made a habit of complaining about how her current situation "doesn't match what's in my head."

Of course it didn't. She was highly competitive and wasn't meeting her revenue goals. She easily slipped into complaining and then working around the clock to do it all herself. In our coaching sessions, she started to practice pausing and stepping back to look around to her colleagues. They had goals too, didn't they?

Her head-down focus precluded her from seeing the obvious—she and her colleagues could either work as independent agents, or they could work as a team. Shelly learned the importance of pausing to open up space and connect with her colleagues. Instead of attempting to wrestle down her reality to match what was in her head, she could more easily see what was right in front of her. Her colleagues' energy and goodwill in working together allowed the rising tide to lift all boats.

Despite the speed, increased complexity, and chaos of the world, leaders in all walks of life—from the boardroom to the factory floor to the softball team—need to be able to work with their own reactions under the pressure of continuous competing priorities. They'll also still need to set a clear vision and inspire others to support it. And they'll need a willingness to explore creative solutions while motivating everyone's best efforts. All of this requires keen self-awareness and practice.

In the chapters ahead, you'll meet a number of leaders who've used the practice of pausing to great effect. There's Paul, whose communication style didn't engage his team. You'll learn how, after soul-searching, he shifted that dynamic. Then there's Marc, who exhibited the presence of mind—along with the engaged support of his team on the shop floor—to pivot in the 2020 pandemic and create a new line of business.

Jean, who had already long been on the road to conscious leadership, exudes the power of pause as she walks the shop floor engaging with her team, deepening a culture of care in her Midwestern manufacturing shop. Dave realized the extent to which we "all have these kind of reflexive, conditioned responses that are limiting, so we confuse being busy with being productive"—an important insight to his financial institution.

You'll also meet Rand, who realized his need to grapple with his own internal mindset and—like Shelly—had to confront what was in his head versus what the marketplace was asking of him and his business.

For all those among us who lead and who feel compelled to bring a new future into being, we'll need not only new, more effective skills to navigate the perpetual whitewater. We'll also need to show up, embody confidence, and engage others to join us. The leaders who share their stories here are on that journey. Welcome.

Leadership Qualities and Skills

> Becoming a leader is synonymous with becoming yourself.
> It is precisely that simple, and it is also that difficult.
>
> —WARREN BENNIS, FOUNDING CHAIRMAN OF THE LEADERSHIP
> INSTITUTE AT THE UNIVERSITY OF SOUTHERN CALIFORNIA

Leaders who are conscious are: *mindful* of themselves and the world around them; *embodied* with an ethic of care, courage, and skillful action; and *generative* in creating the future rather than simply reacting to complexities out of fear. Conscious leadership starts with self-awareness and enough courage to start a shift—first within yourself, then by sharing your perspective, and finally leading by example.

Influence and shaping the future will require self-cultivation through mindfulness, reflection, self-discovery, and deep learning. This high level of emotional intelligence represents table stakes for all leaders who want to make a difference and accounts for 85–90% of the difference between outstanding leaders and their peers.[23] In short, to lead requires one's whole self. And it's tricky.

More than technical skills, leadership qualities are mediated via an internal neural guidance system, what some may call intuition. It's the honing of this mental process that will be required to lead us forward during these times of complexity.

Leadership is not about tricks, or techniques, or previously learned skills or strategies (which can be part of the problem) as much as it is about embodying certain qualities that enable you as a leader to enact the skills to move forward in powerful ways.

One's primary source of power as a leader comes from the qualities that enable a leader to connect, inspire, and engage others to act toward a greater good. Said another way, one's primary source of power reflects the self of the leader—a powerful way of being.

Key *leadership qualities* required for the twenty-first century revolve around the Leadership Pause. They include:

- **Presence**—the capacity to be in the current moment, on purpose with full attention.

- **Curiosity and a learning mindset**—a willingness to put aside what one already knows to be genuinely curious about what might emerge in the next moment. Curious leaders are willing to be moved rather than needing to be right.

- **Connection with self and others**—a deep connection with one's own values allows leaders to more deeply connect with others they lead.

- **Care and compassion**—concern for others and what matters to them, in a spirit of genuine human care, opens up compassion for what it means to be fully human in the workplace, and in life.

Leadership skills most vital for the twenty-first century include:

- **Focusing attentions where they need to be focused**. Increasingly, leaders will need to be able to choose their focus instead of being distracted in order to keep pace with where the world is moving.

- **Working with energy to enact agile decisions and to pivot as needed**. This requires being attuned to one's self and to the needs of the environment and others simultaneously. It sharpens leaders' critical-thinking and decision-making capacities.

- **Listening and engaging in conversations**. Listening defines leadership. This essential leadership skill involves thinking dialectically, since society is in constant flux, and then listening deeply to others—something leaders typically think they already do well. Pontificating is not listening.

- **Developing people**. Being able to mentor, champion, and coach others will be essential to moving forward in this century. The ability to get work done *through* others and *with* others as fellow human beings on the journey rather than being a lone ranger will be a highlighting characteristic of this age.

A Spear in My Chest

> The question of reaching sustainability is not about if
> we will have enough energy, food, or other resources.
> The question is: Will there be enough leaders in time?
>
> —KARL-HENRIK ROBÈRT, SWEDISH CANCER SCIENTIST
> AND FOUNDER OF THE NATURAL STEP

An unlikely radical with a soft Southern accent and easy manner, Ray Anderson nonetheless is one of the most visionary businessmen of the twentieth century. When I first learned of his story, I was fascinated. As the founder of Interface, a global commercial flooring company that he started in 1973, Ray embodies the qualities and skills of a conscious leader.[24]

Ray started his career in the textile industry. It was on a business trip to England in the early 1970s that he discovered the novel carpet tile (carpets at that time were created in long rolls). An astute businessman, he'd been watching the changes in office infrastructure in the US and anticipated the coming shift to an open-plan approach. By 1973, he'd founded Interface to bring the concept of free lay carpet tile to the new open office spaces in America. Little did he know that he'd started a revolution in commercial flooring—and in awareness-raising.

It was later, in the early 1990s, that one of his architectural customers inquired, "What's your company doing for the environment?" Beyond confirming that Interface followed the law and had taken basic steps to reduce interior air contamination, Ray realized he couldn't answer this question. In fact, he was provoked and stymied by his inability to answer the question of sustainability and what Interface should be doing. He grew increasingly alarmed and created a company task force to address Interface's environmental impact. Later, when invited to address the task force at its kickoff meeting—a speech he didn't want to make—he was at a loss.

Around that same time, Paul Hawken's book *The Ecology of Commerce* fortuitously happened across his desk.[25] Hawken—a serial entrepreneur, ardent environmentalist, and founder of garden supply company Smith and Hawken—wrote passionately about how businesses were laying waste to the world's natural resources. Desperate to respond, Ray devoured Hawken's book. His experience was nothing short of transformative—a "spear in the chest" moment that dramatically shifted his perspective on business and sustainability.

That spear awakened in him an urgent need to set a new course for Interface. He charged his engineers with determining the quantity of natural materials that Interface had extracted from the earth to produce the company's income that year. His engineers estimated that Interface had used 1.2 billion pounds of raw materials, mostly oil and natural gas, that was later incinerated to produce $800 million in revenue. Ray was staggered.

Within the year, just as he was retiring at age sixty as the founder and CEO, Ray announced to his employees and customers that he was setting out in quest of sustainability. Ray explained: "I gave that task force a kickoff speech that—frankly—surprised me, stunned them, and then galvanized all of us into action."

Never a tree hugger, Ray said in the speech: "I'm a husband, a father, and an industrialist. Some people call me a 'radical' industrialist, but I want to assure you that I am as competitive and profit-minded as anyone in this room."

The central theme of the speech was that, together, he and all those at Interface would climb Mount Sustainability to "take nothing from the earth that is not rapidly and naturally renewable and do no harm to the biosphere."

With this leadership move, Ray shook the foundations of the petroleum-intensive carpet manufacturing industry. He declared that Interface was committed to becoming the world's first environmentally sustainable and restorative business, an initiative he christened Mission Zero. In early November 2019, Interface met its commitment to Mission Zero success ahead of the original 2020 target by reducing impact in three key areas of business: factories, products, and suppliers.[26] Today, every flooring product—carpet tile, rubber sheets, etc.—that Interface sells is now carbon-neutral across its full life cycle. "Mission Zero is the embodiment of Ray's vision for Interface and for the world," said Interface CEO Jay Gould. "Ray's dream incited a movement toward sustainable business and thoughtful consumption. His legacy lives on through the fulfillment of Mission Zero and the work Interface and others are doing every day to endeavor to create a carbon negative future."

Why did Ray take such a stand and go through such an arduous process? It had to do with his learning orientation, his willingness to be challenged and emotionally pierced that tapped into his sense of purpose, and his embodied commitment to living out his purpose for the greater good.

Twenty-First-Century Leaders

We know that developing effective, competent leaders has never been more important or relevant. With all the rush and busyness of our times, the constant distraction and taxing on our attentions, and the bigger commitments leaders must make for our collective future to survive, the pause is essential. And it's as close as our next breath.

Who we are as leaders, and the skills we bring, will likely need a bit of tuning as our identity shifts and changes. What got us here will no longer take us where we need to go in this complex world of constant flux and change.

Like Ray Anderson, when we find our current situation formidable, it generally isn't so much a description of the situation at hand—though none would argue the case—but rather a description of who we are and our interpretation of it. In fact, our responses to increasing complexity are directly correlated with the identity we have built over a lifetime. As a lifelong learner, Ray leaned into the situation with a willingness to be changed. In turn, his choices not only changed but also transformed an entire industry.

We too will be called at times to let go of our identity and expand who we know ourselves to be in order to deal more effectively with this new, complex, and rapidly shifting world. From the PTO chair to the CEO, how will you navigate the future as it unfolds?

What will be required of you? Where will you focus your attentions? How will you make the shift?

• • •

YOUR VUCA EXPERIENCE AND
THE DIFFERENCE YOU WANT TO MAKE

Allow yourself ten minutes to complete this reflective practice. Allow yourself to feel your body's sensations, as well as whatever emotions arise as you work.

List your top five VUCA (volatile, uncertain, complex, and ambiguous) stressors in the following space. Don't think too much—just write.

• • •

Reflect for a moment on your answers and tune in to your body's sensations as you sit with your responses. Notice any tension or tightness, movements like pulsing or streaming. Keep breathing and letting any tension go with each outbreath. Make a mental note of what's showing up below the surface.

Look up and around. Take a deep breath. Bring to mind something that makes you smile. As you slowly exhale, let yourself feel into these new and different sensations. List three words that come to mind about your current state.

From this new state, reflect on the following questions and make notes for later.

- What's the difference you want to make? Why?

- If you make that difference, what will life be like for you?

- How will making this difference influence your feelings? Your interactions with others? The future?

• • •

Lessons from Whitewater Rafting the Royal Gorge

My husband and I took our honeymoon vacation to the Royal Gorge canyon in southwestern Colorado a few years ago. We were looking forward to whitewater rafting down the Arkansas River to take in all the beauty.

After purchasing tickets, we were each issued the standard bright orange life jacket, a turquoise helmet, and a two-sided oar. We were told in no uncertain terms by our guide, Joe, to "keep your eyes on me at all times."

A crisp coolness greeted us as we boarded the raft. The smell of damp earth and lush vegetation hung in the July air. As we drifted down the river, we could see the water picking up pace and its live energy roiling. Our senses were heightened as we heard rumbling sounds up ahead, followed by the voices of those ahead of us—shouting and screaming.

Suddenly, the rapids were upon us. The spray, foam, and the raw energy and churn of the water was breathtaking and frightening. Once in the throes of the rushing water, there was no stopping, no resting, and no taking a break. As our guide shouted, we pulled and paddled, trying to shape the raw kinetic energy upon us. It was pure chaos—stressful and exhilarating. There was nothing to do but to learn, on the fly, in the moment, how to navigate down the river. Thank God for a great guide.

As quickly as it started, the rushing water came to an end. We were through the rapids for the time being. Calm waters held us and our raft while we caught our breath. We drifted and shared our respective stories until the next set of rapids was upon us.

Conventional leadership—how it used to be anyway—involved time to prep, create a plan and execute it, and review. After a brief rest followed by short bursts of chaos, the process unfolded again. Those days are gone, just like the rapids on that hot July day. The new pace of change comes with higher demands. The time for rest and reflection is all but gone. What worked yesterday is not likely, in fact is highly unlikely, to work today. Living and leading in perpetual whitewater requires a different way of seeing the world, different qualities and perspectives and new navigational skills.

As we explore new leadership practices and skills to steer by, as your leadership path unfolds like the fast-flowing water, it'll be wise to remember—as teacher Jon Kabat-Zinn has said, "You can't stop the waves, but you can learn to surf." Some leaders become so distracted by the volatility and constant change that they become overwhelmed and react to events, like a guy in the raft just ahead of us who was overwhelmed by the rushing water and flipped out of the raft more than a few times.

Others become so cowed by the uncertainty and ambiguity, they become paralyzed for fear of making mistakes. Still others don't want to miss anything and want to do everything, so they lose their focus and energy. Their efforts are scattered to the wind.

When complexity is high and variable, the future will require greater clarity of vision and a sense of what's appropriate for that moment. As leaders begin to surf and read the complex shifts in the seascape of what's emerging, new practices and skills will be essential in order to move with agility and pivot as needed.[27] Learning to surf can transform the tensions of VUCA into the skillful leadership qualities of vision, understanding, clarity, and agility.

Those leaders who take up the challenge to pause will capably man the tiller and steer through the complexity and uncertainty to chart a way forward for their organizations.

The Leadership Pause

We're naturally drawn to leaders who embody Core Presence. They are authentic. They actively connect with others and lead from heartfelt values with sincerity and conviction. They're calm under intense pressure and accountable for their choices and actions.

They've committed to cultivating a deeper understanding of themselves as leaders and are open to facing the deep truths of who they are. They lead with care. These conscious leaders are cultivated. They aren't born that way.

As humans we can easily get snagged up in the details of unfolding drama. When you're freaking out, others will pick up on your freak-out energy and get pulled into your vortex like a magnet. And because energy is contagious, you'll spread it around and contribute to breakdowns, thus reinvigorating the vicious cycle of feeling overwhelmed. Your presence will be perceived as stressful.

Facing your own reactivity, turning into it, and grappling with the realities of the current situation can begin simply—with a pause. Taking a pause to breathe, to notice, and to feel the energy of the moment.

When we've begun to consistently practice pushing pause, it becomes easier to lean into whatever the situation at hand might be, without feeling pulled into it, and to drop the storyline that keeps our stresses high and our energies low.

With the rush and busyness of our times and constant distractions taxing our attention, to pause is essential. And it's as close as your next breath. In fact, as Buddhist nun Pema Chödrön—author of a classic, *Taking the Leap: Freeing Ourselves from Old Habits and Fears*—shares, "When we pause, allow a gap, and breathe deeply, we can experience instant refreshment. Suddenly we slow down, look out, and there's the world."[28]

Too often we even have a clue about what to do, yet we fail to pause and open space for ourselves to listen deeply and to respond to our own best instincts. It requires a willingness on our part to commit, be uncomfortable, and stretch beyond our current capacities.

William James, the father of modern psychology, reinforces the need for emerging leaders to commit to such training: "The faculty of voluntarily bringing back a wandering attention over and over again is the very root of judgment, character, and will ... An education which should improve this faculty would be the education par excellence."[29] For those who choose to play in a bigger game in this life, it's a fundamental aspect of the long game to train your attention.

Paul's Skillful Navigation

Paul is a hulk of a man—tall and wide, with a booming voice to match. At the time I first met him, Paul was the CEO of a small business, Prosort Services, that he had built up through sheer will and hard work. It all began in his garage (yes, really). He systematically built his business over the next twenty years and employed more than one hundred people. By all the usual standards, he's a successful guy.

Yet, Paul was frustrated and stuck. "Why don't they just listen to me?" he asked with exasperation about his leadership team. There was a real disconnect between Paul and his team that was taking a toll on everyone.

Paul couldn't understand. Why weren't his employees responding in the way he'd anticipated—by just following his direction? He'd been to Vietnam, where people had listened to him and even trusted him with their lives.

What could he be doing so wrong that people in Chicago, at his own company, resisted him?

In taking a closer look, it became more apparent why his employees weren't willing to simply follow Paul:

- He barked orders and didn't ask them for input. Of course, they hadn't been drafted to the front lines.

- He didn't stop to listen to their respective concerns. He believed he had all the answers.

- He didn't slow down to see if his requests were reasonable. They often weren't.

- He focused all his energies on them, their responses to him, and their work. He didn't have much of a life outside his 24/7 work pace.

- He didn't show them his heart—the reason he was in business in the first place.

It soon became clear that coaching Paul would be a bit longer engagement than expected. We had work to do.

First steps first—Paul was living with the outdated belief that leadership is about directing people to take action quickly and with minimal discussion. This model had given him excellent results in the military and when he first started his business. However, his team had contributions to make that didn't involve the intensity of combat. He needed to develop a new set of leadership skills.

As a leader, Paul felt torn between feeling grateful for the opportunity to grow his business and the tension that he experienced with his team. He'd come to doubt his leadership capacity. Though Paul staunchly believed in his product and his ability to make things happen, the push to develop himself personally as a leader, embrace cross-cultural diversity, and cultivate collaborative relationships with his leadership team proved to be an opportunity *and* a stretch.

We started with a pause. A small step, perhaps, yet critical for anyone truly wanting to make a difference. He agreed that, when he was in conversation with any member of his staff, he would pause before speaking.

He would pause to listen to what they were saying and clarify by asking questions. He'd pause and ask those in the group who had not shared their opinions what they were thinking. He'd pause to ask his team if they had a solution to the problem before directing them to act.

Paul shifted his leadership with the simple pause, and his influence grew. Trust sprouted like a new spring flower. His staff became more engaged, and the mood at the shop began to shift.

His increasing willingness to pause and his openness to "not knowing" what was best—and instead to listen and learn from his team members' experiences—cleared the way for more generative, innovative thinking.

Today, where will you begin to experiment with the power of a pause?

RECAP

- The trifecta of technology, busyness, and comfort reinforces a vicious cycle of feeling overwhelmed.

- Multitasking is a myth, and continuous partial attention creates constant crisis.

- Conscious leaders are mindful, embodied, and generative and must learn to navigate in perpetual whitewater.

- A key leadership skill in the attention economy is to train our attention. It begins with a pause.

- One's primary source of power reflects the *self of the leader*.

CHAPTER 2

Pause into the Moment: What Is Pause?

Tell me to what you pay attention
and I will tell you who you are.

—JOSE ORTEGA Y GASSET, SPANISH PHILOSOPHER,
AUTHOR OF *MAN AND CRISIS*, 1962

As a leader, you steward energy—in your company, organization, or even in your own family. You will inspire or demoralize others by how well you work with your own energies and by how well you focus, galvanize, invent—even renew—the collective energies of those you lead.

Amid the hustle and bustle of our globally connected, complex world, we're all challenged to be superheroes, superbosses, and superleaders.

We try to juggle so many responsibilities and opportunities that we're easily caught up in the activity at hand, losing sight of what's important at any given moment. Even if we *do* know what's important to us, our energies tend to spread out across our lives like bits of confetti floating in the wind. We're often unsure even how to collect ourselves.

The Sacrifice Syndrome

As a leader, you inevitably deal with the *power stress* that's created by a combination of high responsibility, constant self-monitoring, and addressing the myriad of crises that exist in day-to-day leadership. These can leave even the hardiest leader physically, mentally, and emotionally drained.

If you don't deal with this power stress, you may fall prey to what leading business consultant and best-selling author Annie McKee and her colleagues call "the grip of the Sacrifice Syndrome."[1] This vicious cycle of overmuch is fueled by being highly responsible, which can rouse passionate emotions involved in helping and serving—feelings such as concern, interest, resentment, and fear. All of that caring can result in mental, emotional, and physical fatigue. The sacrifices involved in putting others first (the team, the project, the community, etc.) without taking time for self-renewal will take a toll on you, depleting your energies. You find yourself trying to give more, while having less to give. The Sacrifice Syndrome is in full swing!

In addition to dips in self-confidence and momentary lapses in judgment as the strain wears on, the impact of this cycle can infect others too, resulting in energy drain and strained relationships. Dissonance, then, becomes the default reaction.

The antidote? Being fully engaged in a present-moment state that requires you to be physically fit, mentally focused, emotionally connected, and spiritually aligned with a purpose beyond the immediate interest at hand.

In other words, to cultivate the power of pause.

Learning to Pause

It's a funny thing how we learn the essentials in life.

My dad, Roger, taught me about the pause and about leadership as a result of two factors: his lifelong severe stuttering and his attempts to cope with it, and his courage to act on his convictions.

Dad—a lovable, rebellious farmer boy—didn't let the fact of his stutter stop him from being captain of his high school football team or president of his class. He was the life of most parties and a rambling storyteller who'd give you the shirt off his back if he thought it'd help you out.

When I was young, he quit his job as an electrician to break out on his own as an entrepreneur, founding Roger Johnson Construction Co. to build custom homes. By the time I was in high school, he'd become involved in local politics. This led to him winning the election for supervisor in our local township in central Illinois, a position he held for sixteen years.

He compensated for his speaking impediment in three ways: 1) working harder; 2) making 'em laugh; 3) drinking with the best of them. Alcohol loosened his tongue, endearing him to the locals. This resulted in dad being a hardworking, funny, and functional alcoholic.

Two memories stand out, though the activity of each occurred numerous times over the years.

Typically, late at night after not coming home for dinner, he'd show up inebriated and plant himself at the kitchen counter. There were two black Naugahyde stools there, and if by chance I'd walk in as he sat down, he'd begin to ramble on about how no one respected him.

Now this would be enough for a fluent sort, yet with his stutter—which did relax as he drank—it took forever to get his words out. On top of that, did I mention he was a storyteller? He'd become upset if you didn't sit through his entire story—at least twice. It was there that I learned a few things, not the least of which was to pause to listen.

You see, I believed him: he didn't think anyone respected him. He carried the shame of his impediment deep inside, compensating for it by transforming others' stares and whispers into a source of strength. Yet it took a toll on his own self-respect.

It didn't matter that his daughters respected him—actually adored him. What mattered was that he wanted to be fluent, to relate and connect. He dismissed the influence he did have on others, not fully owning his own power.

My enforced pause while sitting at that counter, listening despite not wanting to, taught me the power of listening deeply to the concerns of others—to their heart.

Years later when he sobered up, it was that heart that won him the local election, that heart that led for the next sixteen years as he maintained township road district highways and bridges, assessed real estate property values, administered a general assistance program to qualifying residents, and developed the community.

What Is It to Pause on Purpose?

To pause is to intentionally train your attention on purpose,
to direct it where you will.

The most fundamental skill for effectively leading one's life, not to mention a family or a business, is to learn to pause. In fact, psychologist and best-selling author Dan Goleman says, "Though it matters enormously for how we navigate life, attention in all its varieties represents a little-noticed and underrated mental asset."[2]

Simple? Yes. Easy, no.

Let's experiment for a moment. If you've ever tried this, you'll know exactly what I'm pointing to here. Even if you've played already, it's worth doing again. Go ahead and read the paragraph in the following box first and begin the practice.

● ● ●

BREATH PRACTICE

○ Pause a moment, closing your eyes. Tune in to your breath where it's most vibrant for you—at your nose, mouth, chest, or belly—picking it up and following it through a full cycle of inhalation and exhalation.

○ When you're ready, breathe in a nice, full breath and hold it at the top for a brief three-count, then allow a long, slow, and complete exhalation out through your nose.

○ Be fully present with your breath, allowing breathing to happen.

○ Sense your breath exiting your nose. Feel into your chest and notice your torso settling. At the end of your last exhalation, notice how you feel differently than before this practice.

○ What changed?

○ Repeat this practice three times.

○ Identify three words that describe how you feel different.

○ Now, close your eyes and repeat the process . . .

● ● ●

Directing attention itself changes and regulates the condition of our entire nervous system. Energy follows our attention.

What did the pause reveal to you? Were you able to stay with your in-the-moment experience or did you pop out too soon? Did you feel twitchy? Notice an urge toward action?

Whatever three words you chose to best reflect your experience with pausing just now, those you made a note of, didn't happen simply because you took a breath.

You take many thousands of breaths every day, on average something like sixteen breaths per minute, or 23,040 breaths per day.[3] Whatever shifted did so not because you took a breath, but rather because you directed your attention to the sensations of your breath, and—more generally—to the sensations that are *constantly present in your body*.

By experimenting with a breathing pause, you shifted your attention from *cognition* (like the reading and meaning-making you're doing in this very moment) to the *present-moment sensations* that arise in your body—a process called interoception. You could repeat the breath pause with your full attention and you'll likely notice similar, potentially amazing results.

Pause into Present-Moment Sensation

The insula, a brain region deep in our cerebral cortex, has a lot to do with your present-moment sensations.[4] It effectively maps your attention to your internal organs, sending signals to the heart and activating neurons in the cardiac circuitry that indicate how well people can sense their heartbeat. This noticing your heart beating has even become a standard way of measuring self-awareness.

Somatic marker is neuroscientist Antonio Damasio's term for sensations that tell us when a decision feels right or wrong.[5] This bottom-up biological circuitry telegraphs its conclusions through our gut feelings, typically long before top-down (cognitive) circuits come to a reasoned conclusion. The ventral prefrontal cortex (vpfc) is key to this circuitry and guides our decision-making when we face complex decisions—such as where to live, if or who to marry, what job will best suit us, or leadership choices in uncertain times.

If, however, you noticed your attention zooming elsewhere during the pause practice above, you won't be surprised to learn that such wandering is a common phenomenon. In fact, it's a typical human experience. Researchers tell us that it's the nature of our minds to wander . . . a lot, about 47% of the time; thus only about 53% of the time are our minds in the moment at hand.[6]

While it's true that we tend to put a high value on goal-driven attention over a wandering mind, research also suggests that a wandering mind—especially when you're wandering on purpose—serves to address issues that are on the back burner of our minds and not immediately of concern. A mind adrift can get your creative juices flowing. Remember back to a time when you were out on a walk—or putzing in your garage, or even showering—and you were hit with an amazing idea about how to work with your team, or an insight into your golf game, or an idea for a new product or service. That's the power of the wandering mind.

The good news? We could say that a wandering mind, on purpose, is a kind of choice to pause.

Goldfish

Currently, there's a popular notion that our human attention span has now dropped down to seven seconds. That's slightly less than that of a goldfish, which clocked in with an eight-second attention span.[7] Whether the goldfish comparison is true or not is less important than that it underscores the fickle fragility of our attention. "The true scarce commodity," says Microsoft CEO Satya Nadella, will be "human attention."[8] Easily distracted, we experience the *felt sense* of urgency that has become increasingly common and perhaps reflects our unintentional yet habituated avoidance of the present moment.

Mindfulness teacher Pema Chödrön speaks of it as "a deep-seated tendency, almost a compulsion, to distract ourselves, even when we're not consciously feeling uncomfortable. Everybody feels a little bit of itch all the time. There's a background hum of edginess, boredom, and restlessness." She further declares, "We have absolutely no tolerance for uncertainty."[9] I've personally found that to be true. Sitting in the kitchen on those late nights years ago, feeling out of sorts with my dad's ramblings, all I wanted was some semblance of certainty that all would be well despite my dad's suffering.

In this age of increasing complexity, directing attention toward where it's most effective is a primary task of leadership. Psychologist Dan Goleman offers three areas of attentional focus that are critical for leaders, who would be well served to be nimble with each.[10]

1. *Inner focus* involves attending to your perceptions—like those sensations you were just noticing, including your emotions and intuitions, your thoughts and underlying value—that inform your decision-making.

2. *Other focus* extends outward to your human-to-human interactions.

3. *Outer focus* attunes to the larger forces at play as you navigate the world. It is especially important as complexity increases.

Training our attention has never been more important. Leading well hinges on capturing and directing the collective attention of everyone involved and expanding that attention to the larger context. We know that where a leader's attention goes, others will follow, whether expressly stated or not. As Goleman says, "When leaders choose strategy, they're guiding attention."[11]

First, a leader must catch herself to intentionally direct her attention in the moment. Mindfulness is—as Jon Kabat-Zinn, a leader in the movement to bring more mindful awareness to life's situations, describes in his classic book *Full Catastrophe Living*—"paying attention, on purpose, in the present moment and non-judgmentally."[12] Mindfulness is a powerful force multiplier. The pause is an essential linchpin around which the flywheel of attention moves.

To lead in today's attention economy, with its constant barrage of information, will require you as a leader to hone your navigational skills in the waters of complexity. Of necessity, you'll move to direct others' attention toward the bigger picture of your endeavors.

What Exactly Is a Pause?

Life is a dash. Pause in the present. Enjoy this moment.

—J. R. RIM, AUTHOR

To pause is to interrupt an automatic and typically out-of-awareness behavior such as a thought, an action, or even an emotion—to open up the space to see what the present moment will hold.

But what truly constitutes a pause? Is it simply a momentary pause of breathing? Are there periods of taking a pause, like taking a gap year between high school and college? How long does a pause have to be in order to be official? And does it matter if it's official?

To pause is to choose to step back temporarily—to slow down and intentionally disengage with whatever's at hand. With a pause, we're no longer moving toward any goal but dropping into the unfolding moment at hand.

It's actually quite simple. So simple that it's easy to dismiss the importance of a pause. Yet in a pause is where we mindfully discontinue whatever we're doing—thinking, talking, planning, walking, worrying, eating, writing (as I'm doing now)—and become fully, wholeheartedly present, attentive, and aware of all around us: sounds, sights, smells, and our internal experiences. We're often physically still, though not always. It's when we pause that the world becomes alive right before us.

If the point of a pause is to more fully inhabit this moment—whatever the activity—then a pause could come in many sizes and forms, lasting for an instant, for hours, weeks, or even for seasons of our lives. For example, we may pause when we notice we're feeling agitated or tense, choosing to get curious about the feeling that's arising right then. Noting and naming our feelings, as neuroscientist Antonio Damasio says, allows us to weigh our choices to make effective decisions.

We may pause in conversation, letting go of what we were about to say in the meeting or at the dinner table, to genuinely listen and be fully present with another person.

We may pause when we're suddenly moved or delighted or saddened, allowing the feelings to play through our heart.

We may pause to reflect on a decision, considering the ethics of a choice.

We may pause to listen deeply to the movement of Spirit in our lives, that something bigger than we are enervates our neurons, jazzes us up, and moves us in the direction of our bigger selves.

We may pause to notice what's typically overlooked or not seen.

We may pause to notice the play of light in the trees one afternoon.

We may pause in the midst of a meditation to let go of thoughts and reawaken our attention to our breath.

We may pause before stepping into a work retreat, or before stepping out of daily life to attend a spiritual meeting, or before spending time in nature. We may take a longer pause, like a sabbatical from work for a few weeks or months.

PAUSE . . .

○ reflects and reveals our embodied way of being, more commonly known as our patterns and habits.

○ is essential to developing the qualities of leadership as a conscious leader.

○ allows us to tap into the natural rhythms of our life and to notice the subtleties.

○ is a portal to greater resonance with all of life.

○ requires us to slow down and be here, outside of the confines of time.

○ connects us to the divine breath, the Ultimate Inspiration.

Pause Has Many Faces

One afternoon when my dad was visiting and doing some construction work on my home, I noticed it in the sky and couldn't wait to share it.

It was a beautiful late-summer day. A smattering of showers had passed through a bit earlier. The double rainbow glimmered, looking like a foot-bridge across the expressway into another land. I ran to get my dad so he could see it too. While I was at it, I grabbed a nearby neighbor who was stepping out to get her mail.

As we each leaned on the rail at the edge of the roadway—staring in wonder at such natural, kaleidoscopic beauty—I felt joyful. As the rainbow faded, we each left with smiles plastered on our faces and a feeling of being a bit more connected to one another.

Of course, when we pause, we don't know what will happen next at all—like watching that rainbow. But by intentionally disrupting our habitual behaviors, we open ourselves to the possibility of new and creative ways of responding to our wants and fears. To pause is a generative, life-giving moment.

Pauses, by nature, are time limited. Yet when we resume activity—especially if our pause has been intentional—we'll be more present to the concerns at hand, with greater ability to make choices to extend the moment. By experimenting with pause in its various forms, you can play with the rhythms of your life, noticing how they take shape and texture your experience, attuning to your own sensations and not simply to external forces over which you have no influence.

Pauses clearly come in any number of sizes and shapes. There are **momentary pauses**—like the rainbow—that allow us to slow down to attune our inner sensations and our natural rhythms to those of the world around us.

Then there are **short**, **daily pauses** that you can knead into your day to create spaciousness for reflection. Think of reflection time, prayer time, quiet time, get-in-the-flow time—otherwise known as daily practice—or a **micropause**. Or your daily pause may include a walk around the shop floor—as it does for Jean Pitzo, CEO of ACE Metal Craft—during which she touches base with, and generally greets, her employees each day.

Weekly pauses can allow us to refresh and renew, like when I'm out in my garden on Saturday mornings futzing around. I'm in heaven. I experience a sense of renewal by being outside and engaged in the dirty details of cultivating life. One client treks to his weekly golf game early on Friday mornings, while another enjoys casting his fly over the water at his favorite flyfishing spot. At work, a pause may be like my weekly Sunday afternoon pause, during which I spend thirty minutes reflecting on last week and planning for the week ahead.

Last, there are **planned pauses**: monthly, quarterly, even yearly pauses that provide spaciousness to be off the grid, attuning oneself to life's natural rhythm and flow. We might think that vacations are in this camp, and they may be, though it depends upon the intention. This past year, a good friend who is a senior sales executive at a tech company joined us for a ski vacation. "This is the pause I've been looking for," he exclaimed as he expressed relief at being both off the grid *and* with people he cares about to recharge and renew.

Consider billionaire co-founder of Microsoft and philanthropist Bill Gates. For many years, he has escaped alone twice each year to a secret cabin in a cedar forest in the Pacific Northwest for what he calls Think Week. Off the grid, he reads, reflects, and ponders what he cares most deeply about. Innovations on the future of technology and global health have been just a few of his results.

To mindfully pause is to interrupt your automatic reactions to life's events and the stories that flow from those reactions. Pausing allows your mind to take a break so you can be with life as it is versus how you'd like life to be. Pausing is also part of a larger cycle of work and renewal—a rhythmic flow of life. Pausing is not merely a good idea. It's a required nutrient like air or water or food.

Benefits of Pausing

The benefits of practicing a mindful pause span key areas of our lives: our overall health and wellness, our cognitive thinking and analytic capacities, our social and emotional intelligence, and our ability to bring the benefits to work in service of leading well.[13]

HEALTH AND WELLNESS

- ⬆ Resilience
- ⬆ Immunity
- ⬇ Reduced Stress and Emotional Reactivity
- ⬇ Reduction in Chronic Illness

THINKING AND COGNITION

- ⬆ Awareness
- ⬆ Focus
- ⬆ Mental Flexibility and Agility
- ⬆ Working Memory

SOCIAL AND EMOTIONAL INTELLIGENCE

- ⬆ Self-Awareness
- ⬆ Self-Regulation
- ⬆ Empathy and Compassion
- ⬆ Perspective-Taking

LEADERSHIP

- ⬆ Critical and Divergent Thinking
- ⬆ Listening and Holding Space
- ⬆ Agility and Decision-Making
- ⬆ Engagement and Collaboration

Why Don't We Pause, Anyway?

We don't take time to pause because of its weighty baggage. Take a look at the definitions below from Merriam Webster:

Pause (poz)

- a temporary stop, delay, wait, or rest, especially in speech or action
- a cessation of activity because of doubt, or to cause to hesitate or be unsure as if from surprise or doubt
- to make a brief stop or delay; wait; hesitate; rest; linger or tarry

As you can see, pause tends to be associated with uncertainty, doubt, and hesitation. Not exactly what you want more of as a leader. It's as though our very use of the word, and how we've come to think about it, might be getting in the way of committing to the simple practice of pausing.

Plus, let's face it, we're mostly in the habit of blasting through our days and not pausing to inhabit our moments. The opposite of pausing is:

- getting caught up in being a "human doing," as if being busy is a badge of honor;
- overthinking, which takes us out of the moment and thrusts us into our heads;
- checking activities off a list and not being fully present;
- relating to the world as if it is full of things and objects (e.g., my kids, my work, or chores versus relating to the world in the present moment as it unfolds); and
- constantly either avoiding or rushing around.

To pause, in whatever form, is to accept the powerful invitation to step out of our automaticity. It is essential for leaders. Take my client Nick, who said, "At first, a 'mindful pause' sounded to me like a squishy, overused synonym for group hugs and undisciplined leadership. I couldn't have been more wrong. I'm very thankful that I was open-minded enough to listen, read, and learn the science that's foundational to the pause. It's made a huge difference in my ability to be present."

Taking up the challenge to commit to practicing pausing on purpose creates the conditions for learning *and* for leading.

• • •

PAUSING AND ATTENDING

Before you begin this practice, read the script that's here. Then set a timer for three minutes.

- Sit, back straight, shoulders relaxed.

- Close your eyes.

- Attune your attention to your breath, wherever it's most vibrant and full: at your nose, your chest, or deep in your belly.

- See if you can keep your attention initially focused on your breathing cycle for three minutes.

- You're simply observing the experience of your own breathing and then coming back to your breath with your attention each time it wanders (it will, trust me on this front).

- When your alarm goes off, continue to sit for a few moments and reflect on what occurred. Curiosity is your friend.

continued

What was your body's response? Were your shoulders up and high? How's your jaw—tight or relaxed? What other body sensations did you notice?

Where did your mind go? To all the to-do decisions of the day? To your next project? To a family concern? Blank?

Did you notice emotions surfacing? Anxiety about that last-minute order or project due? Irritability with a colleague or spouse? Excitement at a new opportunity? Unsure?

Simply observe what occurred without self-judgment about whatever came up for you.

You're developing a new muscle—the muscle of attention. Jot down some of your experiences in the space below.

• • •

Pausing into Story

Our lives are composed of experiences that we string together to form a coherent narrative or story. We all have stories that encapsulate our sense of identity and our place in the world.

In fact, we cannot *not* tell stories. The trick, however, is to know when we're in a story and to be able to "see" it as just that—a story. Not me, myself, or I, but the narrative that keeps me hanging together.

Our stories are embodied in us—often, or even usually, invisible to us—and they reveal our core values, beliefs, and the actions we're capable of taking. Depending upon how aware we are of our stories and how attached we are to them, we either suffer or find great freedom. If we're aware of the story that's holding in place our identity as a leader, we say that we're conscious of it. Yet, it's more often true that the stories we live in, live us instead. Even our leadership stories.

Here's what I mean. For example . . . let's go back to Paul, that booming leader who didn't think his team was listening to him. Paul's story about his own leadership was largely shaped by his time leading troops in Vietnam as a young man. His gruff, barking manner worked there. It moved his men to move into action. Dodging active combat fire generated a deep bond of care between them. Back home on the mainland, however, barking orders at his current employees—well, that didn't work so well. It didn't show his employees "care" at all. Quite the opposite, they were afraid of him.

The emotional underpinnings of life and death that he'd experienced in Vietnam were driving his current meaning-making and his decisions about "working with people." Those strategies were running his primary internal operating system. And all without his conscious awareness—his behavior was totally invisible to him. If you'd asked him, and I did, he'd have told you that he cared deeply about his employees, articulating in great detail what he valued about each of them. Yet, no one else could see his prosocial feelings because his behaviors were running on the story of his old operating program.

• • •

Pausing interrupts our automatic patterns of thinking—those that drive our behavior and reinforce our old operating system.

Though we like to think that we're in charge of our own minds, that's not accurate by a long shot. It's more accurate to say that our minds run us, quite literally.

The thoughts that we think over and over take up prime real estate in our daily lives and eventually become who we are.

Our stories—perceptions, sensations, and emotions—manifest as survival strategies that run us unless we: 1) learn the skills to identify and attend to them, 2) acknowledge that we're experiencing what we're *actually experiencing* despite what we think we *should* be experiencing, 3) own our stories as part and parcel of what it means to be human, and make decisions based on our best judgments at the time. Only then will we be able to reflect, analyze and evaluate, and determine if our stories are still serving us and the greater good. And if so, great. If not, we can learn to ask, "What new story would be of better service?" and then go about creating it.

Our Different Selves

Our *experiencing self*—otherwise known as our default mode network—operates automatically, attuning to our sensations.[14] It's superfast, intuitive, out of our awareness, and imperceptible to us. Our experiencing self is efficient and autonomous. It requires little energy because it's focused on the moment, though admittedly highly prone to biases and error.

Meanwhile, our *narrative self* creates stories to make sense of what we've experienced after the fact. This story typically confirms our point of view, our story, and our identity. The experiencing self needs the partnership of the narrative self to more carefully, slowly, and with effort make good choices, because the experiencing self is often incorrect and can cause lots of mischief.

Generally speaking, since we typically make decisions and choose actions based on what we already believe we know, we tend to not spend too much time thinking about alternatives.[15] Instead, we assert what we already think we know.

For example, when you meet someone, it takes mere seconds to have a fully formed opinion of them, their attitudes (Is he kind or aggressive? Is she approachable or distant?), and to garner a sense of whether you'll get along with them or not. With lightning speed, your brain operates with limited data points.

Once we have an impression formed, one based on our experiencing self's history, our narrative self gets busy weaving and integrating our impressions and our recollections into a coherent story that makes sense of what we call self—our identity, values, and needs. Our narrative self deposits the story, with all our working strategies to support that story, into the context of our relationships, our work, our life. And we'll act as if the narrative is so and believe it. It doesn't have to be accurate, complete, reliable, or true. It's enough that it hangs together, seems right, and allows us to deal with the world around us. We feel confident and competent.

Relevance for Leaders

Paul saw himself as a strong leader—involved, taking charge, and making all decisions on his own. As a result, he believed his people would know he cared about them. These were elements in his story of what it meant for him to lead. When he focused narrowly on incoming information (they didn't listen) and analyzed the day's situation all evening in his home office, he confirmed the accuracy of his belief. The disconnect came when his conclusion didn't reflect what was actually going on out on the shop floor.

Not only are *our* stories often inaccurate, limited by our own perspective, but our vision of the entire picture or whole can be eclipsed. Our perspective, experiences, and memories are often biased, despite *what we think we know*.

For Paul to drop his storyline, to push pause into the moment on the shop floor, and to be able to see what was there all along, was itself an act of courage. A radical act. A vulnerable act. A leadership move.

• • •

PUSH PAUSE PRACTICE

1. **Pause**—Take a time-out to recognize your situation and steal a temporary break from your thoughts and feelings, especially stressful ones.

2. **Take a deep breath through your heart and down into your center**—Shift your focus first to your heart and then down to your center just below your belly button, and feel into your physical sensations.

3. **Invoke your intention for the moment and remember a positive experience with your intention**—Make a sincere effort to activate a positive experience and feeling.

4. **Ask yourself, "What would be a better alternative right now?"** Ask yourself what would be an efficient, effective attitude or action that would de-stress your system. Listen to the answer.

5. **Pause again to note any changes in your experiences or perspective**—Quietly sense any changes in your body, thoughts, or feelings, and sustain your attention there as long as you can.

• • •

Donna's Pause

Bright, direct, and engaging are words I'd use to describe Donna. She was in the midst of incredible personal changes in her life that were amping up her stress levels. She couldn't figure out how to do life any differently, and she felt unmoored. So she did what she knew how to do—she worked even harder.

As a result—like many professional women—she went overboard and was at the edge of burning out. She needed an effective, immediate challenge to her way of working with herself.

To help Donna deal with her experience of crushing stress in her life, I taught her a standing pause practice. While pausing may sound easy, when you're hardworking and engaged, with even a smidgen of competitive spirit thrown in, well . . . let's just say that getting Donna to pause and notice what was actually going on in the moment was like stopping a freight train!

That said, by standing—and noticing she was standing—Donna learned that she could feel the weight of gravity in her feet, connecting her with the solid ground beneath. Standing tall on an in breath, feeling into her verte-brae, she could sense the power and dignity of connecting with what she cared about.

To her credit, Donna accepted my challenge. She committed to incorpo-rating several standing pause practices into her day, three times each day for 60–90 seconds—feeling her feet and noticing anything else that came up. This practice wasn't easy for Donna.

In time, however, she began to see patterns in her interactions, notic-ing how she'd react in particular situations. She didn't like everything she saw. Donna began to slow her pace down and listen to the person directly in front of her, instead of getting caught up in *their* past behavior or *her* automatic opinions of them. This practice produced greater personal satis-faction, despite how difficult it was for Donna when they didn't simply "get to the point."

Together with 360-degree feedback, Donna came to the realization that "my listening, well, it's a huge issue. I don't listen well. I tend to come to solu-tions and don't allow people to finish their thoughts or sentences. I have high expectations and strong opinions on how to do things, and I believe that my way is probably the correct way. Yet this tendency of mine is getting in the way of my leadership. I don't allow others to try and even fail. If I did, then they'd have to figure things out, which in turn would make me a better delegator. And, in terms of developing people, the way I can improve is to allow them to work their way. It seems like I'm in a vicious circle." Indeed, she was.

By practicing grounding herself, literally, and then responding via the pause, Donna was able to receive new information. She decided to take more space to become a better listener. She learned to connect with her team members in a more personal, authentic, and effective way.

As she experimented with a variety of pause practices, Donna was able to shift from *reacting* to *responding* to other people. Her team members began to find her more approachable and engaging. At the end of our work, she reported a decrease in her stress and greater satisfaction in her work.

Pause for Time and Space

With a pause, our world slows its frenetic, often invisible, movement. We can breathe unencumbered. If we look around us, we'll see no story of expectation or demand. It's spacious. Jon Kabat-Zinn, the founder of mindfulness-based stress reduction (MBSR), talks about this state as "stepping out of time." According to Kabat-Zinn, time "is measured as the space between our thoughts and the never-ending stream of them . . . Since the present is always here now, it is already outside of time passing."[16]

Eminent futurist Ray Kurzweil speaks of this notion of time in his classic book *The Age of Spiritual Machines* as the Law of Time and Chaos. Kurzweil writes that our subjective sense of time passing is regulated by the interval between what we feel to be "milestones," or notable experiences, and the existing "degree of chaos."[17]

When you go on vacation (milestone event), likely having not been at that location previously (an increase in chaos since it's all new and novel), time seems to move more slowly. When you're back home (familiar territory) and return to work, however (less chaos because you know your routine), time moves more quickly. Enough of these routine days in succession and you'll have the sense that your days are disappearing, years flying by like vapor.

Of course, babies and small children have scads of milestones in their development. Because the intervals between them are short, our childhood time seems to move slowly, often recalled with a dreamlike quality. As we get older, the intervals between our significant events lengthen and result in our sense of time moving quite quickly.

Short of actually creating a steady stream of novel, noteworthy experiences—whitewater rafting down the Colorado River, skydiving in New Zealand, or even dining at Zagat's highly acclaimed Zia's Trattoria in Chicago—you could simply choose to pay attention to your ordinary moments, making them all quite noteworthy.

By paying attention in such a way, even to the apparent chaos at work, you'll begin to notice the timeless quality of the present moment.

You'll likely not only begin to destress but also to notice the vividness of your life: the play of light through the morning window, the autumn colors, the quality of your child's voice, and the pungent scent of your coffee.

You may be thinking, *How pollyannaish! What about all the deadlines, decisions, and distasteful coworkers that I have to deal with?* You can even bring a sense of wonder to those difficult events, much like a small child would. In doing so, you'll likely notice a richness to your ordinary moments, and time will begin to slow.

Okay, well what about those moments when we're pressed for time and feeling the urgency of the moment clicking away? If you pause to bring yourself fully present, you'll notice a net gain of time because you'll experience the fullness of each moment—even if it's unpleasant or challenging. In truth, our stories often get in the way of what's actually occurring or what needs to be completed.

The more you practice making some bits of time in your day to *not do*, the more your whole day can become *nondoing*—simply noticing what the moment holds for you. That is, it's suffused with an awareness grounded in the present moment and therefore outside of time.

Do it, I dare you. Pay attention to your ordinary moments, even the seemingly unpleasant ones. Go a day without your watch or iPhone and focus your attention on the ordinary in each day, each hour, and each moment.

• • •

PAUSE PRACTICE: BELLY BREATHS

○ As you go through your day today, simply stop, drop your attention to your breath at your belly, and take three deep breaths.

○ You have no other agenda other than to pause.

○ Look up and out at your surroundings. What do you notice? What's the quality of connection you notice with yourself? With others?

○ Do this practice three times throughout the day and reflect on this practice as you complete your day. Answer the question—*What did I learn?*

• • •

SCOPE Signposts

The Leadership Pause invites you to choose to commit to a deliberate practice of pausing to direct your attention—plain and simple. Pausing supports self-awareness, which is *the* key component of emotional intelligence and powerful, conscious leadership.

It can be useful to identify signposts to follow when we're learning something new, especially when it's something we think we already know—like breathing or pausing.

Reflecting on what it means to pause, SCOPE emerged as an apt acronym to serve as a guide as you continue reading and exploring.

You're likely accustomed to thinking in terms of a scope of work or the scope of the proposal or project. Scope—originating from the Greek term *skopein*—means to observe, examine, or aim at. It's related to a second Greek work, *skeptesthai*, which means *to watch,* or *to look at.*[18] SCOPE here is composed of various components of pause that, when you check in with yourself, will aid you in exploring how pausing can support you in your leadership.

It's essential that leaders cultivate the ability to self-observe and accept the reality at hand. From there it's possible to self-correct to keep what's important to you center stage. Using SCOPE questions as a guide, you'll be able to self-generate the energy and mood you need to grow your leadership presence.

SCOPE includes five components of pause—Space, Connection, Openness, Pace, and Energy—all interwoven like a braid. In each chapter, you'll see questions related to each of these SCOPE components. They're designed to support deepening your relationship and practice of *The Leadership Pause*.

Space

Have you ever longed for more space in your day so you didn't feel rushed, or put-upon, or crowded? If so, you're tuning in to the necessity we have for space.

As a senior vice president of client services at a professional services firm, Amy struggled with space. She regularly booked her calendar back-to-back-to-back, not allowing adequate "passing time" from one meeting to another. Meetings were jam-packed, last-minute cancellations frequent, and tensions often ran high. When she experienced a lack of space, she found it harder to navigate meetings or to notice what was unfolding in a conversation. Amy often felt rushed and cramped.

Three key practices supported Amy's ability to use the pause to shift her energy, mood, and overall day. Practicing an "on-the-spot pause" focused her attention on her breath, allowing it to settle her central nervous system and her busy mind. Within 20–60 seconds, her cortisol levels would drop and she'd become more fully present to herself and others.

Amy is also a distance runner, so she has incorporated pausing into her daily run—tuning in to her body's sensations, as well as the sound of her footfalls and the beautiful environment around her. Running has always nourished her, yet adding a pause to the process has deepened her sense of renewal.

Later, calendaring bits of time for "space and time for myself" allowed her to slow down and find her natural energetic rhythm. Over time, she reported a greater sense of spaciousness and an increased awareness of what was the most important task or project to attend to. By creating more space, she not only improved her productivity, but the tension in meetings subsided and more creative time for projects opened up.

Connection

Pragmatic, focused on outcomes, and perhaps detailed to a fault, Nick is wicked smart and funny. A former military officer who spent five years on a navy submarine, he attended business school and worked as a consultant for a large management consulting firm before taking a position at a national, purpose-driven nonprofit.

I met Nick when it was strongly suggested that he take advantage of executive coaching to address blind spots in his leadership. He was all about the business and came off as verbose, arrogant, and detached from his colleagues. His perfectionistic tendencies were reinforced when others didn't quickly come to his conclusions. He thought they were "imbeciles" and "not very smart."

After a 360-degree assessment that highlighted some of these challenges, I taught Nick a basic centering practice that is a particular orientation to the pause. Centering involves aligning one's head and heart to be congruent in action. He was so "up in his head" that he didn't know what he was sensing or feeling—not to mention being clueless to what others on his team might have been experiencing.

But Nick needed to feel himself—his sensations and his emotions—because only then could he tap into his softer heart, the one that had him working at the purpose-driven nonprofit in the first place.

He also took on another pause practice, "catching himself" getting triggered and caught up in believing that his view was *the* accurate truth. Nick was a keen student, so catching himself helped him develop a sense of curiosity about his teammates. He learned to check his assumptions, to listen more effectively by actively inviting questions, and—in time—he began to connect with his teammates. Others started to feel his interest and began to feel more connected to him too. Work projects began to flow more easily.

Openness

Urgent, laser-focused, and competitive, Paul had used his driving energy to build his company. His strategy was great for getting the job done. But now, he was spewing negative energy all over the place. His controlling, micromanaging behaviors came with limited openness to others' ideas.

My first step with Paul involved simply listening deeply to his concerns. He was frustrated at the train wreck that was his life. Since he worked around the clock, he was typically tense and allowed himself little time for rest and renewal. Though he agreed it would be a great idea to feel more energized, he wasn't initially open to new actions. His basic self-care habits were evident in his poor diet and sleep routine. They only reinforced his attempts to control his environment versus controlling himself.

Then I taught Paul to pause by dropping his attention to his feet, which focused his energy down, cleared his mental cobwebs, and reduced his tension almost immediately. Being more alert then created space for him to open his thinking and consider trying some new behaviors.

From there, I challenged him to actively create open space in his calendar. Could he choose to leave the office at five p.m. instead of seven thirty p.m.? Could he allow for an evening off to *do* nothing? I soon learned that he loved Southwestern art, which filled his office and home. He also loved motorcycles—building and rebuilding them, and riding cross-country. Creating more open space to engage these interests began to replenish his energy.

In the time we worked together, Paul chose to create more open space for his own renewal, reversing his vicious overwork cycle into a vibrant, positive cycle of good energy. He dropped weight and committed to a "normal" day's work.

Pace

Darek—a general manager at a global environmental company—was mentally quick, likeable, and action-oriented. Yet he moved and spoke so quickly and his orientation was so "next, next, next," that he could only observe what would move things along with greater speed. Others felt rushed and pushed around. His pace kept him from being an optimal performer.

In our coaching, Darek focused on working with his pace, slowing to pause, feeling his feet on the ground (yes, really), and noting the support of gravity.

Darek needed to slow down to "see" what was going on around him versus simply reacting to each moment as if everything were a crisis (some were, some were not).

We began with a simple pause practice—catching himself when he became defensive and noticing his triggered reactions.

Over time, catching himself became a bit of a game, and he was able to ask himself, *What pace is required in this situation?* As a result of his pause practices, Darek did, in fact, learn to slow down and listen to his direct reports and to his own best intuition. He became more present to others in conversations and was able to delegate more effectively. He had found his leadership rhythm.

Energy

Bright with energy, Debra's creative tendencies lead some to see her as eccentric, jumping from one thing to another, wild with ideas. As a former actor turned facilitator and leadership coach, she works with organizations teaching processes that allow them to flourish and grow their businesses. She thinks big, is open, and acts quickly—a natural entrepreneur.

In conflict situations, her tendency is to see both sides and harmonize them. Her highly creative approach to problem-solving allows her to see options others often miss. And, though others sometimes view her as disorganized in her thinking and actions, she is engaging and funny. Working with Debra is transformational.

The impetus for our work together was the significant loss of her father; they'd always been close. Debra was having a stellar year in her business, though at quite the cost. The loss served to slow her down, yet slowing down is hard for her. Her typical MO is overdoing and overextending herself to serve and support others. Yet now, more than ever, she needed support herself, as she was back-to-back with client work that took a toll on her energy. In fact, her energy deficit was not only slowing her down but was also getting in the way of processing her grief. It was even scaring her a bit.

Our initial work involved Debra zeroing in on her physical sensations. When she did, she noted how fatigued she felt. She also became aware of how she continued to overfill her calendar, in effect reinforcing her tendency to push herself and deplete her energy stores instead of allowing her natural rhythms to energize and inform her.

This awareness in hand, she made structural changes to her calendar and to a morning routine, which was centered around working with her energy. In turn, she began to allow herself to feel her loss more deeply and to reengage herself around questions of identity and purpose.

Components of "Pause"	No-Pause Observable Behaviors	New Pause Actions
Space	• Fill up time completely • Leave no time for "new" or a flexible shift to occur • Back-to-back meetings • Last-minute cancellations • Try to fit too many actions into a small space	• Create small bits of time to "do nothing" • Practice mindful breathing one time per hour • Develop a practice listening to music while doing nothing else • Become comfortable with "having time"
Connection	• Detached and distant • Overly focused • A sense that life is happening "out there" • Can feel safe, though also lonely	• Complete tasks and acknowledge that to yourself • Spend quiet moments with yourself • Become curious about specific moments of each day—e.g., other people, nature
Openness	• Controlled, predictable, reliable • Closed, rigid, tight • Overly open, yet has difficulty with follow-through • Uncomfortable with receiving from others	• Explore the unknown on purpose • Gently acknowledge accomplishments • Ask for support • Receive acts of support from others (massage, dinner, etc.)
Pace	• Move and speak fast • Next, next, next orientation—rushing • Only observe what will help move things along more quickly • Check watch frequently	• Slow down speed • Play with various speeds—e.g., operate at 25%, 50%, or 150% of regular speed to get to know and choose • Ask what pace is required in this situation?

Energy	• Overdo it, overextend toward others	• Zero in on sensations of energy in the body
	• Difficulty sitting still or sluggish and sedentary	• Note times when most energized and feeling alive
	• Too focused, or the opposite, too flighty with ideas	• Notice both external and internal events and the impact on energy
	• Inattentive, focus is outward	• Focus on internal experience
		• Focus on values

• • •

CALENDAR YOUR PAUSE PRACTICE

One simple way to get started is to formally calendar a time to pause. Yep, put it in your calendar. This may seem silly—frivolous, even—but it works. It works because you're in the process of fine-tuning a skill, one your body already knows how to do.

If you take the time to book an appointment with yourself, in your calendar, you're recommitting each day to pausing. You're not scheduling over it because you're too busy. Instead, you're intentionally shifting gears from deathly exhausting habits to life-giving practices.

And, if you're ready to be bold, schedule a second time to pause in your day.

Or schedule thirty minutes instead of fifteen. This will allow for more transition time to arrive in the moment, to feel the spaciousness, and to step into the next moment with a flexible mindset.

• • •

RECAP

- Power stress is costly for leaders

- Energy follows attention

- To pause is to step out of automatic reactions

- Pause has many faces:

  · Momentary
  · Micro
  · Daily
  · Weekly
  · Extended

- Pause is composed of the five elements of SCOPE:

  · Space
  · Connection
  · Openness
  · Pace
  · Energy

CHAPTER 3

Catch Yourself Being Yourself: Pressure

To be good at stress is not to avoid stress, but to
play an active role in how stress transforms you.

—KELLY MCGONIGAL, HEALTH PSYCHOLOGIST AT STANFORD
UNIVERSITY, AUTHOR OF *THE UPSIDE OF STRESS*

S pending more money than we earn isn't sustainable over time—we all
know that. Yet that's exactly what many of us do day in and day out
when it comes to our life energies, especially when we're under pressure.

We're on deadlines. We experience urgency. We get caught up in a whirl
of life that's all about productivity and performance. This pace can seem so
ordinary that we don't tend to notice when we're depleted, because in that
state our reasoning and rationale seem sane.

Yet such constant go-go-go isn't sustainable. No way, no how.

Take Paul. You might remember that when I met him, Paul hadn't yet
learned to pause. He believed it was essential to work sixteen-hour days with
his cell phone attached to his body, to bark at his staff, and to skimp on
essential self-care habits like getting enough sleep, eating a healthy diet, and
getting some moderate exercise.

He lived his life as if all that mattered was getting the work out.

His workload was unsustainable for any human for any length of time. Though stress typically causes people to overengage with work—fearful that they may not be performing well—tipping across the line into burnout results in disengagement and feelings of despair.

Paul had slid down the slippery slope into burnout, a state resulting from chronically high and unsuccessfully managed stress.[1] He felt disconnected from his employees, despite his firm belief that he was building a strong community culture at work. He felt out of control, working 70–80 hours per week. There was no room in his life for rest and renewal, nor for any pleasant moments, places, or people.

Instead, he was exhausted, overweight, and grumpy. The messy moods of cynicism (everyone's out for himself) and pessimism (the worst will happen, there's no hope) had taken root. When those two moods show up, they reinforce worn-out, embodied patterns of behavior in a never-ending cycle of ineffectiveness and self-judgment.

Cynicism and pessimism have become so much a part of our collective narrative that we can easily get caught up in focusing on all that's wrong with our jobs, other people, or the national political and economic landscape—all while feeling utterly hopeless to shift it. Then it's a short distance to slipping into self-doubt and blame, with negative assessments shaking self-confidence. Additionally, we're not at all sure others are trustworthy—the negativity blinding us to possibilities for something different.

To be clear, none of these strained, conditioned ruts occurred overnight. Such is the slow impact of burnout that saps our energy in bits and drabs. Burnout occurs as a result of not regularly pausing to reexamine what's important, revising commitments, and renewing our energies.

Like Paul, you may find yourself on an all-consuming, energy-draining treadmill leading to nowhere. You may be feeling dull and exhausted, wound up tight and anxious, or numbed out and flat.

And like Paul, who learned the importance of pausing and listening in a new way, you too can learn what it takes to switch from living with too much pressure to moving into powerful, decisive action. One early step for Paul involved observing himself in action, followed by completing an inventory of his life habits and practices.

• • •

YOUR TURN: CHOOSE TO PAUSE

Choose to pause, maybe for a morning or afternoon or weekend, and reflect on the following questions. They'll help you get started in taking an honest look at your current habits. Are they serving you? Exhausting you?

○ When was the last time you took an afternoon to yourself?

○ Are you getting at least seven hours of sleep, five days a week?

○ Once at home, what automatic habits kick in? Dinner with family? Glued to electronics? Spending time with friends?

○ Are you getting any exercise each week?

○ What's the last fun event you participated in? How did it impact your mood and energy?

• • •

Leaders and Today's Complexities

To lead in today's stress-filled VUCA environment—a world of increasing volatility, uncertainty, complexity, and ambiguity—requires agility, skill, and a willingness to "not know" and not be attached to set outcomes.

It will require, as it did with Paul, facing and letting go of a few tired, worn-out adages first:

1. Performing and producing are the ultimate endgame.

2. Leaders alone must have all the answers.

3. Emotions should be kept out of decision-making—period.

4. Productive work is defined by time and hours in the office.

Being willing to hold such beliefs lightly will enable you to shift gears more quickly and efficiently in response to changing circumstances. Paradoxically, only when you're able to pause to see and settle into the moment is when you'll begin to accept that the current situation's reality is inherently unpredictable and uncontrollable. Only then can you begin to relax even in the midst of high pressure and stress. Michael—the chief human resources officer for a large foundation—discovered the value of holding these beliefs lightly after the foundation implemented a mindfulness program in a culture that was back-to-back-to-back with meetings (maybe like yours?), with no one ever fully present to any one of them. "By learning to start each meeting with a pause, the proverbial reset, we gained the biggest benefit right out of the gate—pausing, breathing, and focusing. We start every single one of our meetings like this now so everybody arrives fully to the meeting. It's contagious!"

Stress Is Bad, Isn't It?

> If you are perpetually in a pinch, you are not your best self;
> you neither feel good nor perform well.
>
> —ROBERT POYNTON, AUTHOR OF *DO/PAUSE* AND IMPROV TEACHER

An erroneous inherited belief that we all share has had an enormous impact on how we work with pressure and stress. You'll probably never guess it because it's pervasive and ubiquitous in our everyday sense-making of life.

Stress is bad.

Note how your mind might be racing rapidly just now to defend this "truth," tapping your own life and leadership experiences for confirmation. *Stress is bad, and you know it!* You wouldn't be alone, nor could you be blamed if this were your initial reaction.

The stage for viewing stress as bad was set back in the mid-1930s when Hungarian doctor Hans Selye had an insight while in his lab.[2] He'd been injecting lab rats with hormones from cow ovaries to identify what happened to them as a result. Whatever he concocted and injected into them sickened the rats, who all exhibited a variety of physical symptoms and became ill. In the end, they all died.

The great insight, the big aha?

Maybe the rats weren't becoming ill due to any of Selye's concoctions but were becoming ill as a result of what they were experiencing. So, he shifted up the experiment and began to subject the next cohort of rats to extremes of heat and cold, forcing them to exercise and then denying them rest, and nearly drowning them. Those actions resulting in heightened physiological reactions: their immune systems became compromised, and all attempts to fight or to get away stopped.

The results? The same. Within a few days their immune systems shut down entirely, and they died.

His rats were not exposed to regular, day-to-day stress but to the worst possible kind of stress: unpredictable, uncontrollable, and devoid of meaning.

Selye coined the term *stress* to describe what he was doing to the rats and how their bodies reacted. As a doctor, he reasoned that his "stressing out the rats" was akin to the accumulated wear and tear of life's events on human beings—not unlike some of his former patients who suffered from illnesses like severe allergies, heart disease, and cancer. He surmised that after the initial shock, resistance followed, then exhaustion, and finally death. It was only a short distance from there to claim that "stress is the response of the body to any demand made upon it."

This broad definition set the stage for the predominant view of pressure and stress today—*stress is any situation that requires action or adaptation, period.* This included not only severe or traumatic events but nearly everything in daily life. In this way, we've come to know stress as synonymous with simply living our lives.

Dr. Selye later toured the world, receiving funding for a newly developing area of stress research, and—even later—he was awarded the Nobel Prize for his work. He became known as the Grandfather of Stress. Over time, he expanded his broad definition of stress to distinguish between good stress (eustress) and bad stress (distress). But the proverbial stage had been set, with the lights turned up on the unfolding play of stress experiences. The name of the stage play? *Stress Is Bad.*

Psychological Stress Survey

The stress saga seems to be confirmed by research supported by the American Psychological Association's (APA) findings from its Stress in America survey.[3] Since 2007, until the most recent reports in 2019 and 2020, each year has shown that money and work were the top two sources of significant stress—67% and 65%, respectively. These were followed by family responsibilities (54%), personal health concerns (51%), health problems affecting the family (50%), and the economy (50%).

More specifically, 75% of adults reported experiencing moderate to high levels of stress within the past month; 53% reported trouble sleeping, resulting in ongoing fatigue; and more than 60% reported struggle with irritability, anger, and decreased levels of energy and motivation.

The APA's 2020 survey was different, given the devastating impact of the global pandemic. Considering the traumatic physical and emotional toll of increased stress, nearly half of adults (49%) reported negative behaviors: increased tension in their bodies (21%); "snapping," or getting angry very quickly—what I call getting triggered (20%); unexpected mood swings (20%); and lots of screaming and yelling at loved ones (17%).

The majority of adults in 2020 cited healthcare (66%), mass shootings (62%), climate change/global warming (55%), and immigration (47%) as significant sources of stress. Remarkably, three in five (60%) said that the number of issues America is facing in the future is overwhelming to them. And, of course, all these numbers include those who find themselves in leadership positions—perhaps like you. So, yes, of course, stress is bad. How could it not be?

Your Stress Response System

Your stress response system is your body's built-in, factory-loaded mechanism for dealing with pressure, stress, and threat. Like a zebra on the savanna who has caught wind of a lion on the prowl, once you perceive a threat, your biological survival system kicks in to high gear. Floodgates open in the central nervous system, and stress hormones—adrenaline, cortisol, noradrenaline, oxytocin—begin their cascade through your body, directing you toward actions that provide safety and connection rather than certain death (at least that's how it can feel).

Your heart rate increases, your pupils dilate for greater visual acuity, your hearing becomes sharper, and your peripheral vision increases as you scan the environment, searching for additional trouble. Whether you're aware of it or not, your digestion slows to allow blood flow to your major muscle groups so you can escape the danger at hand.

Your thinking becomes momentarily hyperfocused, overridden by the threat of the moment. In time, if the threat persists, you'll become irrational and overwhelmed, with your judgment impaired. You see, your brain can't tell if the lion in pursuit is real or not.

Sounds like a typical day at the office, yes?

This biological process activates your sympathetic nervous system to rev up the energetic gas to up your system. The trouble is, unless you're on safari, you're not likely out on the savanna fearing the lion's approach. Instead, you're in the office or the boardroom, or at a child's soccer game or the PTA with screaming parents. Your centuries-old fight-flight-freeze-appease reaction isn't required in any of those situations, despite how unpleasant the circumstances may be. Your old biological reaction—your perception involved—may be hindering your best performance. That's because perception is biology. As Chilean biologists Humberto Maturana and Francisco Varela write in their book *The Tree of Knowledge*, perception is a continuous process of "bringing forth a world that manifests itself in *all* our actions and all our being"; it's the process of living.[4]

The antidote to our body's overreaction—outside of the context of a real, life-threatening experience—is to invoke the relaxation response on purpose, activated by your parasympathetic nervous system, which is akin to putting the brakes on your reactions. By intentionally pausing, you can invoke the relaxation response by attuning your attention to your breath, sensations, and full-body experience. Pausing allows you to be with "what is" right now. It enables you to ask yourself, *What's required in this situation?*

Pushing pause allows you to reset and recalibrate the stress hormones coursing through your body, reestablish critical thinking, and relax into what is actually occurring instead of reacting to your fear of what might be happening. Big difference.

My Bias at the Time

As a result of my work at the Employee Resource Center, an employee assistance program—which would now be called Corporate Wellness—I'd been hired to teach a stress management course in Chicago at a large, well-known financial institution. The predominant view of stress at the time defaulted to that of the Godfather of Stress, Dr. Selye—stress is everywhere and an outcome of simply living life, so there's no way around experiencing it. Traditional cognitive interventions reinforced the prevailing belief that stress was bad.

To be stressed was to be skewed in a negative direction—needing to get ahold of, loosen the grip on, or "manage" your stress reactions because that trifecta of fight, flight, and freeze were believed to be the *only* stress responses. In fact, *fight, flight, freeze* was the commonly used phrase to describe stress and the one I'd come prepared to help people address at the bank.

Except that in the prep for this work assignment, I found that I had a problem—one that shook me up quite a bit and reflected my own drive for results. Ironically, it taught me a lot that I hadn't planned on learning.

Let me tell you how. Remember, I hadn't learned the incredible power of pausing yet.

Stress and Itchy Bumps

I'll admit to being driven and self-competitive—like many leaders with ideas about where to go and how to get there.

Over a few weeks during one August, I developed a set of painful, irritating, and embarrassing symptoms: ugly red and rash-covered, constantly itchy legs. Not jumpy or achy legs, but itchy legs—itchy to the point of flaming red bumps that screamed at me and kept me up at night scratching.

These symptoms went on for a few weeks. Despite application of topical creams, I couldn't stand it any longer. I consulted my doctor.

I was convinced I'd developed an allergy or at least was having an allergic reaction (both good guesses, by the way, but wrong), even though I could think of nothing—nothing physical, at least—that was different in those few weeks. No new detergent, no hiking trips to confront lurking poison ivy, no nothing.

After conducting a series of allergy tests—thankfully I wasn't allergic to anything—the doctor concluded that I was suffering from the effects of contact dermatitis, an unpleasant and painful situation that typically remits after two to four weeks with treatment. This explained my symptoms.

The doctor's diagnosis? Chronic stress!

I was not happy. I was convinced she was wrong! You see, I was decidedly not stressed—that was the story I told myself anyway. The good doctor recommended a stress management program for me, which I thought was absurd since I was just then about to begin teaching such a course at the bank. I went on my way, pointedly focused on filling the Benadryl prescription but not addressing the underlying stress.

It took the itchy bumps just shy of a month to clear up, and all the while I was befuddled at my doctor's recommendation. With the wisdom of hindsight, I could later see that working two jobs while completing an advanced degree, purchasing my first home, and moving in just a few weeks beforehand had placed me high on the stress scale.

However, I couldn't "see" my experience because:

1. The story I was telling myself was that I could and should handle it all. So I didn't view myself as stressed out. I believed stress was a sign of personal weakness.

2. I believed that all my hard work, extra hours, and focus would prevail. I was quite attached to my belief about working hard, though I couldn't realize it then. This contributed to my body's manifestation of stress symptoms.

3. I hadn't taken the time to reflect and listen to what my body knew to be true—I was experiencing overload, and my body needed more attention from me. Contact dermatitis sure got my attention!

Shortly afterward, I ran across *Full Catastrophe Living.*[5] This book, later a primer for the mindfulness classes I was trained to teach, supported Jon's approach of simply "pausing to being with" whatever arose relative to stress versus attempting to manage it. I experimented with this approach and soon found myself hooked. Thus, I began a new leg in my journey of working with stress and using it to grow my leadership.

Only recently, however, has emerging science offered new insights into what happens when we meet up with pressure and stress. It seems we're physiologically wired for more than these three possible stress reactions.

Beach Balls and Building Awareness

As part of a leadership training team working with a global energy company, the possibility that there's more to our stress reactions became apparent. The company had grown from a small family-owned business in the Pacific Northwest to a worldwide player in the energy industry in just a decade.

Our team was called in to assist two hundred senior leaders to integrate the business cultures of their very different businesses worldwide, entailing a massive culture shift. To learn from one another, these leaders needed to cultivate a common language to be able to make and fulfill their commitments to one another, their customers, and their vendors all while staying competitive.

This yearlong internal program included two major weeklong conferences that bookended the year. In between, we met with teams of seven to nine leaders on a biweekly basis to support them in making the shift. Todd, a great experiential learning facilitator and colleague on the project, introduced everyone to a fun beach ball exercise at the outset of the first conference. Picture two one-hundred-person teams competing against one another for the fastest time in moving the multicolored beach ball across the room. There were only three rules:

1. Everyone had to touch the inflated ball as they passed it up and down conference room rows.

2. No holding the ball.

3. The ball couldn't touch the floor.

How would they work together to secure the best, most competitive timing? Would they be willing to be beginners at this new task? The exercise required cooperation, enthusiasm, and ingenuity to be successful together. In this silly, low-stakes learning game, reactions were varied. Some participants were strikingly competitive, blasting the beach ball past three or four others, only to have to return it down the line so everyone could make contact, costing them precious moments. Others hung back, reluctant to participate, and allowed others to do the work—all against the backdrop of loudly shouted advice.

I'll never forget Todd's admonition about learning—"You have to catch yourself being yourself to win." This catchphrase became our mantra, since our job as coaches on this project was simple, though not easy. We were to coach these leaders not only in learning about new ways to integrate their product and services or how to cultivate a culture of excellence and care. We were to coach them into new ways of being as leaders.

As simple and silly as this beach ball game was, it opened up the space for leaders to practice learning as beginners—observing their own automatic reactions and behaviors (bossy, overly competitive, hanging back, or offering no suggestions) and taking responsibility for the impact they were having on the team.

Catching Yourself Being Yourself

The range of what we think and do is
limited by what we fail to notice.

—R. D. LAING, SCOTTISH PSYCHIATRIST

To pause is to notice what's typically overlooked or not seen. Despite popular opinion, we're not so great at seeing ourselves clearly as human beings. There's even a name for this tendency: *confirmation bias*. The concept is that we search for, interpret, favor, and recall information that supports our prior beliefs, values, and ways of behaving.

It's invisible, and it can kill your leadership.

Catching yourself being yourself, and combating personal confirmation bias for the sake of transformation, requires self-awareness and clear-seeing. Remember Todd's comments earlier: you have to catch yourself being yourself to win.

Discovering where you put your attention and what you're truly up to each day goes a long way to increasing your self-awareness, which is an essential aspect of emotional intelligence. Noticing your mood and your current way of interacting with others, observing the types of questions you ask or not, and sensing the emotional tenor of a meeting will sharpen your self-awareness (key to change) so you have the choice to create new ways of working with yourself and others.

What's So? So What? What Now?

Observing "*what's so*" (like, right in front of you) is the best starting point. It helps you to let go of all you make up about the world (remember my contact dermatitis!) and be present to what is directly in front of you. It's also the first step to move into a more powerful way of working with your life energies to flip the switch from pressure to power to create better outcomes.

But don't be fooled. To observe "what's so" in how you address and work with your stress, and then to ask "So what?" isn't about giving up, acquiescing, opting out, or being a worn-out doormat. It is responding effectively to the question, "What now?" by saying, "I give up my resistance to what is. I'm choosing to quit fighting with myself about reality." Not easy, yet necessary and vital as a leader today. Once you do that, you can begin to close the gap by developing new skills, sensibilities, and actions. You'll begin to learn to surf on those monstrous waves of complexity.

● ● ●

A DOSE OF DAILY STRESS

○ Let's try an experiment here. Push pause now—take a deep, slow breath and feel your breath on the inhalation.

○ Recall a *daily stress* from your own life. Make sure it's junior sized, or about a 5 on a 1–10 scale. For example, something like standing in line for your first cup of coffee at Starbucks or sitting in traffic en route to work—that kind of thing.

○ As you bring that daily stress to mind, let yourself tune in to what occurs in your body as you do so. Perhaps you noticed an uptick in heart rate, tightness around your eyes or jaw, or sweatiness in your hands. Remember, you're simply noticing—not changing anything.

○ Then shift your attention and tune in to your emotional response, subtle though it might be. A mild irritation or annoyance arises. Nothing, sadness—it's all fair game.

○ Then shift again and tune in to how you're thinking about this experience and talking to yourself about it. This line is too long. What's keeping them anyway? Or, Don't these people know how to drive? I have a meeting, and I know I'll be late.

How we think and talk to ourselves, even in those small daily moments, reveals how we view stress.

Our self-talk matters. A lot. Tuning in to all these dimensions is key to how you'll work with stress, as you'll soon see. Learn the skill of catching yourself being yourself to shift your mindset, mood, and your effectiveness in life and leadership.

● ● ●

Signature Stress Styles

I've been drawn to assessments of all kinds since I was a kid, in hopes of trying to make sense out of people in general and myself too. I'm fascinated by the patterns that inevitably emerge when we take a stab at objectively observing how we behave, without judgment and instead with curiosity. Our patterns are distinctive ways that we express ourselves. We embody the patterns, only to have them show up as the strategies we use that run us unconsciously— that is, until we can identify and shift them with conscious awareness.

Difficult, pressure-filled situations we find ourselves in can reveal our patterns, which is why it's essential to catch them. Plus, I find it comforting to know that my quirky traits and unique behaviors are not so unique after all and that I share patterns with scads of others. You likely do too.

By tuning in and noticing your signature stress pattern—how would you show up in the beach ball game?—you can learn to shift it to transform your stress and grow your resilience. Then you'll be on your way to dealing with pesky people, airy beach balls, and tricky decisions with ease and presence.

How? First off, and most accessible, is to catch yourself *doing that thing* you do that keeps you from handling life's stresses and intensities well. That thing has become a habit, it has a pattern, and it's become embodied as a strategy. For example, that thing could look like:

- needing to be in control all the time;
- not caring, or being indifferent;
- freaking out like your hair is on fire;
- a screaming Mimi, barking orders; or
- shutting down at the first hint of tension.

For example, if you say you want to reduce your work stress, but you won't stop working sixteen-hour days because you're too afraid of negative repercussions or you're too nervous about stepping in and making a request for some time off, you're clearly out of alignment with what's important to you. And that awareness, my dear reader, is gold.

Why? Because by catching yourself being yourself, you're expanding your self-awareness, which will allow you the space to shift out of old patterns and into new practices that can work more effectively for you.

Consider your reactions to each of the following:

- You knew Josie planned to move. You just didn't think it would be so soon! You weren't prepared and now you're facing a setback of at least three or four months. You wish she'd been more forthright about the timing. It all seems to be spinning out of control. Agh.

- You didn't see this unexpected news coming at all! You've felt pretty on top of things here lately, so to receive it is a total shock to your system. Your good faith in John just flew out the window, along with your energy. What will you do now?

- You've been anticipating a great response to your proposal, yet you're now noticing that you're feeling anxious because they have not gotten back to you. You keep wondering, "What'll happen if we don't get this big project? I mean, we've been counting on it, nurturing it for the better part of twelve months." You're on edge, with self-doubt creeping in and eating away at your confidence.

Just reading these scenarios, how're you reacting? Did you notice an uptick in your heart rate? Are your thoughts racing, thinking back to that tricky conversation you had last week? Are you feeling irritated or flush or thinking "Get me outta here!"?

Wouldn't it be nice to get a bead on what others have done in these types of circumstances? You know, so that you could learn from their experience. Though common, these stressors can undo us, with each of us reacting with our own signature stress reaction. Do you want to learn yours?

When you identify it, it'll likely be familiar to you and evident to everyone around you. Knowing your style can make life much easier because it opens up the possibility of greater choice and agency.

Here are a few questions to consider that may shed light on your signature stress reaction:

- How do you deal with the unexpected?

- How important is it to you to have control over outcomes?

- How often do you feel nervous and stressed out?

- How do you work with others who irritate you?

- How often do you feel overwhelmed?

• • •

Find Your Signature Stress Style

Styles	Behaviors and stories	What we tell ourselves and questions
The Defender Push against	Forward energy, questioning, offended, fight, overtly reactive, and externalized Concern with self or important cause can be seen as possible bullying or hotheadedness Stories include: blame; lack of accountability; overt anger; and irritation It is all about me Lack of empathy Driven by a Higher Power Certainty	1. I know I'm right about this—they're just oblivious. 2. I get hot under the collar really fast and need to let others know it—but that's just the way I am. 3. When stress is high, my patience is low. 4. I don't know why people don't take more accountability for themselves! 5. They aren't listening to me; they don't understand me.

continued

| The Pleaser **Move toward** | Appeasing, conciliatory, brown-noser, dislikes conflict, hides stress reactions by being nice

Concern with other party and mollifying them; can be seen as manipulative

Stories include: acquiescing; moving to make nice; all someone has done or is doing for you; feeling fearful, anxious

Loses self in others; needs to be helpful

I don't matter

All empathy while other feelings don't register | 1. I don't like conflict, but I do like everyone to be happy all the time.

2. I find it difficult to admit that I'm irritated or stressed; I often feel resentful.

3. I hide when I feel fearful because others will be mad.

4. I like to help others out, and I don't understand when they back away

5. Don't show feelings, so others will be comfortable and let me help them.

6. When I feel nervous because others might be upset, I rush to fix it. |
| The Avoider **Pull Back** | Avoidant, internalized stress, hangs back in conversation, can be seen as unapproachable

Concern with staying safe, disengaged, and not overly emotionally taxed

Stories include: "I gotta get out of here"; "Don't bother me with that"; doing something else versus doing what's at hand (ground for addictive behavior) | 1. I don't like to be bothered by others' concerns too much.

2. Others overwhelm me with their emotionality.

3. In stressful times, I find myself looking for other things to do: drinking, eating, working out, or hobbies.

4. I notice my whole body pulling back when there's lots of stress and I tend to disengage from others.

5. I tend to get lost in my own thoughts about how things should be, and I can tend to blame others. |

| The Paralyzed

Freeze | Shuts down, masked face, confusion, panic, dissociates from moment, lock down, may be seen as out-of-it, unreliable, distant, unsure what to do so may do nothing—passive

Stories include: "I was paralyzed"; confused; terrified | 1. I notice I zone out when tensions around me are high.

2. I get confused fairly often about what to do in stressful situations.

3. I often feel panicky and stuck.

4. I can be overly conscientious at times because I'm trying to make sure I get it right.

5. My body goes into total lockdown, and I can't take action. |
| The Challenger

Open,
Inclusive,
Responsive | Mindset of rising to the challenge

Focused but not fearful

Recovers and learns from stressful events, building resilience

Confident and courageous

Experiences flow states of absorbed concentration

Seeks social connection

High peak performance | 1. We're all in this together.

2. I can identify my moods/feelings, and I feel confident about handling stressful situations.

3. I listen to my body's wisdom to guide the way I handle stress.

4. I can catch myself in stress-inducing thoughts and shift them.

5. I enjoy the way I feel when challenged—it gives me a chance to grow and learn. |

To discover more about your signature stress style, you can take the following quiz: https://www.quiz-maker.com/QB60XTZ.

• • •

Formation and Transformation

Our identities form early in life as we attempt to discover how to survive and thrive in our family of origin. As kids, we learn to steer our specific circumstances to get what we need. We're shaped and validated by using our stress style and strategies over and over to secure the essentials we need.

Those early winning strategies became embodied in us: he's the clown, she's the smarty pants, he's the jock, she's the science nerd, etc. Eventually, it's how we come to define who we are. Our way of being and engaging with the world becomes evident. We call it our personality or identity.

Our deepest human drives for safety, connection, and dignity feed the relentless, automatic, and lifelong process of constructing and defending ourselves. The rub is that we don't know we're doing it. It just seems normal, and though it is a normal developmental process, it's invisible to us.

Typical strategies for progressing in life include *avoiding* what we don't like, what doesn't feel good, or what doesn't work well—such as embarrassment, failure, and shame. Conversely, we learn to seek out and become attached to behaviors and actions that do work well. We vociferously cling to them because they work.

Biological at the core, this dialectic life tension exists between attachment and aversion. It precedes all our behaviors and actions.

Faced with any threat to our real—or imaginary—identity, our signature stress styles become more pronounced and include tightening up or battening down the hatches, numbing out, distracting ourselves, or keeping busy and working harder. I know the latter pattern. It's my old go-to strategy. Remember, I didn't think I was stressed, because I didn't want to believe it.

Obscured, our identity requirements—our personality—run the show and sabotage our effectiveness as leaders. This is true whether the stakes are big (running for election, taking your business public), small (conversation with a loved one), or somewhere in between. Once you can learn the skill of catching yourself being yourself, you can choose to let go of those older strategies that no longer serve you.

To catch yourself is to turn a spotlight of attention on your typical strategies to unveil the anatomy and learn the contours of what's worked and not worked in your life and leadership. Consider the words of my client Dave, a credit union CEO who'd been working to catch himself: "We all have reflexive behaviors that can be limiting or even harmful—or at least not particularly productive in terms of what's important. It's pausing that interrupts my reflexes and behaviors so I can reflect, listen, and organize my thoughts instead of following my inclination to not allow others room to speak. Pause allows for a better, more true exchange with people."

Your strategies are at the source of who you are and what you do—for good or ill—and reveal your readiness to step into what you're willing to take a stand for in your leadership.[6]

Catching Myself on the Aikido Mat

When I started toying with practicing aikido, which looks like a choreographed dance, I was sure I'd never learn the steps. The mere thought made me uncomfortable.

I'd received feedback from a business coach about my leadership. After having reviewed my 360-degree assessment and observing me in action, she offered me an assessment. She was frank.

"You need to develop some fierceness in you," she said. "You're simply too nice, and it's not serving you or your leadership. You need to get into a body-based practice. I'd suggest aikido."

I was a bit stunned at her directness but not surprised by her feedback. There was some part of me that absolutely knew she was on to something. She was on to me. The feedback smarted in the same way that a needle's initial prick can smart when having blood drawn. Yes, she had drawn blood.

Yet I trusted her, so I set about finding an aikido dojo near my home.

The modern Japanese martial art of aikido, with deep roots in the samurai warrior tradition, is a comprehensive system of throwing, joint locks, striking, and pinning techniques coupled with training in traditional Japanese weapons such as the sword, staff, and knife.

I settled on Tokushinkan Dojo near my home. The big plus was the teacher, or sensei. She was a five-foot-two-inch female who was powerful and fierce. Just what I needed.

Observing a few classes evoked an internal stirring of possibility within me. Much like the woman observing Sally in the classic movie *When Harry Met Sally*, I knew beyond words that "I'll have what she's having."

In time, I became enamored with all of it: the sensei, the quiet power of the practice, the ability to move with energy and intention—to "see" and even create openings.

In terms of catching myself being myself, that occurred right from the start. I was moderately athletic in high school, and I've worked out regularly for the better part of my adult life—so my confidence stepping onto the mat was moderate. "How hard could it be?" I wondered.

After doing aiki warm-ups for proper body alignment, we moved to wrist stretches and then to forward and backward rolls. While struggling to competently do a backward roll, I quickly realized that aikido would be more challenging than I'd first thought.

The first basic technique for a white belt is Katatekosatori Kotegaeshi, a cross-hand wrist grab. It looked easy enough in the static setup and demonstration. Yet in slow, dynamic practice, I became frustrated and flush—my fears had been activated.

I was surprised and embarrassed as my frustration took the form of an uprush of tears. Catching myself being myself meant coming face-to-face with my "already knowing" mind, my long-held expectation that new things came easily to me, and my competitive spirit. For the first few years of practice, this triad of reactions was commonplace and left me competitive enough to want to continue and tame my body's initial reactions, yet also wanting to hide in a hole of humiliation.

Practicing pause on the mat in order to collect and center myself has proven foundational to my aikido life—as important as learning this first technique.

• • •

PAUSING TO CENTER

Centering builds the muscles and skills of being present, open, and connected to life and what we care about. Practicing centering provides an antidote to the daily violence of our modern times. We develop ourselves by practicing centering consistently when the stakes are low. Then, when the stakes are high, we can readily access our most resilient, creative, resourceful self.

○ We practice centering by first bringing our attention to our breath and pausing to notice "what is so" in the current moment. Feel the weight of your body pressing down into your seat and into your feet. Let your attention follow this downward press, finding a sense of ground, support, and solidity.

○ Extend yourself up, drawing yourself up into the full length of your torso, so that your head and neck are directly aligned with your spine.

○ Relax your jaw. Relax your shoulders, letting them drop as if the soft parts of your body are a silk shirt hanging on the coat hanger of your skeleton.

○ Take a couple of breaths, following the breath with your attention and feeling the settling in your nervous system as you release tension.

○ Sense the space behind you. In front of you, left and right.

○ When you are ready, take a breath or two and open your eyes.

• • •

RECAP

- Stress isn't bad; stress can build resilience

- Pause cultivates awareness

- Catching yourself being yourself provides freedom

- We all have a signature stress style

  - Defender
  - Pleaser
  - Avoider
  - Paralyzed
  - Challenger

- Centering builds the muscles and skills of being present, open, and connected to life and what you care about

- Letting go is part of the growth process

SCOPE—SPACE, CONNECTION, OPENNESS, PACE, ENERGY

S – How much space do you give yourself each day to see yourself in action?

C – When was the last time you gave yourself permission to relate deeply with someone else?

O – How well do you share the burden of a task?

P – When have you ever moved at less than the maximum speed?

E – Do you notice your energy and your self on a regular basis?

CHAPTER 4

Learning and Growing Embodied Trust

Trust is a feature of the fundamental fabric of our social lives.

—FERNANDO FLORES, CO-AUTHOR OF *BUILDING TRUST*, PHILOSOPHER,
FORMER MINISTER, SECRETARY GENERAL OF CHILE

I f you've been wondering why you'd bother to pause and tune in to this whole "catching yourself being yourself" thing anyway, you'd be in good company. Kevin Cashman, global leader of CEO and Executive Development at Korn Ferry, asks, "Why would pragmatic, hard-charging, achievement-driven leaders pause to accelerate performance and growth?"[1] He then goes on to answer his own question: "It is exactly what is needed to sort through complexity and then drive performance to the next level . . . *in today's world, the doing needs to be new and different.*"

The doing does need to be new and different. *Yet, none of us can think our way into a new way of doing. We need a new way of being.* In today's rapidly changing times, leaders have little guidance to follow. The stable scaffolding of yesteryear is crumbling away. And, with no singular "right" answer at hand, learning to cultivate skills to read the environment is a prerequisite for leaders to create history, if they will.

As leadership expert Warren Bennis has said, "Letting the self emerge is the essential task of leaders."[2] As a leader, you must first come to know and experience this within yourself. It requires courage to turn and face situations head-on, grapple with them, learn, and allow yourself—as Ray Anderson of Interface did—to be deeply moved, and to reconstitute yourself anew in order to choose the best response to the new challenges that lay ahead.

Learning

> Learning is almost synonymous with life itself. The learning process is the process by which we grow and transform ourselves from who we are to who we want to be.
>
> —DAVID KOLB, AUTHOR OF *EXPERIENTIAL LEARNING*, AMERICAN EDUCATIONAL THEORIST AT THE WEATHERHEAD SCHOOL OF MANAGEMENT, AND CREATOR OF KOLB LEARNING STYLE INVENTORY

Conscious, masterful leadership is needed to successfully address the extraordinary challenges we face today. So conscious leaders must be active learners. Decades of research on learning, studied and articulated by leading educational theorists such as Piaget, Dewey, Kolb, and Dreyfus, reveal a common four-step, cyclical process that encompasses what it takes to learn nearly anything:

1. We experience something.

2. We observe it, reflect on it, and get feedback.

3. We interpret the results, generalize from them, and assign some sort of meaning to the experience.

4. We move to take action, informed by our conclusions, and the iterative cycle repeats itself.

Simply understanding this learning process can dramatically improve our willingness to learn and our effectiveness across teams and organizations. When we've taken on learning something new—like training on a new accounting system, investigating climate science, or taking up tango with your spouse—our old strategies and beliefs about what's possible can easily get in the way. That includes learning how to lead.

Our society hosts few places in which we provide current or emerging leaders a training field on which to *develop mastery*. For most of us, our only opportunity to develop and practice leadership skills is in the very setting in which our actions have real, often substantial consequences for ourselves and others. That's a bit like putting an athlete or musician into competition all day, every day, without ever providing space to reflect on their mistakes and improve their performance to hone their craft.

Most leadership training—in fact, most education of all kinds—takes as its starting point the conveyance of new information, based on the premise that knowledge is power. Books, teachers, models, new ideas, and simulations and advanced training are great places to start when learning something new. This is what's called *acquired learning*. Its focus is *horizontal* and occurs as people work to beef up their knowledge base and sharpen current skills to become better at what they do. If we use a technology metaphor: acquired learning occurs when we download data into our heads, like we'd download new applications and data onto a computer to expand what the system would be capable of enacting.

The problem, however, with this type of learning is that it's the place most training stops—and with it, most learning stops too. The book is shut, the instructor is long gone, and we return to our day-to-day lives, proceeding pretty much like we did yesterday. How many times, for example, have you learned a new idea and even known "what to do" but found yourself unable to actually do it?

A second way, the way of *adaptive learning*, builds on one's early learning foundation with the goal to transcend it. A newly upgraded inner operating system supersedes what came before. Few adults, unless foisted into learning as a result of a crisis, ever upgrade their own sensemaking beyond the equivalent of the basic Windows version. Resistance to change is high, even among leaders, so to deliberately stretch to learn new perspectives and grow new capacities that might fundamentally shift how and why they do what they do, or—more importantly—who they are, can be daunting.

However, it's exactly this vertical type of learning that can expand the mind itself by growing it to evolve to the next level of complexity. And, like high-performance athletes or masterful musicians, those leaders who do choose to train will experience similar discomfort when stretching beyond their current limits.

Back to the leadership training. Despite all the cool takeaways and swag you brought home last week from the latest conference you attended, your learning is likely now just a faint memory. Certainly, you might use the input at the weekly trivia night, but you're not really able to take new action in any way.

It turns out that simple exposure to new ideas is necessary but not sufficient to enable us to take new action. "A cultural overemphasis on cognitive learning has atrophied our natural somatic intelligence," says my colleague Amanda Blake—"somatic" being the rich wisdom of our biology.[3]

Recent neuroscience research sheds light on why this is so, exposing the limitations of purely intellectual learning—horizontal or vertical. Quite simply, it has to do with our neurobiological makeup and how our brains change through attention and practice.

A third approach to learning—the most accessible—is to develop an *embodied approach to learning*. It's unlikely, however, that you've experienced this kind of learning before, at least not in any formal setting. Typical leadership development focuses on teaching people what to do through models and ideas versus developing who they are.

Embodied Learning and Deep Listening

Learning how to learn is one of the most powerful
ways of dealing with the changes of today's world.
In this time of accelerated change, learning to learn
gives us a competitive advantage.

—RICHARD STROZZI-HECKLER, PHD, AUTHOR OF *THE LEADERSHIP*
DOJO AND FOUNDER OF THE STROZZI INSTITUTE

With the rapid pace of change and an increasing demand for flexibility, *learning how to learn* is a master key to powerful engagement with the world. Learning happens in our bodies through practice. This type of learning is full-bodied, accesses all our senses, and is developed via intentional focus and practice over time. As a result, new learning becomes embodied, or "automatic"—integrated into one's life to the point it becomes a "new normal."

Embodied learning is less about acquiring knowledge, a process in which the focus is on the input of information (i.e., teachers talk and students are required to listen), and more about being able to quickly, pragmatically, and effectively shift gears, roles, or positions to pivot one's direction toward a defined outcome. In other words, embodied learning enables you to take actions previously unavailable to you and to know what right action to take in a given situation because you've upgraded your inner operating system yet again.

The doing can only be different if the being is different. The neural guidance system that successful leaders use to listen deeply—their gut feelings, a knowing intuition—gauges trust, creates resonance with others, and taps into current reality to take effective action, which is something not accessible with a cognitive shift alone.[4]

Intuition, which is often denigrated as an unreliable soft skill, is the ability to accurately listen, read, and respond to direct, unmediated sensory and emotional experience. It's more precise to say that intuition is a *power skill* that's body based and can be developed. It first begins by situating the body as the essential place of learning, action, and—ultimately—of transformation.

Because sensation and emotion move much faster in our bodies than our conscious awareness, building receptivity to your senses gives you a greater chance of getting intuition to work on your behalf. Spindle neurons help, operating to create a specialized superhighway that moves information from various parts of the brain to others. They're located in the prefrontal cortex near the insula, which—if you'll recall—is involved in feeling ourselves as humans.

One way you can improve and deepen your intuition is by shifting gears, pausing, and directing the focus of your attention to what's emotionally significant to you. In other words, to reflect on what you care about. Intuition is a whole-body process and a reliable source of wisdom, knowledge, and information. It hinges on what's important to you, because that's where your attention will go. Remarkable as it may seem, what you focus your attention on literally grows and shapes your brain over time. Since it's impossible to take in every sight, sound, smell, or internal rumbling that you experience, your attention functions like a gate, allowing in some information and editing other information out. Directing your attention really does matter.

When you repeatedly focus on a thought or action, the electrical and chemical connections between the involved brain cells strengthen. In this way, frequently trafficked ideas and behaviors are reinforced.[5] They ultimately become an intrinsic part of your behavioral and biological identity: who you are, how you perceive the world, the actions you can take, and—quite literally—the structure and function of your brain.

As a result, long-held beliefs, expectations, and actions take shape as your strategies to deal with life. They literally take on a physiological shape and become embodied, so that the very structure of your brain reflects the life you've led up to this point. By attending to your full experience—sensations, emotions, and the meaning you assign to them—conscious thoughts are manifest in your physical structure: your gestures, movement patterns, and your very presence reflect your history up to the current moment.

Learning on the Mat

One of my favorite books, even before I started practicing aikido, was George Leonard's book *Mastery: The Keys to Success and Long-Term Fulfillment*. A journalist, George started on his aikido journey in his forties, as did I, so I felt an immediate sort of kinship with him.[6]

In *Mastery*, Leonard integrates the wisdom of aikido practice with an applied practicality that brings learning off the mat and into life. I was struck by how he made the connections from the physical practices on the aikido mat to golf, business interactions, and leadership—as if they were all one. In some ways, they are. As I came to learn, the secret sauce to success is about how one shows up to learn. It makes all the difference in winning at golf, business endeavors, daily life, and leadership.

To explain the inevitable ups and downs that learners experience over time, Leonard speaks of four energetic learning "rhythms" on the path to mastery, though only one will take the learner all the way there.

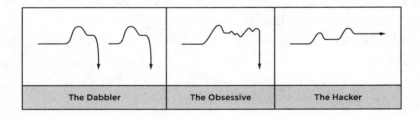

To be a **Dabbler** is to start out with great enthusiasm and love of novelty. But once the initial excitement subsides, the Dabbler will drop the activity to find the next new, exciting thing. That racquetball racket collecting dust in the corner, the pottery wheel in the basement, and the banjo in the closet are all evidence of the Dabbler's approach.

The **Obsessive** starts out strong but can become frustrated when her efforts don't produce outcomes quickly. No longer feeling as though she's learning, she'll double down and work around the clock, only to burn out, drop the activity quickly, and leave without looking back.

Hackers get the gist of things quickly, yet, because they're satisfied with basic competence, they tend to hang out on the plateau of simply practicing. They're not stretching or challenging their level of competence. Since they're not really committed to mastery, they practice just enough to get by. Occasional hobbies—that once-a-year ski trip, or the yearly music jam with college buddies—are examples of this rhythm.

Recognizing these common rhythms serves to normalize the learning process and can help us clarify those skills we're serious about mastering versus those that will be pleasurable hobbies or activities.

Leonard strongly warns against believing in the fantasy that learning is one continuous flow of peak moments. If you'll recall, I got caught up in this belief early on too. I'd expected aikido to be easier than it was.

Leonard refers to the fourth orientation as the *Mastery* approach. Elite performers demand mastery. They know that learning takes energy. According to Leonard, "A human being is the kind of machine that wears out from lack of use . . . we gain energy by using energy."[7] In reality, it's about getting on the path and staying on the plateau—practicing for the sake of practice itself. This harnessing of energy to stay on the plateau is what sets elite performers apart from others. They revel in the secret sauce. By staying on the path of practicing for the sake of practicing, they improve. As Leonard says, "The real juice of life is to be found in how it feels to be alive."[8]

As I mentioned earlier, I was as surprised as anyone that I "took to" aikido as I did. Truth be told, I fell in love with the ritual: bowing upon entering the dojo, changing into my gi, bowing again when I stepped onto the cool mat, lining up to sit seiza, warming up, watching our sensei teach the moves, and then practicing with partners. Her loud hand clap would have us sitting again, only to resume instruction in quiet. I loved the paradoxical nature of aikido practice, at once very intimate and human—grappling or striking, turning and throwing—yet sacred too. I had a felt sense of the long lineage of practice I'd stepped into. Despite the bumps and bruises, I felt alive!

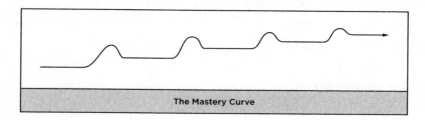

The Mastery Curve

In any practice you take on—a martial art, an artistic endeavor, a sport, writing, or speaking—your intention to step onto the path of mastery is what makes all the difference. By intention, I'm invoking what Richard Strozzi-Heckler speaks of as the "faculty of your imagination" and what Leonard calls the "intentionality that fuels the master's journey. Every master is a master of vision."[9] This vision is all about your purpose and your willingness to linger longer in the tension that lives at the edges of goalless practice and alluring goals that come your way.

Catching Myself in Action: 1 is 1

I've always loved a good plan. Part of me finds great satisfaction in checking off those square boxes on my Action Item List. I'm sure it's the feel-good squirt of dopamine that makes me so happy!

Really, though, a good plan helps us juggle our daily commitments and move the ball down the proverbial court. Effective leadership involves taking responsibility for our commitments and our results, and, assuming we're taking real action versus simply getting caught up in mere activities, a good plan can work. We know this.

Our collective tendency these days, however, is to try to plan too much stuff into a day or an hour. We cram. We juggle. We finagle. We think we have more time than we do. We think we're being smart—efficient, even. At least, that's my modus operandi. It doesn't work, though. Instead, it creates mischief. Sometimes high-priced mischief.

At first, you may recognize it internally—a bit of worry creeping into your brow as you juggle all your commitments. You wonder what will get dropped from the list today. You imagine who it will impact as your thoughts turn to damage control.

Unchecked, a not-so-subtle impact begins to show up. You may notice it as your gut gripping or a sudden drop of energy and increase in fatigue. It can also show up interpersonally as unmet expectations and disappointments.

Finally . . . the old cram-it-all-in strategy fully explodes, and, well, you likely know the end of the story: overcommitted, overscheduled, and over-worked. Breakdowns unfold right before your eyes—such as that tardy phone response eight days late, the late report for the boss, the forgotten bill unpaid (oops, a late fee), or the "it slipped my mind" response to your neighbor's Big Birthday Party.

There is another way, however. **1 is 1. Number two doesn't exist until one is complete. Let me explain.** I've heard this dictum often from our aikido sensei. "*1 is 1,*" she admonishes us on the aikido mat—"2 doesn't even exist until 1 is complete."

On the aikido mat, *catching myself* meant noticing how my tendency to cram-it-all-in shows up in my techniques, my moves and timing, and the twenty-two-count jo kata.

The jo is a wooden staff typically used by peasants to fight the samurai, since they didn't have access to steel-bladed swords. A jo kata is a series of moves—a form—that's practiced individually, and then with a partner, to embody new and more effective moves of attack. It's there in the kata that I rush, impatient to get on to the next move. I anticipate too much. I stop rather than flow. I value efficiency, yet with my impatience I create inefficiency and use more energy than is required.

It's there in the kata that I find myself having to pause to pay close attention, to slow down, to actually *be in* the particulars of the move, and to wait for the moment to open and reveal the next right action. I've learned that so much more space is available in each move if I am actually in it fully. 1 is 1; 2 doesn't exist until 1 is complete.

How we show up on the mat is how we show up in life. Another way to say it: how we do anything is how we do everything, including our leadership. Leading consciously is about taking responsibility for our results and for what we create on the mat of life. If we can catch ourselves and then practice 1 is 1, maybe we'd all be able to find the space and flow in *this* moment to enact the plans of the day with flow and ease.

Bodies under Pressure: Tuning In and Transforming Stress

It's good to know how you react under stress and intense pressure. Knowing your automatic reaction is the starting point to growing your leadership. (If you have not determined your signature stress style yet, you may want to return to chapter 3 to glance at it now).

The benefits of catching yourself being yourself and learning about your own signature stress reactions—those worn-out strategies you override that have you defending yourself and making excuses—is to move into a place of greater choice. No longer will the old strategies keep you from being your best self—tripping your trigger, taking you out of the moment, and leaving your head spinning. Instead, you'll be clearheaded, on point, and able to make moves in the right direction with confidence.

Did you know that your physical body is first to register pressure—not your thinking mind or even your feelings? It's true.

Consider the following examples of how pressure showed up before these leaders registered it.

- Dave begins to talk faster and louder in a leadership team meeting, not making eye contact with his team while continuing his long-winded soliloquy.

- Debra notices her jaw is tight and tender, her breath is constricted, and her fists are clenched when leading an executive team process. She's surprised.

- Nick is all heads-down, with his face twisted in concentration as he moves across the room. His people think he's mad and uninterested in them. He thinks he's smiling.

- Darek moves so quickly and is so "next, next, next"–oriented that he's easily agitated and defensive. He received feedback that he's abrasive and that working with him is difficult.

In a tiny portion of the midbrain of your cerebral cortex, the *insula* registers internal sensations in your body that you're likely unconscious of at any given moment. It serves an integrative function, receiving sensory input and "reading" the body's current physiological state. It has emerged as a crucial component to understanding what it feels like to be human.

Whether you're aware of it or not, your biological system typically experiences pressure as a threat to your system. *Neuroception* is the term for your body's automatic, immediate, and implicit responses to danger, perceived or real.[10] A perceived threat might be a real one—like absentmindedly walking out into oncoming traffic while talking on your cell phone, noticing the cars, and then adjusting to step back to the curb.

Or a perceived threat might have no real substance, yet it activates your biology as if the threat were real—like that zebra on the savanna running from the lion in pursuit. It might sound something like, "OMG, I forgot to send that email by five p.m. last night, and I know the partner is going to be upset!"

Your biological response mirrors your *perception* in each of these cases, not your *reality*. Another way of saying it is that *biology is perception*. From a brain science point of view, we're biologically wired to take care of life's pressures and stresses: to stay safe, connected others in our tribe, and to protect our integrity. We've evolved different, primarily biological, capacities to work with our perceptions of stress and threat.

Immobilize. Think back for a moment to the meeting last week in which the junior partner's biological system registered threat. Highly conscientious and likely overprepared for the meeting, her jaw froze in place, rendering her speechless as she stepped to the podium. This deer-in-the-headlights reaction immobilized her for a brief moment. Under extreme or traumatic levels of stress, it's even possible to slip out of touch and into an internal dissociative response, in which someone might seem confused or less aware of what's going on around them.

Mobilize. Reflect on a recent moment in which you overreacted emotionally to someone at the office or your partner. Even simply recalling this moment is likely activating the most commonly talked about stress reaction—fight or flight—right now. It relies on the activation of your sympathetic nervous system—the proverbial pressure on the gas that gets your energy up and moving. You might knock someone out or make a snarky comment as a way to fight back. Or you'll flee by avoiding the person. Or, short of that, you may begin to shut down and disengage from them. Your breathing speeds up, your pupils dilate for increased vision, and the flow of blood shuts down to your viscera, shunting it instead to your large muscles to ensure you can move quickly away.

Connect. Remember a time when you reacted to a threat by moving to appease or mollify someone in hopes of "making nice," reducing intensity, or staying safe. Or you might have felt moved to connect with others to share your experience, whether of grief, loss, or joy at the moment. This stress reaction is tied to the neuroanatomy of your face, head, and neck, where low-grade tension is often expressed. The use of gestures and body language signal your wish to connect with others, increasing empathy and mutual self-soothing.

Challenge. At first blush, this response may look like a hybrid of the Mobilize and Connect reactions.[11] But looks are deceiving. The biology of the Challenge response is just that—a response, not a threat at all. This response also prepares you for action, though because you're not registering threat, your blood vessels stay relaxed. By not constricting your blood flow, more energy literally moves through your body and increases the likelihood of better performance.

While threat reactions sensitize the brain to future stress, Challenge responses set you up—with the cascading of resilience-boosting hormones— to grow your resilience as you learn from stressful experiences. Some studies reveal that performance isn't enhanced by an absence of a threat reaction but rather by the presence of a Challenge response. Challengers are interested in learning, and strong emotions support the neurobiological conditions for learning.[12] The key to how you handle pressure is how you think about your own ability to work with stress. In other words, your best renewable resource for dealing with stress is to know what you care about and to know your own signature stress style; then you can learn the skills to shift and to embody a Challenge response instead.

Skydiving High

Unquestionably, when your survival is at stake, these same biological changes come on strong and you may find yourself reacting in classic stress fashion. However, McGonigal's research reveals that when stressful situations are *less than life threatening,* our body and brain shift into a different state—the Challenger state.[13]

In my twenties, I started actively skydiving—jumping out of planes on weekends, much to my mother's chagrin. I loved the thrill of getting right to the edge of the door of the plane, looking down on the drop zone, and then letting go into freefall. Doing so activated the same chemical cocktail in my system, and I felt the "excite and delight" aspect of the Challenger stress. It may be familiar to you, too, if you find yourself regularly rushing to meet a deadline, beating the clock on a project, or get excited watching a close game on the court.

Similar to a fight-or-flight reaction that mobilizes you into action, the Challenger response indeed amps up your energy—yet it'll actually help you perform better under pressure too. Your heart rate will still rise, and your adrenaline will still spike to provide more juice to your muscles and brain.

Yet a Challenger response differs from a fight-or-flight response in a few crucial ways.

You feel focused but not fearful. A different ratio of stress hormones cascades through your system, raising the growth index of your stress response—including higher DHEA (dehydroepiandrosterone) levels, which determine whether your stressful experience is strengthening you or harming you.[14] Additionally, a Challenger response helps you recover and learn from your stress.

Contrary to what you might expect from top performers—from surgeons to performance athletes to martial artists to video gamers and musicians—they don't report feeling physiologically calm under pressure, and neither will you, if you hold a Challenger view of stress. Rather, you'll experience a strong Challenge response, the kind of stress response that gives you greater access to your own mental and physical resources. High performers often report being in a flow state while engaged in highly enjoyable activities and completely absorbed in their craft or skill. They don't talk about being stressed out, because they've learned how to harness their biological energy stress to work in their favor. High confidence, enhanced concentration, and peak performance are the results instead.

Your stress response—driven by the neurohormone oxytocin—can also motivate you to connect with others. It's a complex hormone that fine-tunes your brain's social instincts, and its primary function is to build and strengthen social bonds. Elevated oxytocin levels make you want to connect with others, and they create a craving for social contact via touch.

When your oxytocin levels are high, you're also more likely to trust those around you, since your brain's reward centers become more sensitized and responsive. It's been called the "tend-and-befriend" hormone, but it involves much more than social connection. McGonigal calls oxytocin *chemical courage*—"This hormone doesn't just make you want to hug. It also makes you brave." It dampens fear responses in your brain while suppressing your instinct to freeze or flee.[15]

Unlike the fight-or-flight reaction—also known as "defend-or-pretend," which is primarily about self-survival—the "tend-and-befriend" response motivates you to protect the people and communities you care about. Importantly, this stress response gives you the courage to do so, and it even strengthens your cardiovascular system by supporting heart cells to regenerate—certainly different than "It'll kill you!"

By design, your stress response has built-in hormones that help you recover from the mental and physical aspects of stress and increase your brain's neuroplasticity, or your ability to learn from stressful events. People who release higher levels of these hormones during pressured experiences tend to bounce back faster, with less lingering distress and improved resilience.

However, recovery isn't automatic, which may not surprise you in the least. When you've had one of those high-intensity, can't-wait-for-a-break days, you've possibly felt agitated, with a variety of reactive emotions straining to get your attention—so much so that you may have trouble *not* thinking about what happened. That's a sign, one you can now welcome, that your brain is busy processing what occurred and rewiring itself to learn from and remember that very experience. Your discomfort and mild agitation after the stressful event are the feelings of new neural pathways of learning that are growing.

Taking Yourself On

When I ask clients who take on the catching-yourself process as a way to work with stress, most will start by telling me what they *thought* or *felt emotionally* or *did*. All of those things are important, though not useful—not yet anyway. You'll get the most leverage in your learning if you first tune in to your body's sensations. Why there? Because, as you can see, they're happening in real time. Like, this very moment—now.

By learning to consciously register incoming sensory data, you can transform experiences of pain and distressful emotions—including disappointment, distrust, contempt, and hate—into empathy, trust, and compassion. Those who are better at reading sensations connected to emotions or one's gut feelings—such as a quickened heartbeat, a flushed face, or slow breathing—score higher on psychological tests of empathy. This intuitive capacity has become increasingly important for leaders.[16] A "scholarly review of gut intuitions concludes that using feelings as information is a 'generally sensible judgmental strategy,' rather than a perennial source of error as the hyperrational might argue."[17] In short, tuning in to your senses will produce, in a nanosecond, an emotionally relevant context for you to make your best decisions.

You can train yourself to consciously notice your reactions and your sensations, which will give you a short leg up on the other guy for any decisions you make.

In particular, there are five areas of focus—temperature, pressure, movement, location, and level of energy—that you'll want to start by practicing in low-stakes situations in order to jump-start your ability to consistently transform your reactivity into response.

For example, you might happen to notice varying *temperatures* in different parts of your body—your hands might be cold as you prepare for that stressful meeting this afternoon, though you're generally warm.

Pressure can take the form of tightening or contracting muscles, like those around your eyes, mouth, shoulders, or hands. You may notice that your stiff neck is becoming more painful, even to the point that you're ready to call the massage therapist.

Or, you may notice *movement*—the pulsing of your blood in your heart, or the streaming of your breath at your belly, which are both examples of inner movement. *Proprioception* is noticing where you're located in space at any given moment: noticing where your left foot is as you read this, or how you're holding your pen. The sensory intelligence in proprioception signals where you're located in space and impacts your mood and connection with others. Last, what's the *energy* of a sensation you're having—perhaps listless, hyper, or queasy?

Pausing on purpose, even momentarily, will allow you to tune in to yourself and turn up the volume on your sensory self-awareness. Your ability to catch yourself being yourself and tune in to your sensations will support you in making finer distinctions around your emotional experiences. Being skillful working with your emotions will impact your decision-making confidence and how you handle situations—whether taking an important stand or seeking support rather than blowing up, withdrawing, or opting out—to find the best choice in working with your team.

As you become more familiar with your biological cues in response to stress, you'll be able to respond best by asking yourself what part of the stress response you most need at that moment: fight, flight, escape, connection, or meaning. To be good at stress is not to avoid stress but instead to catch yourself being yourself and play an active role in transforming your stress and your leadership.

• • •

TENSION AND RELEASE: PROGRESSIVE MUSCLE PRACTICE

The point of this pause practice is to tune in to your body. There's no goal here to do it right or better than anyone else (who's watching anyway?) or even to feel less stressed. Instead, the point is to notice what's happening for you in your sensing self. You might want to read through this page before setting aside 5–7 minutes to do the practice.

◯ Tense and hold each muscle group for 5–10 seconds, feeling into and noting your sensations before releasing the tension on an exhalation. Give yourself the full 5–7 minutes for this practice. Be curious.

◯ Begin with your face—moving to your eyes, dropping down to your cheeks, and releasing your jaw and mouth before moving out to your shoulders and down to your arms and hands.

◯ While breathing in, expand your awareness to include your torso and ribs, then down to your hips and your bum in the chair. Sense gravity in your entire body before shifting your attention to your thighs, then move down to your knees and calves, feeling into your heels, the soles of your feet, and last, your toes.

○ When we're stressed and tense, we tend to get caught up in our minds. We're either way out ahead of ourselves—with our anxiety rising—or stuck back in a past situation, ruminating and replaying it over and over again. Emotions will arise too, so don't be surprised.

○ For this pause practice, there's no shifting of anything. Instead, it's about pausing to pay exquisite attention to each muscle group, energy, and sensation. Do this without judgment, merely noticing with detached awareness.

○ What do you notice? Are you tired, in pain, or hungry? Are any particular physical bugaboos showing up for you, like shoulder pain, headaches, gastrointestinal issues, or sleeping disturbances?

○ What mood are you in now? Crabby, rushed, calm, anxious, optimistic? How long is your fuse now?

○ What's the tenor of your self-thoughts? Are you moving toward a relaxation response, or are you beating yourself up and adding stress? This could sound like, "I should've known. I was such a (name your critical voice)."

○ How's your decision-making? Impulsive, thoughtful, numbed out? Are you pushing too hard, ready to give up, procrastinating, or moving along at the right pace?

• • •

Relevance to Leaders

If every time you faced intense pressure, a difficult conversation, or a tough decision, you punched someone, fled the scene, or avoided dealing with any of it by ordering an extra glass of wine, you'd run out of energy reserves very fast. You'd have spent all your energy over minor concerns, and—as a leader—you'd have wasted your stress response.

Dr. Kelly McGonigal, a professor of health sciences at Stanford, was once a true believer in the saga that "stress is bad." That is, until she ran across research that indicated that high stress levels increased the threat of dying by 43%—*but only for those who believed that stress was harming their health.*[18] In fact, those who didn't buy in to the stress-is-bad belief had the lowest risk of death in the study.

As you might imagine, that fact got McGonigal's attention. She went on to develop a popular course called The New Science of Stress, in which she teaches that—contrary to popular opinion—we humans have adapted our stress responses over time to function more effectively in modern life. We're no longer at the mercy of our fight, flight, freeze, and appease biology.

According to McGonigal, "The energy you get from stress doesn't just help your body act; it also fires up your brain."[19] Adrenaline wakes up your senses—your pupils dilate, your vision becomes more acute, and your hearing sharpens. Your mind stops wandering, and less-essential priorities fall away. The biology of stress can create a state of concentrated attention that gives you access to more information about your physical environment in a heartbeat.

A cascade of chemicals—a cocktail of cortisol, adrenaline, and testosterone—provides a rush familiar to adventure enthusiasts of all stripes (and entrepreneurs). As it surges, it increases a sense of competence and power that makes you more willing to pursue your goals.

You Can Train for This

As a leader, it's important to know that stress is a natural, biological state *designed to help you learn from experience.* Different types of stress, you now know, produce different reactions. That meeting that went sideways over a decision, or social stress, may increase your oxytocin so you move *toward* others rather than *away* from them. Deadlines and stretch goals can skyrocket your adrenaline and increase your energy and focus to drive results.

Without actively committing to proactive practices, in the face of intense day-to-day pressures: chaos, a felt lack of control, and even social mayhem can result. In aikido we train to "seize chaos" in the face of multiple attackers. It's called a randori, and it's great training for leaders.

Principles of Aikido, Randori, and Life

Randori means to "seize chaos" and to bring to bear, in the process, the four foundational principles of aikido. Of course, the principles are also applicable for leaders:

1. **Keep one point**—stay focused on what matters most, your core work.

2. **Keep weight underside**—stay grounded in yourself and connected to your core values and concerns.

3. **Relax completely**—you'll trust yourself and rest in your mission the more connected you are to your core values.

4. **Extend ki (energy)**—move with intention in the direction of your commitments.

In a randori (attack from multiple sources), depending upon one's rank in aikido, anywhere from three to six attackers come at you with full energy—striking and grabbing at you in order to distract you from your goal of staying alive.

To survive in a randori is the ultimate test of one's ability to move in and through the chaos, requiring an embodied understanding and integration of the four aikido principles. We train to see, move, and respond versus react and freeze. Ideally, the mind is free, relaxed yet alert, and aware of space, place, and timing—a state otherwise known as Mushin, or embodied presence. O Sensei—the founder of aikido—moved with deft energy, blending with the natural energy of his attackers in order to move them across the mat to where *he* wanted them.

Randori always comes 20–30 minutes after the end of a high-intensity, grueling demonstration. This loosens up one's reactive, embodied shape to ensure that one's pure, full essence shines through in the randori. A few years ago, early on a sunny Sunday morning, six of us were testing for our black belts. The dojo was full to capacity—about twenty-five fellow aikidoka had come out that sunny December day for the demonstration. While the others were testing for *shodan* and would face four attackers, I was testing for *sandan*—third degree—and would be up against a few more. I'd just spent twenty minutes demonstrating weapons work. I was cooked. I sat at one end of the long, gray mat for a few moments facing off with six attackers, my training partners.

First, we faced the kamiza at the front of the dojo and bowed with respect to O Sensei and other teachers in our long lineage of practice. We then turned to bow to our own sensei. Last, we bowed to one another across the expanse of the mat.

I paused to breathe in deeply, focusing on one point to presence myself. I settled into my now warmed-up body and relaxed as much as I could that chilly morning. My mind started to race, requiring another deep, settling breath. Despite pausing, I felt a buzzy anxiety mounting in my chest in anticipation of the loud slap on the mat that would quickly move us all into action.

The job of my fellow aikidoka was to give me their most sincere attack; mine was to lead, move, deflect, throw, find, or create new openings to move through. The slap was sharp and intense, "*Hajime!*"—the loud Japanese exhortation to begin. In a blink, we were all up and moving—bodies were swirling fast in my direction!

At one point, I looked up to see a six-foot-five-inch man coming in to crack the head on my five-foot-five-inch body, his loud *kiai* startling me. I pivoted out of range, only to be confronted by someone throwing a punch at my midsection.

The intensity, the noise, the exhilaration! It's easy to get caught up in the chaos—to have someone grab and hold tight, and to find yourself fighting, struggling, and getting caught in your own web of resistance instead of simply surrendering to the moment and moving. That's why we train—to be alert and responsive instead of simply reactive. We train to pause and center while in motion.

Avoiding getting stuck in a corner and jammed up, which I knew could easily happen, required me to hold the awareness of the bigger picture in my mind—not just to see what was right in front of me but to continue moving and leading. The endless supply of attackers continued, tiring me out until the final *Yame* (Japanese for "stop") was shouted and my demonstration test was over.

A key phrase, frequently heard in my years of practicing aikido, is "Own the mat!" Translation: the mat is your life and your workplace, so step out and own it—learn to move within it, to make your impact, and to live well until you die.

If you've ever been caught up in a project and felt the apprehension of deadlines, flowcharts, and logistics, you've likely felt the physical uptick of rising anxiety—an urge to know more than you can possibly know at that moment and a fervent wish for it all to be over soon. To be flexible, fine-tuned, and resilient as a leader, know that you, too, can train your body and mind to respond to each stressful situation by best using your energetic resources in any context. It doesn't have to be on an aikido mat!

RECAP

- The doing can't be different until the being is different
- Learning occurs through the body and can grow trust
- Responses to stress and pressure
  - Immobilize
  - Mobilize
  - Connect
  - Challenge

- The secret sauce to success is how you show up to learn

- Mastery requires practice

- Principles of aikido, principles for life
  - Keep one point
  - Keep weight underside/ground yourself
  - Relax completely
  - Extend ki (your energy)

SCOPE: SPACE, CONNECTION, OPENNESS, PACE, ENERGY

S – How often do you feel pushed into a corner each day?

C – Have you made decisions, only to realize later that they made matters worse for your team?

O – Are you open to others' feelings while in a difficult conversation?

P – Do you make decisions quickly, with little thought as to whether they're the best decisions?

E – How often do you end the day saying, "I'm exhausted"?

CHAPTER 5

The Power of Mindset

To rid yourself of old patterns, focus all your energy not on struggling with the old, but on building the new.

—DAN MILLMAN, AUTHOR OF *WAY OF THE PEACEFUL WARRIOR*

I n its first fifteen years, Stagen Leadership Academy grew in its mission to "raise consciousness through business." Working with a select group of leaders committed to long-term personal growth, those leaders produced exceptional personal change that then cascaded through their organizational cultures and produced a ripple effect of influence.

Stagen flourished, if by flourishing we mean "achieving success." However, Rand Stagen—who founded the academy in 1999—soon discovered that those leaders that Stagen had served, together with the close-knit team Rand had built, were focused on another, broader definition of flourish: "to reach a height of development and influence," a definition that lay at the foundation of the tricky conversation that lay ahead.

Rand described the act as no less than a staged intervention. Interventions typically include multiple people stepping up to share how they've been impacted, usually negatively, by the behaviors of the one on the receiving end of the intervention—in this case, Rand.

Here, however, the general emphasis was skewed in a positive direction: to grow the academy's impact in the world, not necessarily to grow the business into a huge, revenue-generating consulting machine. To grow impact would require expanding Stagen's reach rather than staying in the narrower niche space they'd carved out in the marketplace.

Stagen's clients, community members, and the Stagen leadership team had their collective fingers on the pulse. They knew that the long-term work of growing leaders for the future, a process they call *decading*, needed to be more accessible in the world. In effect, their feedback sounded something like, "You're being selfish by not letting more people have the great food at this buffet table of learning." Rand's response to the candor of the conversation, the pressure? "I got enrolled around the idea that it was time to scale the impact of the business by growing our impact, so I said, 'Yes.'"

Yet, he pulled back, shut down, fought with himself and his team, and generally spent his energy. He stalled, offered excuses about competing commitments, and procrastinated in taking committed action toward this expansive kind of growth. By the time he wrestled the dragon down, he described himself as a "hot mess, fully dysfunctional, and resistant."

According to Rand, "What it came down to was that I was not ready to really start implementing the change necessary. First, I had to surface why I was hesitant and afraid of the change, which I didn't really understand. This included addressing my personal frustration and all sorts of conflict and processing within our own team. Only then did I gain clarity for myself."

In short, Rand says he "wasn't ready, psychologically, to really, genuinely start working on changing the direction of the business. It took me three years to process through my own resistance to change, even change I agreed would be a good idea."

Talk about a pause!

How do you respond to the challenges and pressures that you face today?

It's important to be attuned to the myriad of ways you, as a leader, grapple with stress and play with pressure. If you're unaware, as Rand was initially, you're at the mercy of whatever underlying patterns, mindsets, and old strategies are driving your actions. Those patterns may or may not support your being your best self as a leader.

The key? Pause to investigate your mindset.

The Power of Mindset

The expectations we hold in any given situation reveal our most deeply held unconscious mindsets—those interior patterns of thinking and feeling, those frames of reference that we have about ourselves and others.

Mindsets are the mental foundation for living our lives.

Like a camera lens, our mindset filters how we see the world, coloring what's possible—or not—through its prism. The effect we expect to see is the effect that we get. Think about that.

Carol Dweck, a world-renowned psychologist at Stanford, has been studying the phenomenon of mindset for years.[1] In her decades of research on achievement and success, she has found that one's mindset makes all the difference.

Mindset encompasses those interior patterns of thinking and frames of reference that we hold about ourselves and others: our core beliefs, attitudes, and expectations that all influence our way of being in the world.

Dweck found that, regardless of the baseline ability Mother Nature happened to bestow on any one of us, nurture (effort and attitude) can produce extraordinary gains in capacity. With a "fixed"—aka "acquired"—mindset, we tend to believe that basic qualities like intelligence or talent are fixed traits and are, alone, what ensure success—without effort. Mistakes are avoided, and feedback from others isn't sought or utilized as a means to course correct. And as a result, those with a fixed mindset can spend lots of time documenting their smarts and talents—which are believed to be in scarce supply—instead of developing them.

For example, remember meeting that guy who goes on and on with great bombast about where he went to school on the East Coast? Or the woman who catalogs her soccer achievements from college fifteen years ago in excruciating detail over dinner? Of course, nothing is wrong with their stories. Except that they likely reflect a fixed mindset, where talents are reified and reinforced, leaving little room for growth—especially when it comes to leadership. As tensions increase and pressure around performance amps up, those with a fixed mindset will become increasingly reactive and fall prey to their old strategies and automatic ways of thinking, feeling, and behaving.

The practice of pausing can support the shift to a more fluid, or "growth," mindset. With this mindset, basic abilities can be developed through dedication and hard work, because good brains and out-of-the-box talent merely serve as a starting point. By slowing down to take a beat instead of being fixed in the past, leaders can create an engaged love of learning and grow the resiliency essential for significant accomplishments.

Unlike a fixed mindset, in which one acquires and adds new knowledge to an already existing way of making sense of the world, a growth mindset transforms and expands the mind by stretching it, challenging it, and evolving to a more expansive level of complexity. Like an athlete who knows the burn of pushing his muscles to make them stronger, the leader who trains and grows her mind also knows the discomfort of stretching beyond her current mental, emotional, and embodied limits.

Contrary to popular opinion, as we develop throughout our careers, we don't tend to become more adept or proficient but relatively less so, despite our experience and "expertise."[2] This notion, at first blush, seems counterintuitive. Yet, research by psychologist Anders Ericsson and his colleagues—who have studied performance across a wide variety of fields, from the arts to the sciences to athletics and music—has found that gifted performers are always made, not born.

Mindset isn't just an individual thing, by the way. It shows up at work too—in organizations, in hiring, in talent selection, and in the culture. In a study from 2014, Dweck and her colleagues at management consulting firm Senn Delaney explored mindset in organizations. Cultivating a growth mindset was a key factor in creating better agility and innovation, as well as in developing an engaged, collaborative, committed, and truly trusting workforce.[3]

It's All in Your Head

The phrase "it's all in your head" is typically accompanied by a tone of derision, indicating that the problem or situation at hand is not real. Consider the *placebo effect*, a phenomenon in which beneficial effects of a pain medication cannot be attributed to the properties of the treatment but are instead attributed to the patient's belief in that treatment. Neurobiological research of the past three decades has shown that the placebo effect, or expectation to heal, engages areas of the brain that activate the physiological effects that lead to healing outcomes.

Yet, it cuts both ways. Mindsets and associated expectations can also lead to what's called *nocebo*, or negative effects. When told an injection may hurt, some patients reported heightened pain responses. Similarly, patients told about the mere possibility of a medication having negative side effects may experience increased negative side effects.

The work of Dr. Alia Crum at Stanford speaks volumes to these effects.[4] Her research suggests that one's mindset can influence the benefits of particular behaviors—from a decreased caloric impact of a milkshake to the positive exercise benefits of simple housekeeping tasks. One of her most significant findings has to do with *demonstrating how one's stress mindset makes a difference in one's experience*. Her findings were quite surprising, as you will see.

Are you stuck in a stress mindset? One that filters whatever stresses come your way into intractable views and ways of being? Maybe even a mindset that says "all pressure and stress is bad stress"? If so, you're not alone.

We all experience day-to-day stress—you know, traffic jams, heightened political frenzy, coworkers who drive you crazy, and conversations that fall flat—but the notion that all of it is bad is antiquated. Yet, it may be embodied in your mindset too.

One's stress mindset is the extent to which one holds the belief that stress has enhancing consequences (referred to as a "stress-is-enhancing mindset") for various stress-related outcomes—such as performance and productivity, health and well-being, and learning and growth—or holds the belief that stress has debilitating consequences for those outcomes (referred to as a "stress-is-debilitating mindset").[5]

We've learned that believing that "stress is bad" is both factually inaccurate and counterproductive. It's *inaccurate* because the research shows short-term stress often promotes positive mental and physical outcomes. Good stress can be a powerful catalyst for growth. It's *counterproductive* because simply believing the thought "stress is bad" leads to a stress mindset that undermines the ability of your body and mind to deal effectively with the stress you face.

Believe it or not, altering the "stress mindset" of participants in a study in Crum's lab changed their biological response to stress. Again, *biology is perception*.

Participants in Crum's study were subject to a mock job interview, in which the interviewer offered ongoing feedback to improve participants' interview skills. The rub? All the feedback was critical and designed to evoke stressful reactions in participants on purpose.

However, before the interview began, each participant watched one of two short videos. The first opened with a positive message—"Most people think that stress is negative . . . but actually, research shows that stress is enhancing"— and detailed positive effects such as enhanced performance and higher overall well-being. The second opened with a negative message—"Most people know that stress is negative . . . but research shows that stress is even more debilitating than you expect"—and went on to detail effects such as poor health, trouble with performance, and negative mood states. Both videos were designed to elicit participants' biological responses to a stress.

After the test, saliva samples were taken and analyzed. Crum was measuring two stress hormones, both of which are released by adrenal glands and essential to our well-being, though for different reasons. *Cortisol* improves the body's ability to use fat and sugars to energize while suppressing other functions that are less important when under stress: digestion and growth, in particular, DHEA (dehydroepiandrosterone), which supports your brain's growth and speeds up healing.

What's significant is the ratio between the two stress hormones— cortisol and DHEA—and how it impacts the long-term consequences of stress, or what's called the growth index of a stress response. High cortisol levels reveal reduced positive outcomes, including depression and immune system suppression. High levels of DHEA are linked to reduced risks of stress-related symptoms like heart disease and depression. The higher the growth index—indicating higher levels of DHEA—the more people thrive under stress, including a greater ability to focus, improved decision-making skills, and greater resilience.

The other question asked by Crum's research: Would a simple pre-intervention video, with an even simpler belief statement about stress, impact the growth index after the mock interview? Amazingly, it did. All participants had a post-interview rise in cortisol, yet those who had seen the stress-is-enhancing video had higher levels of DHEA than those who were primed with the stress-is-debilitating video and experienced a diminished biological response and performance. Somehow, simply holding a belief— even temporarily—made it so.

Viewing stress as a helpful part of life—stress-as-enhancing—rather than as harmful—what Crum called stress-as-debilitating and other researchers have called stress-related growth—is how stressful experiences fundamentally change individuals for the better. This seemingly simple adjustment in outlook can result in a multitude of benefits: the development of mental toughness, heightened awareness of new perspectives, strengthened priorities, deeper relationships, improved work productivity, and even a sense of mastery and a greater appreciation for a life.

Mindsets are powerful.

But how does a person change their mindset? Is it like flipping a switch? Or is it more involved? Crum was determined to find out. In a second, two-hour stress management training, she designed ways for more than two hundred participants to choose a new stress mindset. After reflecting on how they themselves experienced stress, they were taught a simple process to shift to a new mindset. The first step was to simply acknowledge the stress and notice how it felt in their body. Next, they were to acknowledge that their stress was a response to something they cared about, which begged questions about their motivation, what was at stake, etc. Last, they were encouraged to make good use of the energy of their stress rather than simply trying to manage it—and certainly not to waste it!

Three weeks later, the participants—who for the most part had bought into the stress-is-bad notion—were working with their stress more effectively and reporting less anxiety and more energy, creativity, and connection with others. Six weeks later, their gains had been maintained when compared with results reported by a wait-listed control group for the program.

• • •

PAUSE TO REFLECT ON MINDSET

Set aside some space to complete the following exercise, and give attention to take an honest look at the core mindsets you hold. Complete the phrases to help uncover what matters most to you. Take your time.

In a world in which being right, being smart, performing at all costs, and making stuff happen are highly valued, it's easy to be hard on ourselves and spin out into judgment. Use this exercise with patience. This will allow space to honestly examine what's up for you.

○ What top three beliefs impact your decision-making?

○ Which stress mindsets do you operate from most often? How's it working for you in your life and leadership?

○ Take a few minutes here to simply sit. Breathe.

Our bodies (including our thinking capacity, our ability to "feel" into others' concerns, and our ability to take effective action) require rest to recalibrate our psychobiological systems and renew ourselves for the sake of meeting the challenges of the day, so take another pause to fully recalibrate.

• • •

Relevance for Leaders:
Pressure Promotes Growth

What's the secret to getting good at stress? At handling pressure?

It's cultivating resilience—as defined in the Oxford Learner's Dictionary, that "ability to bounce or spring back into shape after being stretched, bent, or compressed." This is where a growth mindset can expand and even transform your mind by stretching it, challenging it, and evolving to a more expansive level of complexity.

If you've ever felt stretched too far, bent out of shape, or pressed into a ball of roiling stress, you'll know the internal longing to bounce back and "feel like myself" again.

The good news is that we can develop resilience by making good choices within what Dr. Dan Siegel has called the Window of Tolerance.[6] The Window of Tolerance describes a zone of emotional arousal within our nervous system in which we're able to function most effectively. When we're within this zone, we're typically able to readily receive, process, and integrate information and otherwise respond to the stresses and demands of everyday life without much difficulty.

Under too much stress, however, we may experience hurt, anxiety, pain, or anger that brings us close to the edges of the Window of Tolerance. This can be uncomfortable.

Under too little stress (or prolonged overstress), we may become numb, exhausted, and stressed out—and act with poor boundaries. Generally speaking, however, our present-day mindset has strategies for keeping us within this window. The following diagram demonstrates the ebb and flow of an optimally regulated nervous system within the Window of Tolerance.

Operating within the Window of Tolerance works for coping on a day-to-day basis. We handle what comes to us without losing our cool or sinking to the bottom of the emotional heap. Yet, what helps us get really good at stress—alternatively described as "stress hardiness"—is to work close to the edges of our Window of Tolerance so that we're expanding and growing the breadth of the window and taking more of life in, without doing damage to our overall well-being.

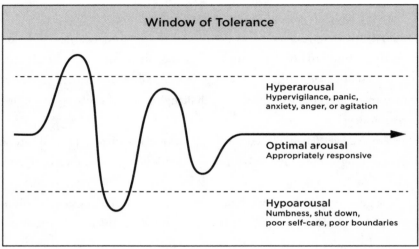

Window of Tolerance developed by neuroscientist and psychiatrist Dan Siegel.
Graph obtained from: https://subtleyoga.com/tolerating-everything-but-the-kitchen-sink-blog/

Getting Good at Stress: Recognize-Renew-Reflect-Return-Rewire

Those who are resilient in the face of life's struggles hold the notion of stress differently. For them, a stress-is-enhancing mindset (versus stress-is-debilitating) alters their moods to reflect openness and possibility.

Rather than a threat, they believe that adversity is a normal challenge and part of life. They don't use their energy to resist change. They believe they have choices to make, and they make them. However aware they are of their mindset and mood, they instinctively follow a process that expands their window (making it look as if they simply were born that way!).

These stress-hardy, gritty, resilient sorts **recognize** the situation they're in and know that it might be tricky.

For example, it may come in a flash for you to realize how fatigued you are in the middle of the day. Or, you may become aware that you're tired of fighting: the kids, your partner, the deadlines, life. Or, you notice that something you love to do—golf, garden, or grandkids—well, none of it sparks your interest at the moment.

Those filled with grit and resilience recognize the need to **renew** their physical body by pausing, slowing down, and breathing to calm down their emotional reactions.

Later, they just might catch a nap or go to bed earlier.

Then they can **reflect** on the details of the situation at hand from a calmer perspective. They then choose to **return** their attention to what that situation calls for at the moment.

And in doing so, they're expanding the edges of their Window of Tolerance and rewiring their brains for greater resilience.

• • •

GROW YOUR WINDOW OF TOLERANCE

We can work within our Window of Tolerance to expand our emotional capacity and become more resilient. This involves working at the edges with both conceptual (mindset and mood) and embodied (physical) practices.

Pausing to notice what's occurring at the moment it's occurring results in building your capacity to tolerate strong sensations without slipping into automatic actions to avoid discomfort. It's central to becoming more resilient.

◯ In this pause practice, you'll examine how you can shift your perspective to increase your resilience. Our mindsets, perspectives, and moods are, by definition, quite subjective (despite those moments we *know* they're the truth).

continued

○ Settle into your body now, deepening your connection with gravity regardless of whether you're sitting or standing. Bring to mind a stressful moment, one that's personal somehow, and rate the level of stress from 1=low to 10=high.

○ As you continue to allow your breath to continue (no extra effort here), simply turn the dial up on your stress, just a degree or two, with just the right amount of challenge (rather than threat), and linger at the edges of the stress for a few extra beats. Then with another breath, and on purpose, return the dial back to a state of physiological coherence—in which your energy is operating within your Window of Tolerance.

The more you practice this when the stakes are low (your job is not in danger, your kids are simply being kids, not monsters), the easier and more quickly you'll recover when you're hyped up, frazzled, or taken by surprise. Exposure, exaggeration, and repetition at the edge of your Window of Tolerance—your comfort zone—is how you'll build your resilience.

You can do this practice alone, though asking a trusted other to review your experience afterward will provide a boost to your learning.

• • •

Catching Yourself: An Upside

It's so easy to get caught up in one thing—and then the next thing, and then the thing after that—and fail to notice what shows up in an ordinary moment.

We fail to pause out of habit that the next moment will be more of something—more interesting, more significant, or more juicy. We do this often.

For those of us who've been educated in the US, with a strong press for productivity and efficiency, we're trained to focus on the next thing, then the next thing, and then the next thing. Even the liberal arts college I attended supported this behavior. With such an outward, forward, and future focus, we fail to notice so much—particularly the extraordinary amid the ordinary.

Take, for example, my experience at the local Starbucks. I'd dropped in to grab a quick coffee before my early morning meeting. The line was long, at least eight people deep. I glanced at my watch, an inner rev starting at my chest.

If I wanted coffee, and I did, then I'd choose to wait. I chose. I took a breath and remembered that "catching myself" here meant dropping my impatience. That settled me down a bit, and I began to look around at others in line.

They were in line at the coffee shop ahead of me. She, a petite young blonde woman with expressive eyes; he, an older, slight man—perhaps a Greek or Italian immigrant—with broken English, twinkling eyes, and a smile the width of his face. While ordering himself breakfast and coffee, she remarked, "Louie calls me his daughter," telling the woman behind her and in front of me about wanting to find a way to help Louie to see better because his eyesight was particularly poor.

The woman ahead of me, obviously as touched as I was, suggested the name of a community resource for free eye exams, which the smiling "daughter" excitedly put into her iPhone, exclaiming that she'd call later that morning after picking up her young son from school.

While awaiting the coffee and breakfast sandwiches, the "daughter" pulled out money to pay for their meal. Yet the resourceful woman beat her to it, stepping in to pay for their breakfasts with a $20 bill, saying "thank you" to them both as she took her coffee and moved quickly toward the door. "She just bought us breakfast, Louie—how lovely! Thank you," the "daughter" said. Louie smiled his warm smile, accepting the directive to move toward the counter to pick up their coffee.

Social scientists tell us that in addition to the person receiving a kindness, the one expressing kindness benefits in the same ways. These benefits include the subjective experience of feeling good due to spiking levels of serotonin—that feel-good hormone that contributes to regulating mood, boosting feelings of optimism and joyfulness, and strengthening one's immune system.

Yet the biggest surprise by far has to do with the fact that the benefits extend to anyone simply witnessing the act of kindness.[7]

This was surely true in my case.

Tears filled my eyes as I witnessed this random, mindful act of kindness. As I added cream to my coffee, I felt my heart opening in my chest. I felt lighter, more connected to my fellow coffee drinkers. I felt inspired and grateful. And though I was unclear whether others had even noticed this small yet amazing act of love, I began to actively search for ways to extend kindness myself in the day ahead. Thank you, Louie and company—you made my day.

RECAP

- Growth or fixed, mindset matters
- It's all in your head
- Your mindset: stress is debilitating, or stress is enhancing?
- Pressure promotes growth: Growing your Window of Tolerance
- You can get good at stress

SCOPE: SPACE, CONNECTION, OPENNESS, PACE, ENERGY

S – Will you take time to check your mindset?

C – When is the last time you stopped to ask yourself, Why do I think this is so?

O – When was the last time you changed your mind?

P – How often do you make a decision without pausing to reflect on it?

E – How does your mindset affect your energy levels by the end of the day?

CHAPTER 6

Presence: Tap Your Power

Power is the basic energy needed to initiate and sustain
action or, to put it another way, the capacity to translate
intention into reality and sustain it. Leadership is the
wise use of this power: transformative leadership.

—WARREN BENNIS, AUTHOR OF *LEARNING TO LEAD*

There's a lot of buzz about the notion of leadership presence. Why?
Because it matters. A lot.

It's important to notice it, cultivate it, and deepen it.

We know it when we experience it. We feel it in others around us. Leaders with this secret sauce magnetically draw us into their orbit, as if by magic.

Leadership presence is decidedly *not* a cookie-cutter kind of thing, nor is it about having a "commanding presence," though one might have that, too. It's not about putting on airs, knowing the secret handshake, or wearing the right attire—though none of those things can hurt. It's not even the timbre of your voice, the steadiness of your eye contact, or the firmness of your handshake. According to leadership expert Sally Helgesen, though "all these things matter, they alone cannot make someone who is unfocused seem like a leader."[1]

Presence is that quality of being in the present moment, taking in the energy of the world around you—whatever that may include—and deeply listening. Peter Senge, systems scientist and founder of the Society for Organizational Learning, has described it as "letting go and letting come"[2]—though my dad used the phrase "easy come, easy go."

Great statesmen like John Lewis and Colin Powell have it. Great actors like Viola Davis and Emma Thompson do too. Of course, it's not just well-known folks who exude presence—that combination of calm comportment, confidence, and warmth that puts you at ease. Your neighbor down the block or your kid's soccer coach or chemistry teacher may have it too. Even those you experience as initially uninteresting or uninviting may later exude calm and authority when fully present—like the Friday night pizza guy, the maintenance guy at the office, or the barista at the local coffee shop.

Leadership presence goes way beyond slick presentations or a glad-handing command of a room. And—though presence can't be manufactured—despite all the hype, it can be cultivated.

Helgesen defines presence as a "bearing, personality, or appearance that is characterized by poise and confidence." It even points to something akin to the supernatural or divine. Presence is the lively combination of a confident and relaxed body, assertive conversational skills, and positive, engaging energy that emanates in a kind of energetic field that attracts others. In short, it's the total package. These qualities together have an aura of power that invigorates presence and serves as one of the best predictors of well-being.[3]

Ultimately, it's about being authentic, poised, and comfortable in your own skin while being willing to be just as you are—warts and all—in any given moment. Leadership presence is, paradoxically, all about you in your full, real, tried-and-true self and also not about you at all!

Simultaneous Awareness

People who give us their undivided attention
most vividly manifest presence.

—FROM "WHAT'S THE SECRET TO LEADERSHIP PRESENCE?"
BY SALLY HELGESEN, AUTHOR OF *THE FEMALE VISION:
WOMEN'S REAL POWER AT WORK*

When someone is fully present, they're confident yet attuned to you and to the entire context at hand. You feel it; it's palpable. You feel seen. They "get you," even at a distance—what Dr. Dan Seigel calls "feeling felt." It's as though there's a spotlight shining on them that somehow extends to you too.

Because it does.

Presence involves the capacity to hold attention simultaneously on yourself, your concerns, and your own sensations while paying full attention to another (or several others) at the same time, in the same moment, and without distractions or abstractions. The distinction of simultaneous attention is important because the neural networks for embodied self-awareness are the same as the neural networks for empathy. In fact, the ability to empathize appears to rest on our ability to unconsciously model in our own bodies what someone else might be feeling in theirs.

This is what enables leaders to listen deeply to what is said and what goes unspoken, to pick up the tenor of the shared energy in the conversational space. How is the leader listening to the situation at hand? Does she listen into what the current situation calls for *now*? Does he embody the presence of mind and heart to lead into action what's called for now?

When you can feel your own sensations while paying attention to another person, they can sense that you're fully with them without having abandoned yourself. Your presence then is "non-sticky," and others sense that you have no secret agenda for them, other than their own. Simply by being present yourself, you provide the opening for others to engage more deeply as themselves too, because presence involves an ability to connect simultaneously with one's self and the thoughts and feelings of others.

In a word, leaders with presence know who they are; they're authentic and we're drawn to them. They actively connect with others, they lead from heartfelt values with sincerity and conviction, they're calm under stress, and they're accountable for their choices and actions. They also devote time and attention to learning, and they cultivate a strong leadership presence that translates into deep, meaningful results.

Leaders who embody presence embody humility. They don't pretend to know everything, and they willingly acknowledge their own shortcomings while embracing the contributions of others. They focus their attention on the present with one eye to the lessons of history and the other eye to the openings of possibility on the horizon. Because presence inspires and motivates, it generates the possibility of building the real, authentic trust required to move into action. Think of Gandhi or Martin Luther King Jr. or Ruth Bader Ginsburg, who each led from a deep well of presence.

Leadership presence is a necessary attribute of conscious leadership that can't be faked, but it can be amplified. It's an invitation to explore the space between, which both reveals and discloses what's important in sharing with another.

When present, we tap into qualities that enable us to connect with others, inspire them, engage with them, and act toward a greater purpose. The more we, as leaders, practice the skills of being aware and present in the moment, as it's unfolding, and cultivating our leadership presence, the more we can create the future for the highest collective good.

How? By training to tolerate, expand, and cultivate capacity for ever more life to flow through us. As my colleague and friend Doug Silsbee has said, "Building our literacy at staying present, sensing the context, and then acting consistently with what the context is asking of us is the art of leadership."[4]

● ● ●

PRESENCE REFLECTIONS

Spend a few moments pausing to reflect on those leaders you believe have strong leadership presence.

○ What do you admire most in these leaders? What about them makes you attune to their presence?

○ What words would you use to describe their presence?

○ What question might you ask that person if you were in the same room together? Why that question?

○ What did you learn from this short pausing practice?

Your Leadership Presence

You're a leader. You hold a vision for what matters to you, and you've worked hard to enlist folks to bring that something to life and make it a reality. Yet it can sometimes feel like the forces of the universe and everyone in it—your clients, your market, your team, and even you yourself—are working against you. Competing priorities, potential obstacles, and inevitable conflict seem to block the path toward the vision you can see but can't . . . quite . . . reach. If you react and become overly stressed out, others will pick up on that energy and get pulled into your negative emotional vortex. The result? Your presence will be described as stressful and sticky.

If, however, you're alert and engaged, clear-eyed and present, others will sense that energy and will be moved to trust you. Leadership presence is an embodied way of being that produces an overall assessment of trustworthy leadership.

Ofttimes, leaders confuse being in charge with leading. Marc Blackman did, at least historically. Marc is the third-generation CEO of Gold Eagle, a Chicago-based distributor of automotive aftermarket fluids and additives for the combustion engine. In his thirteen-year tenure as CEO, his concerns have focused on growth, balancing the necessary investments for Gold Eagle to grow with the overall financial health of a business in which the long-term sustainability of products is dependent upon the internal combustion engine.

Marc says growing his leadership presence involved catching himself being uncomfortable—"I had to know something or had to be right all the time." As he became more comfortable in his own skin, he says, "I could relax and let go. That's when I could really listen and ask others to explain their points of view. By doing that, all of the sudden, we're starting to become better aligned."

Marc's passion for bringing people together is reflected in Gold Eagle's purpose statement—"to protect and preserve the things you love." When panic from the 2020 pandemic hit, the moment required more of the company, and more of Marc, too.

"I'm a consensus-driven leader, yet this intense moment required more," he said. "I had to step up to the plate, and we didn't have a lot of time. I had to really step back, take time to pause and recalibrate myself. I focused my breathing and visualized how I wanted us to address the issues at hand. Ultimately, I had to decide how I wanted to be in it. When I did this, I found it sent me on the correct path."

Given his commitment to conscious leadership, Marc had, with intention and practice, deepened in his presence and become a different kind of listener. "Ultimately, at some point, as business leaders we have to step up and fill the void," he said. "Whether we have to run for office, or we do it in other ways to help this country—business leaders need to step up." By becoming more present to what he was feeling in any given moment, he could respond more effectively to the moment at hand—in this case, the safety of his own people and the community at large.

In the spring of 2020, and with no idea what to expect, Marc and his team went about cutting costs and preparing for the worst. Their first priority was to "keep our people safe." And then, in an effort to do their part to "help society," they dove into learning about product and production requirements in the hand sanitizer market. Instead of high-quality engine lubricants, they pivoted and began producing liquid, gel, and lotion sanitizer. "We ended up being able to do so much more with less," Marc said. "We've surprised ourselves." It's quite possible that Gold Eagle has opened up a new line of business while continuing to fulfill their purpose "to protect and preserve the things you love."

In a later conversation, Marc said, "I find that I'm in flow much more. *I think flow is a function of presence.* It's a function of calmness and confidence, and of really being fully aware of what you're trying to do—connecting with people, in a way, and really hearing and listening."

Leaders with presence—like Marc—radiate warmth, care, and a confidence that buoys a sense that, by following this leader, all will be well. Authentic authority stems from keen self-awareness, which is a key aspect of emotional intelligence and confidence. These leaders know what they are capable of achieving by themselves and through others. They draw from a deeper set of values—those connected to their deepest concerns and longings. In doing so, they tap into their purpose to produce alignment and congruence with what generates life in them.

Triggers: A Hidden Doorway

Masakatsu Agatsu . . . True victory is victory over oneself.

—O SENSEI, FOUNDER OF AIKIDO

In our crazy-fast world, the ability to be present is more critical than ever. We live in a global, multicultural world. Presence is about being human, whether in Detroit or Dubai, and is the result of certain ongoing choices you make, as well as actions you take or fail to take. Presence is a function of directing attention. In turning the spotlight inward to catch yourself being yourself, you'll learn about those sticky patterns of thinking, feeling, and acting that take you out of the present—which, of course, is the only moment in which you can feel, make decisions, appreciate life, or lead.

Your old patterns—those strategies that you developed to keep you safe from harm and connected in life—have done an amazing job getting you to this point in your life. But, truth be told, you're being called to something higher, something bigger, and something that's uniquely yours to do. Admittedly, examining patterns that you had no clue you needed to confront will have you feeling uncomfortable and weirdly out of your skin for bits at a time. But the payoff is priceless.

One surprising way to get there? Observe your triggers—those times, situations, and people that take you out of the present moment. Do you feel the effect of the vagaries of life? At the mercy of others' decisions or moods? Do you find yourself filling your days completely, scheduling meetings back-to-back? Does it feel like you're squeezing every last minute out of your day?

In our Type A culture, we drive hard, we drive fast, and we drive with a near singular focus on productivity. It's easy to get caught up in the vortex of busyness we call business. When we do, however, we increase the likelihood that we'll be triggered by lots of "things" that tick us off, setting off a domino effect of pressure, stress, and tragic stories.

Many of us find that we live in reaction to the ups and downs of life, much to our detriment. When we're caught up in a trigger, our breathing shifts, our muscles tense and constrict, and we quit noticing what's around us, losing sight of a bigger picture. So instead of trying to stop being triggered (to be human is to be triggered—it's as inevitable as breathing), the trick is to turn toward our triggers and come to know them intimately, like a good friend. It's then that you can calm them down to reclaim and redirect your attention and energies to directing the daily traffic—emotional, digital, and interpersonal—of your day.

By being present and willing to investigate your triggers more closely, you'll cease running on empty and open the door to great presence and power.

There really is a better way.

Your Best Self

> We are not here to fit in, be well-balanced, or provide
> exempla for others. We are here to be eccentric, different,
> perhaps strange, perhaps merely to add our small piece, our
> little clunky selves, to the great mosaic of being. As the gods
> intended, we are here to become more and more ourselves.

—JAMES HOLLIS, AUTHOR OF *WHAT MATTERS MOST*
AND JUNGIAN ANALYST

Living in this culture, we tend to think we must be faster (read: beat the "competition"), smarter (read: be the "expert" in our field), better (read: better than the other guy).

But it isn't so. None of this drive, drive, drive is sustainable on a day-to-day basis. Instinctively, you know this to be true. In fact, pause a moment now. Tune in to your breathing and check in on yourself. How're you doing right now?

Pausing first to notice what's going on inside yourself, you'll begin to notice some different truths. Shoulders always up and high? Wow, is my jaw always this tense?

To move faster, play with your pace by slowing down a bit. What happens?

To be smarter, learn what you don't know. Ask inquiring questions to gain insights from colleagues, customers, and your family and friends.

To be better, shift your zoomed-in perspective to a wide-angle view. What do you see from this vantage point? What would happen if you acted from that point of view?

Before you start, however, you'll need an accurate take on what actually triggers you and takes you out of the moment, catapulting you into the cerebral craziness of Type A thinking: "I must be faster, smarter, better—now."

Surprisingly, triggers serve as hidden doorways to the values and beliefs that comprise your mindset, take up residence in your body, and ultimately define your identity. Triggers reflect your already existing mindset to address the increased turbulence of perpetual whitewater. They can usher you across the threshold to a deeper understanding of yourself as a leader.

By surfacing your mindset via the doorway of your embodied triggers, you heighten the self-awareness you'll need to become more deeply present to your best self.

What's a Trigger?

> Often suffering is the trigger, or a spiritual
> teaching or both. Call it readiness or grace. It is the
> beginning of the awakening process.
>
> —ECKHART TOLLE, SPIRITUAL TEACHER AND AUTHOR[5]

If you've ever felt off-kilter or out of sorts or lost your composure and reacted defensively in the moment, you know what it's like to be triggered. It can feel as though something has grabbed you by the throat, effectively yanking you out of the moment and disorienting you.

Two distinctions will help improve your understanding of how triggers might influence your behavior.

A trigger can be direct or indirect. *Direct triggers* are immediate, and we react immediately—like when I had to slam on my brakes to avoid hitting one of the boys on my block who was fielding a ball. An *indirect trigger*, however, is out of consciousness—like when you heard that song from your senior year in high school and memories of your sister on your summer family trip popped up. You called your sister.

Triggers can be internal or external. *External triggers* come from the environment. We notice them via our senses, as well as with our thinking minds. *Internal triggers*, however, are generated within and often take the form of our "inner critic" or that "little inner voice."

Becoming skillful as a conscious leader is being present to how our very identity gets triggered into reaction mode. Being triggered narrows our vision, heightens our anxieties, and throws us off instead of allowing us to stay fully engaged and present to the moment at hand.

There are four domains to consider as we explore and then turn to face our triggers. These domains are interwoven like a braid, yet when we're triggered they can seem indistinguishable from one another.

1. **Mental**: This involves noticing where your thoughts go—perhaps to blame, self-defense, justification, or self-recriminations.

2. **Emotional**: A wide variety of emotions may arise that can be subtle or quite strong—e.g., mild irritation, anger, anxiety, fear, or self-righteousness. Emotions arise in a particular moment in time against the backdrop of a particular mood, which exists on a longer time horizon.

3. **Body**: Sensations such as tension, tightness, constriction, movement, flow, and temperature all offer clues about the strategies that create identity.

4. **Energy**: Flagging, energized, numb, flat, or upbeat are examples of how our life force—our energy—is impacted by mindset and moods in our living bodies.

• • •

PAUSE PRACTICE: TRIGGERS OPEN THE DOOR TO MINDSET

○ Pause for a moment and breathe slowly for a bit, settling yourself.

○ As you pause to catch yourself, you'll inevitably notice what you're practicing, your habits of mind, and the feelings and actions that make you, you!

continued

○ Bring to mind a situation in which you were triggered—a situation in which your automatic reaction to threat showed up in spades.

○ Allow the recollection to be as clear as possible. To pause and catch yourself can stir discomfort and raise questions:

○ What values did the trigger surface for you? What's the belief about how things "should be" that showed up?

○ Can I admit to foibles in my leadership?

○ What impact will it have if I admit to "not knowing"—e.g., not knowing what to do? When to do it? How to go about it? Can vulnerability help or hurt me, my team, my network, or organization overall?

○ What do I do with the emotions that get stirred inside of me?

○ Observe your body's reactions as you simply recall your own reactions. How's your breath now?

○ While we're in the midst of reacting to a trigger, it's likely—whether we're aware of it or not—that some internal line was inadvertently, or even purposefully, crossed.

○ Reflect on what you're learning as you investigate your triggers.

• • •

Your Identity as a Leader

The reality of our ever-changing VUCA world challenges our identity as a leader who can control events or make things happen. Our responses to complexities are determined by our current mindset and our view of stress, or stress mindset—e.g., is stress debilitating or enhancing? When we complain or rant about an experience as "stressful," it's less a descriptor of the actual situation "out there" than it is a reflection of where we're at in that moment "in here" in our own experience.

Increasing complexity activates our natural tendencies to avoid, pushing away what's threatening or unsettling, or to cling to what's worked in the past because ... things shouldn't be as they are, but different. Ultimately, we experience intense situations as grueling because they call into question our sense of *who we are*, our sense of self, our identity. We default to doing what worked in the past and end up reinforcing old identity strategies: he's a problem solver, she's super results-oriented, he's a high performer, she's a networking maven.

Like those CEOs mentioned earlier in Chapter 1, who despite their skills and experience expressed a lack of confidence in their own ability to navigate complexity, your very identity can feel on the line or up for grabs when you're triggered. While knowing that "what got you here won't get you there," it's still amazing how often we cling to what we've known to do instead.[6] Yet, as Jungian analyst James Hollis has said, you're "summoned to leave behind the controlling power of your history and to walk through the doorway to a new power."[7] When new power emerges, it is because the triggers reveal what we care most deeply about. Consider the following examples, each requiring a "leaving behind" in order to move forward:

- A leader asking for greater focus must stop multitasking.

- A leader seeking candor must be forthright herself.

- A leader who strives for excellent customer service must attend to others' needs.

- A leader seeking a global presence must seek out diversity.

- A leader who wants real conversations must stop and listen.

Paradoxically, by practicing pause in any of its permutations, we create the open space to see and accept the reality of the current situation as inherently unpredictable and uncontrollable. Only then can we begin to relax. This more settled acceptance not only allows us to view the situation more broadly, see what we care most deeply about, and notice the bright fulgor at the horizon full of possibilities for new solutions—but it also builds the resilience of leadership presence and power.

Pushing Pause at Work

Darek, the GM of a global environmental company that you met back in chapter 2, was likeable and action oriented, but he had a hair-trigger temper.

When he came to me as a client, his colleagues and direct reports called him "defensive." This accurate truth revealed Darek's need to pace himself to "see" the landscape accurately instead of simply reacting in crisis mode. Coaching Darek over a nine-month period, I had him pause to play with his pace, so he could begin to recognize his triggers.

We began with a simple two-part practice. The moment he was triggered and became reactive, he'd *pause*, catching himself to observe what was going on internally, and then *center* himself by sensing gravity in his body, especially his feet. Darek learned, in a new felt-sense way, that he was chronically tense and exhausted. It surprised him. Then he turned toward his triggers to begin the work of tuning into and recognizing his own emotional reactions. It was these triggers that I suspected were driving his rapid pace. Two beliefs emerged from his experimentation that threaded through his triggered reactions. In fact, they "drove" his reactions.

1. "There's a right way to do this."

2. "I have to work hard—always."

These beliefs propelled his body, his emotions—he was consistently impatient and irritable—and his actions. He was hard-driving, both with himself and his direct reports.

By tuning in to his triggers, Darek recognized that in his deep fatigue, he contributed to the cycle of overmuch, fueling his defensiveness. Not exactly what he wanted, and a relief to know! He committed to a thrice-daily practice of pausing to check in on himself to examine his triggers. Darek learned that he could choose to let go of his triggered reaction to reset his pace for the moment at hand.

Darek learned to slow down and take action steps that were more effective, efficient, and on target. Within a few months his colleagues and direct reports were noticing a difference. He smiled more. He engaged them with questions more readily and incorporated their ideas about where best to move the business. He reported "feeling more clearheaded, better." He was on track to be faster, smarter, and better—on track for optimal performance.

Centering into Presence

> Center is the starting place in the continuum
> of moving through change.

—RICHARD STROZZI-HECKLER, PHD, AUTHOR OF *THE ANATOMY OF CHANGE* AND FOUNDER OF THE STROZZI INSTITUTE

Centering is a bit like tuning in to your favorite radio channel to hear the music. When you're dialed in, your energy is strong and clear, and you can "hear" what's going on in the moment. It's what my friend Renee says—"center is everything." When you're not dialed in, well, there's a lot of static.

When mind, body, and spirit are aligned, personal power—the power to generate competent actions and to experience learning and satisfaction in living life—radiates from within. This state of unified alignment is called "center," and the process and practice of developing this alignment is called "centering."

We begin by bringing attention to the body, or *soma*, the Greek root word that means "the living body in its wholeness." It is in the body that awareness occurs and language begins, it is in the body that emotions and moods and thoughts arise, and it is in body that we move into action. To center in the body establishes both a focus and a place to be with the reality of "what's so" right in front of us.

Centering starts with the biological process of feeling ourselves more from the inside out, a process called *interoception*. It's both a conscious and nonconscious process that encompasses the brain's integration of synthesizing signals relayed from the body into specific subregions—like the brain stem, thalamus, insula, somatosensory cortex, and anterior cingulate cortex—to allow for a nuanced representation of the physiological state of your body. Simply put, centering has a bodily, felt sense about it.

Yet what distinguishes centering from merely feeling the internal happenings in your body—e.g., I notice that my stomach is tight—is that you're actually starting to intervene in such a way that you can organize yourself to allow the maximum amount of life energy to move through you. Then you can make deliberate choices to shift yourself in some way to access the best of who you are.

Centering, then, is a process of deliberately adjusting your physiological, psychological, and even your spiritual state to align first in your body as a whole, then in your heart, then in the greater mystery of life.

Though centering first begins with the body, to be "centered" encompasses more than physical experiences alone. Centering is a way of life—a living, evolving process of self-organization that increases our capacity for awareness, choice, and learning that leads to accountability, action, and integrity. When we practice centering vis-à-vis a pause, we heighten our awareness, expand presence, and open with a capacity to take generative action.

• • •

CENTERING: A CONSCIOUS LEADERSHIP PRACTICE

◯ Start with your feet about shoulder-width apart, with your arms hanging gently to the side and your knees slightly bent. Allow your eyes to soften, and release your shoulders.

○ As you're breathing in, imagine yourself drawing breath up from the ground, traveling along the vertical length of your spine to the crown of your head. Exhale long.

○ With another inhalation, allow yourself to feel the width of your shoulders and the breadth of your hips, distributing your weight evenly as you inhale long and expel your breath out of your fingertips.

○ Inhaling once again, put your attention first on your back side, feeling the space behind your heart and moving your attention through your body on the exhalation, finding the sweet spot of balance.

○ With your three breaths, you've brought your attention to the present and aligned your body in all dimensions. Now drop your attention about two inches below your navel to your center, or *hara*, Japanese for "belly."

○ With a fourth breath, acknowledge that you're centering in the moment, in your body, and now in the mystery of life.

• • •

Shaping and Strategies—Body as Resource

The brain is embodied; the regulation of energy and information flows happens throughout the body.

—DAN SIEGEL, MD AND FOUNDER OF MINDSIGHT INSTITUTE

As kids, we learned to maneuver and finagle our peculiar life circumstances to get what we needed in life. Of course we did. It's entertaining to watch kids engage with the world as they learn to crawl, then to walk, and then to run. Or to listen to how they use new words as they acquire language. Yet the bulk of early foundational learning occurs out of sight via implicit memory.

Unlike explicit memory, which involves a conscious recollection of facts, figures, or events—like that ski trip to Colorado in 2015, your childhood address at 1111 Lake Street, or suddenly remembering that you left your car keys on the back stairs—implicit memory is unconscious yet foundational to all learning. Implicit memory reflects the patterns, principles, and rules that underlie your ongoing, day-to-day experience.

We learn through our unique experiences, and it's implicit memory that strengthens neural pathways and synaptic connections that quite literally wire our behavioral tendencies in place within the neural, biological, and cellular structure of our bodies. Since our brains and body parts are inextricably interwoven in the distributed nervous system of our entire body, this internal wiring manifests in our unique strategies for survival and how we learn to navigate through the world.

The result? Our successful strategies for relating became embodied in the fabric of what we now call our personality. Since we're social animals, we're shaped in response to the context of our day-to-day relationships. It's implicit memory that allows us to make meaning, then, from the underlying patterns that inform our relationships with other humans. As Amanda Blake, creator of the Body=Brain course on the neurobiology of experiential learning, notes: "Like the acquisition of spoken language, emotional learning, patterns of behaviors, and styles of relatedness are not taught, they're simply absorbed."[8]

This also includes the ways that we know ourselves and our expression of skills and talents. Eventually, it's how we came to define who we know ourselves to be—our identity or personality. Who we are has become obvious to the world.

Biological Shaping

As humans, we live in bodies *and* we live in language. Highly intelligent and efficient, your body is a source of learning, mood, connection, and dignity.

The father of American psychology, William James, wrote, "The body is the storm-center, the origin of coordinates, the constant place of stress in our experience-train. Everything circles round it, and is felt from its point of view." He goes on, "The world experienced, comes at all times with our body as its center, center of vision, center of action, center of interest."[9]

Our bodies are designed to ensure that each of us acquires what we need to survive and to make the necessary complex decisions life requires without needing to stop each time to rethink.

It's quite literally our physical body that shapes and structures our interpretations of the world and generates our reactions, from which we can craft our next steps. However, this is not, mind you, one of the typical ways we view what it means to have a body. It's not about having an athletic body or being a patient in need of medical care. Nor is it about being beautiful or desirable, and certainly it's about much more than a transport version of a body. It is the body as a living repository of life: sensation, emotion, energy, and interpretive meaning that are involved in engaging with our day-to-day and moment-to moment experiences.

First and foremost, our attention, particularly attention to the sensory experiences generated within our own bodies, is key to presence and to staying resourceful when the world all around is reeling, uncooperative, and even hostile. The urges, instincts, and intuitions that comprise our strategies reside within the very tissues, sinews, and muscles that, when triggered, enact our old habits and behavioral strategies automatically. Those strategies propel our relationships, connect us with what we care about or not, fuel our curiosity about life, and inform our ability to field both danger and opportunity.

In sum, our identity is an embodied phenomenon. Our early life strategies (yes, we all have them, and they aren't bad) are useful until they're not. Kind of like the way a rubber band loses its stretchiness over time, even though it's done a fine job holding that sheaf of tax documents together until it's safe to shred them. Those who've undergone traumatic experiences and struggle with post-traumatic stress or addictions are quick to provide examples of how their old strategies have quickly outlived their usefulness when they meet with new challenges.

Needless to say, we shape ourselves around our deepest drives for safety, connection, and belonging. Those drives feed a relentless, automatic, and lifelong process of constructing and defending our identities. We embody a history that's unrelenting in its influence on us. Yet because we act, feel, and perceive only in the present moment, we're like a radar that's constantly scanning for the best future we can imagine.

Faced with a real or imaginary threat to our identity, however, our signature psychobiological tendencies will kick in: we tighten up, batten down the hatches, numb or flake out, or drive harder. Yet in the rapids of complexity, using our old, identity-preserving strategies—while they may be more familiar and comfortable—may make for elusive positive outcomes, however big or small. Invisible to us, our identity needs run the show without pausing for reflection. They'll either sabotage our effectiveness as leaders, or—with awareness and intention—we can learn to use them to transform ourselves, thereby opening up new ways of leading in our VUCA world.

Strategies

Men are born soft and supple;
dead, they are stiff and hard.
Plants are born tender and pliant;
dead, they are brittle and dry.
Thus whoever is stiff and inflexible
is a disciple of death.
Whoever is soft and yielding
is a disciple of life.
The hard and stiff will be broken.
The soft and supple will prevail.

—LAO-TZU, *TAO TE CHING*, CHAPTER 76

One typical strategy for getting on in life includes avoiding what we don't like, what doesn't feel good, and what doesn't work. Again, this strategy is smart until it backfires. Common examples include avoiding conversations, actions, and people that we believe would lead us into embarrassment, failure, shame, and a certain lack of success.

Conversely, we seek out behaviors, people, and activities that we enjoy or find comfort in, and then habitually cling to them—even ferociously so—because they worked, reinforcing our particular identity.

Between what we're averse to and what we're clinging to, our identity, our personality is held firmly and securely in place. Because both avoidance and attachment register in the body, we can pause and attune ourselves to how they show up in us. For example, how we contract and pull away when receiving tough feedback, or how we reach for that next glass of wine or a sweet to mollify ourselves after an intense day at the office.

Our nervous systems are elegantly designed to avoid threats while preserving our identity by reliably supporting our survival *without our conscious awareness*. Our bodies constantly organize around what's most salient to us and what we care about most. Day to day, however, we're constantly buffeted by both the external events, often unpredictable and potentially triggering, and our own internal felt sense and interpretation of experiences. In truth, we're constantly bumping up against our own limits and strategies.

For leaders accustomed to making things happen, these personal experiences offer only an uncomfortable space to thrash about. Uncertainty and a lack of predictability trigger and reduce our resourcefulness when we need it the most, in times that require different ways of leading than we've been prepared for historically.

Yet in *those* triggered moments, when our integrity is off, our strategies are on, and we've lost sight of our way, we can access a portal to understanding and growth that provides insight into how we can learn to react under pressure more skillfully.

Therein lies the opportunity.

Because when we learn to catch, stay, and linger longer at the edges of our identity, where we're uncomfortable and disoriented, we can see the stuff we're made of, quite literally. It's at the edges that resilience grows. We can then choose if and how we'd like to create the future from this point forward, and whether we want to grow into our best selves—what I call the brilliance of Core Presence.

Core Presence: Your Primary Source of Power

> We rarely touch this. We rarely contact this simple moment.
> So used to constant input and excitement, we lack fine-tuning
> into all the subtleties of this instant, the ability to register a
> quiet aliveness without the stirring of expectation.
>
> —TONI PACKER, AUTHOR OF *THE LIGHT OF DISCOVERY*,
> ZEN TEACHER, AND FOUNDER OF SPRINGWATER CENTER

What makes others really want to follow you—your primary source of power—doesn't come from your position or rank but from those qualities that enable you to connect, inspire, and engage with them toward effective action. In short, these personal qualities reflect what I call your Core Presence.

Distinct from leadership presence, which is essential to conscious leadership, your Core Presence—call it that spot of grace, source, essence, soul, or whatever name you care to use—lies at the foundation of who you are, reflects what you care most deeply about, and is what energetically resonates with others. Core Presence is composed of qualities and capabilities that are uniquely your own. It's when you operate from here, to borrow a phrase that psychologist Gay Hendricks coined, that you're living beyond your Zone of Excellence and into your Zone of Genius, fulfilling your purpose.[10] While it *is* uniquely your own, your Core Presence is about simultaneously tapping into something bigger than you that energizes you as you move through the world.

Waiting for Your Soul to Catch Up

Once upon a time, an American businessman was following his dream to go on an African safari. He planned and planned and was loaded down with maps, timetables, and agendas for his journey. He'd engaged men from a tribe to carry his cumbersome load of supplies, luggage, and "essential" stuff.

As the story goes, on the first morning, the businessman and the local men all awoke early, traveled very fast, and went very far.

On the second day, they awoke early, traveled very fast, and went very far.

On the third day, they awoke early, traveled very fast, and went very far. And the American businessman was pleased.

On the fourth day, however, the local tribesmen refused to move. They simply sat under the shade of a nearby tree. The American became incensed, saying, "This is a waste of valuable time. Can someone tell me what is going on here?"

The hired translator answered, "They are waiting for their souls to catch up with their bodies."

This wise tale, shared by author Terry Hershey—an advocate for work-life balance—is instructive on a few levels.[11]

First, even a long-planned and dreamed-of trip became about going somewhere exotic, far away—and fast! Did the businessman even notice what was all around him?

Second, it required a lot of stuff: maps, proper clothing, likely a GPS and camera equipment—all more than one person could carry himself. What's actually necessary for the journey?

Third, the businessman's focus was on arriving at his destination rather than enjoying the journey. His lack of presence and driving charge to keep moving precluded noticing the very surrounding environment he'd come to see. He missed engaging with the interesting people who knew the way, the secrets of the land, and the local customs. His attention was not on the present moment but instead on some imagined future. He was out of touch not only with his body or the needs of others, but his driving pace prohibited him from access to his Core Presence—the source of life and vitality. The local men knew the secret of that source and had to allow their souls to catch up!

As leaders today, how many times have you been out ahead of yourself, such forward focus driving your energy while you're losing connection with your own needs or purpose? With the energy needs of your people? And at what greater cost than a mere slowing down of a trip?

Pausing into Stillness

Stillness is the new axis of learning and leadership.

—OTTO SCHARMER, FOUNDER OF THE PRESENCING INSTITUTE

As you've seen, not all pauses involve stillness. Yet the quality of quiet stillness opens up opportunities for reflection and contemplation. It's in stillness that we can make connection with Core Presence and discover our heart's desire, that deep offering that connects us and our worldly ambitions and institutions. Experiencing that connection will liberate our human energy and help us focus it to accomplish and benefit the greater good. An irresistible force begins to emerge.

Down through the millennia, people have engaged in practices that are inseparable from the experience of simply being alive. Ancient wisdom traditions, be they Christian, Hindu, Buddhist, Islamic, or pagan, have interwoven these practices and experiences of mind and emotion with body movement and sensation to support greater states of aliveness. Such moments point to a straightforward, body-based connection between our personal, direct experiences and those ineffable, wordless ones that tap a greater wisdom or source.

It's in quiet moments, when we still our minds and body, that we can begin to sense what lies just beyond our current everyday "reality." In this heightened state of awareness, insight, wisdom, and mental clarity are more accessible while change ceases to be a thing to be managed or controlled. Instead, change reflects the unending pulse and flow of life, a ceaseless dance of energy in which cause is effect and effect is cause.

Many express and name such experiences as sacred, holy, and deeply meaningful, though they're bereft of words to describe it fully. Exploring your direct experiences of sensation and movement will empower you to surface your deepest and most meaningful truths, what's central to your Core Presence. There you can feel the life stream moving through you as you engage and direct that energy into what matters most to you. It just might be the sweetest experience of all.

> Our true nature is stillness,
> The Source from which we come.
> The deep listening of pure contemplation.
> Is the path to stillness.
> All words disappear into It,
> And all creation awakens to the delight of
> Just Being.
>
> —THOMAS KEATING, "STILLNESS"

Movement and *Mushin*

Students new to aikido learn the myth of the white belt early on in their practice. Traditionally in Japan there were only white belts and black belts. Graying over the seasons, in the movement of being thrown and thrown again, the white belt eventually turns black, symbolizing a student's time and effort training in aikido, the art of peace.

With dedicated practice, the student has also been cultivating *mushin*, a state of unity between mind and body, or "mind without mind." Samurai trained rigorously to cultivate this state of "no-mindedness," or what we might call a state of "flow" or "peak performance" or "embodied presence," in which the mind is free from fixed thoughts or cluttered emotions. It's mushin that supports embodied action free from the interference of the conscious mind. Mushin signifies an absence of something yet with nothing lacking.

It's the space for the next right move to take place based on what's required at the moment. The more "emptiness" there is, the larger the pool of existing possibilities for action. The space of emptiness is full of rich resources.

In my training, it was only after a long period of time—after first learning the basic technique of a move—that I could sense and feel into the space of an attack as it was opening. It took longer still to know, in my body, that it was the *right* time to throw into the *right* space. My fellow aikidoka and I were intentionally practicing together to strengthen our bodies and nervous systems to work with increased pressure and power. We were also each practicing being a beginner in every new move, trusting the space around us as a resource itself.

If you'll recall, my business coach had earlier said to me: "You need some fierceness in you." The intensity of aikido practice cleared openings for that to occur. As someone who started aikido in her forties, however, with a body already entrained to particular ways of reacting under pressure, I found the practice both maddening and exhilarating at the same time.

Ask Rand: Presence and Power

Leadership is the wise use of power.
Power is the capacity to translate intention
into reality and sustain it.

—WARREN BENNIS, LEADERSHIP SCHOLAR

Although trust is not power, it is through trust that we
can acquire the greatest power: not power over others,
but something far more important—the possibility for each
and all of us to realize our full potential—**together**.

—FERNANDO FLORES, CO-AUTHOR OF *BUILDING TRUST*,
PHILOSOPHER, AND BUSINESS CONSULTANT

Working with power means expanding your capacity to do great work without debilitating side effects. It means building on your strengths while illuminating your blind spots. It means being able to bring something to life, to give it teeth. It's what Kevin Cashman calls "authentic self-expression that creates value."[12]

Earlier you met Rand, the founder and CEO of Stagen Leadership Academy. His journey beyond leadership presence and into Core Presence involved what he now calls a "three-year strategic pause." It enabled him to step into greater personal power and to shift into new action toward his purpose. And it wasn't easy.

After his team had their intervention with him, Rand couldn't see any opening—"I didn't know how to explain what I felt, or exactly why I cared so deeply. It was invisible to me at first. I was confused, too, because I wanted to make a change to the business, but I also didn't want to make the change."

Some context. Rand's self-reported winning strategy in his early years was organized around what he *wasn't* when he was growing up: "I wasn't good at sports growing up, and not particularly social. I got bullied a lot." In high school, and later in college, he became "ridiculously good at relationships. My fun, superficial relating was a way to get some validation, to be liked." But being liked came at its own cost; he diminished his presence and gave away his power by saying yes to please other people. In his case, his leadership team. They could clearly see an opening for a more expansive, broader reach for Stagen Leadership Academy than Rand could at that point.

Rand recalls: "For three years I did my own inner work on the leadership journey. It included all sorts of internal conflict, conflict in our team, and lots of processing and frustration." Rand's extended pause required him to learn to listen deeply within himself and surface the invisibles of the long-buried old strategy that lay at the heart of his people pleasing. To hear him tell it, "It was like I had to stay in the extended pause of frustration. Almost as if I was pausing unconsciously, or like my spirit put a pause on me as opposed to me pausing. I became increasingly aware that I was contradicting myself, but I was not yet willing to let go out of my basic fear."

After learning to pause and do the deliberate practices necessary, he began to listen.

What emerged out of that troubling time was an awareness that he had held a belief, at a deep, unconscious level, that if the business were to really grow into a big brand, "we'd lose ourselves in the growth. And while it's taken years to get on the other side, during that pause—which wasn't being still or inactive or dormant at all—we surfaced our Design Principles (practice-based and experienced in community), and our Engagement Principles; everything we do is high-touch, high-intimacy, and personalized."

Rand's Continuing Practice

For Rand, today it "feels that the energy is moving now, because of the pause." He continues to practice on the mat of life and at Stagen Leadership Academy. "What I'm practicing right now is noticing when I get grabbed, emotionally. It shows up for me as insecurity, as defensiveness. So, I'll pause to re-center myself. I've learned how to take the witnessing perspective, observing what's in the moment. And to say, 'That's interesting.' Then I choose something of my own liking."

Many who knew Rand earlier in life might be shocked to learn of his extended pause, as his leadership presence today reflects confidence and power. Rand knows that "all of this [is] happening because I've shifted my inner experience. Yet, what's so amazing is that I literally still have to pause and notice that it's my choice to be firm, assertive. What's not obvious is that I'm using the pause as a part of my capacity to be more at choice every day."

RECAP

- Leadership presence = power

- Triggers are the doorway to presence. Embrace them.

- Centering is a conscious leadership practice

- Shaping and strategies: your body as resource

- Core Presence is your primary source of power

SCOPE: SPACE, CONNECTION, OPENNESS, PACE, ENERGY

S – How often are you quiet, allowing the next moment to come to you?

C – When do you feel most connected, seen, and heard?

O – How comfortable are you admitting, "I'm not sure"?

P – When is the last time you put "take a walk" on your calendar?

E – When are you at your best? Your best self

CHAPTER 7

Pursue Your Energy

Everything is energy. Energy cannot be created or destroyed—
it can only be transformed. Thoughts and feelings are energy.

—ALAN SEALE, AUTHOR OF *TRANSFORMATIONAL PRESENCE* AND
FOUNDER OF THE CENTER FOR TRANSFORMATIONAL PRESENCE

L ife speaks to us directly through sensation, whether we pause to notice
or not. We instinctively experience our life as a reflection of our energy.
In China, they call it *chi*. In Japan, it's called *ki*. *Prana* is the Sanskrit
name for it, while the French call it *elan vital*—the vital force, that impulse
of life immanent in all organisms. It's the literal pulse of life living through
you, as close as your breath.

Typically, when we think of energy, we think of it as the amount of vigor,
vitality, or zest you have, or your quantity of "get up and go." By tuning in
to your breath and the sensations within your body, you'll begin to notice a
whole new world of experience that opens up to you. In fact, your sensing
experiences are inseparable from your everyday experience of being alive and
being yourself. Pausing to direct your attention to sensation and movement

will allow you to drop down out of your head and come into direct contact with the energetic currents of your body. Living here, in your body, translates to being present to your life in the moment as it's unfolding.

We are energy bodies, pulsing with the life force, blood coursing through our veins, breath and oxygen moving through our lungs and distributed throughout our bodies. Though the statement "we are energy bodies" may sound woo-woo, it's profound in its implications. It first acknowledges that we live within a vessel that's teeming with life and exquisitely responsive to the environment. For example, when you notice you're chilly, you may find yourself rubbing your hands together to stay warm—the vigorous rubbing stimulates energy in the form of warmth. If you've been driving and had someone suddenly swerve toward your lane, you know the experience of being jolted to attention, followed by rushing energy or tingling.

Second, that we are "energy bodies" points to the tremendous interplay of biological and chemical systems within our bodies that are constantly regulating the impact of our surroundings and environment. We measure energy by way of blood pressure, variable heart rates, fMRIs, and pulmonary output studies. Our biological systems work in tandem to maintain a stable, homeostatic state: body temperature typically hovers around 98°F, intricacies of the respiratory system keep us breathing without engaging conscious thought, and the digestive apparatus processes essential nutrients to fuel the enterprise of living while eliminating unnecessary waste. When all systems are "on," life flows smoothly, and we may not notice our energy levels much at all. That's because of *neuroplasticity*—the feature whereby our bodies respond, shift, and learn from our interactions with the world around us.

Our limbic system, particularly the amygdala—which is located deep in the midbrain—fast-regulates our emotions while our cognitive system keeps us analyzing patterns, making decisions, and executing on them. It's our capacity for self-organization that regulates the flow of energy and information: if you register thirst, you get a drink of water; if you're cold, you find a coat or wrap to put on. Said another way, we organize ourselves around what's most coherent in our biology.

Self-organization is an emergent property of complex systems, which we are. And, as Dr. Dan Siegel writes, "Every system is perfectly designed to get the results it gets."[1] Over time, our personal and interconnected biological systems first differentiate the various energies and then connect the dots to create the most flexible, adaptive, and optional functioning, called *kokoro* in Japanese.[2] The character, or *kanji*, is translated as the "mind, heart, spirit"—that which aligns your life energy in the radical heart of who you are. Dr. Siegel speaks of the rhythms of energy movement this way: "We become balanced and coordinated in life when we create integration, allowing for the flow of energies between chaos and rigidity" that results in flourishing and thriving.[3]

Quantum physics explains that our thoughts, emotions, feelings, and sensations are all vibrating energies that come together with others' energies at the same frequency, in resonance, to form what we perceive of as reality. One way to get a handle on this is to imagine that you're singing in a choir, with your strong tenor voice distinct and vibrating beautifully. Yet it's in the coming together with others' vibrating voices—the alto, bass, and soprano— that you create the beautiful harmony of Handel's *Messiah*.

Sweet Spot

Over one hundred years ago, Albert Einstein addressed the scientific community of his day. His claim? He passionately presented the idea that everything we take in with our five senses, called exteroception—everything we see, hear, taste, touch, and smell—is energy. We're not solid, dense matter at all; in fact, we're not what we appear to be. Instead, we *are* dynamic movement—every cell in our body a world of its own, with one's energetic resonating directly related to their level of consciousness. "The more conscious a person is, the closer to their potential that person lives, and the more positive energy he or she has available to use."[4]

Our energy rises to a challenge. Too little challenge and we effectively rust out, never reaching our full potential or doing that thing we always wanted to do. But too much energy, rising in the form of stress, and we can literally burn out. In other words, the energetic sweet spot of arousal lies somewhere in the middle.[5]

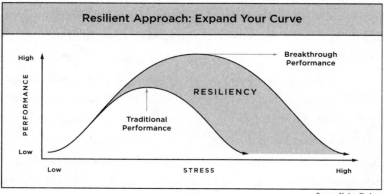

Source: Yerkes-Dodson

In *The Power of Full Engagement*, authors Jim Loehr and Tony Schwartz point out that optimal energy and sustainable performance "requires cultivating a dynamic balance between expenditure of energy (stress) and renewal of energy (recovery)."[6] In other words, the consistent, vibrant flow of energy is a result of challenging—then renewing—our energies, not what typically occurs when triggered into reacting then driving hard at breakneck speed. It's in the dynamic interplay that energetic resilience is cultivated.

The Energy of Aikido

> To live, love, and lead in accord with universal energy
> is to accord the Way in the truest sense. It's not easy,
> and yet leads to the greatest ease.
>
> —GINNY WHITELAW, AUTHOR OF *RESONATE*, BIOPHYSICIST, AND
> FOUNDER & CEO OF THE INSTITUTE FOR ZEN LEADERSHIP

Aikido is a Japanese martial art born out of the samurai tradition and developed by Morihei Ueshiba, or O Sensei (Great Teacher), beginning early in the twentieth century. Though O Sensei was experienced in a variety of martial arts, it was during a visionary experience that he realized that the true way of the warrior was to "manifest divine love" by cultivating a spirit "that embraces and nurtures all things." From that time, O Sensei dedicated himself to creating a martial art that would guide others to an insightful reconciliation of intention and action, expressing itself as a way of peace. Aikido, the art of peace and the way of harmonizing through energy, was born.

Primarily a defensive art, the practice of aikido involves attacks—a strike with a weapon or empty hand, or a grab—that are met by joint locks, throws, and pins. It's all about learning to blend with the energy of one's attacker to subdue and control a situation by redirecting his energy and maintaining flow. It's as if *uke* (pronounced "oo-kay" and meaning "the attacker") and *nage* (pronounced "nah-gay" and meaning "the one being attacked") are one, energies interconnected and both protected from harm.

When I first ventured to explore aikido, I was struck by the energy of the dojo space itself: it was buzzing with a vibrancy difficult to name yet ever present that evening. As aikidoka (those practicing aikido) bowed in and stepped onto the mat to begin their warm-ups, I could feel the energy move through me too.

A dojo is a place of learning and profound transformation. It's there that we train and shape our bodies to move to the pulse of energy within and around each of us. In time, as I trained, I came to appreciate the ritual of bowing to the kamiza (the seat of honor at the front) and then to our partners as an expression not only of respect but also of an exchange of energies. In that resonant exchange with one another lay a permission to train hard with the intention to learn something new: how our life strategies show up in our bodies, how letting go of struggling releases tension and rigidity, how to more skillfully *blend with* instead of *fight against* another's energies to redirect them, and how it's possible to extend energy beyond the physical limitations of one's body.

It was on the mat, over countless days of practice, that the integral principals of aikido began their slow seep into my tissues. Being thrown hard across the mat, learning to roll out of it, and moving quickly to return a strike to my partner proved an ongoing process of self-confrontation—and it was exhilarating.

Left to my own default strategies and my need to "get it right," I might never have returned for the more rigorous training. Yet I was compelled to show up. It was only through practice and momentary pausing to center at "one point," or hara, physically located about two inches below the belly button, that I had any chance of accessing the flow of energy to integrate my mind, body, and spirit into congruent action. While learning to maintain alignment along the core length of my spine in a posture of relaxed presence and dignity and engaging my breath deeply in my belly—only then was I able to cultivate the ability to remain calm under pressure and, dare I say it, even fierce.

Feeling and Emotional Fortitude

> It is in the experience of the lived body
> that we have the opportunity to contact and
> learn from the process of being alive.
>
> —RICHARD STROZZI-HECKLER, PHD, AUTHOR OF *THE ANATOMY OF CHANGE* AND FOUNDER OF THE STROZZI INSTITUTE

Feeling deeply is fundamental to being human—a part of our natural intelligence. To feel is to increase conscious, intentional attention to your direct, in-the-moment experience of life—the energy of sensation, emotions, and mood—as they're occurring. It is this ability to direct attention that is a critical skill for anyone who wants to develop their capacity for conscious, generative leadership.

Feeling more opens the door to becoming more responsive and less reactively bound to old strategies. Emotions are packets of energy that are always in motion. They're not necessarily well-defined and certainly don't exist in a geographical location in the brain. Rather, they reflect our early life strategies and our interpretations and sense-making for how to react in a given situation. As leadership coach and best-selling author Christine Comaford notes, "Emotions have measurable energy and can either foster or negate cell life."[7] Increasing your capacity to handle a wider range of sensations and emotions will extend life. You'll start to see options and possibilities previously invisible to you while you were in the midst of a knee-jerk reaction. The more you feel into your own energy in the form of *sensations* (pulsing, streaming, heat, tension, and lightness) and *emotions* (passion, resentment, joy, anger, grief, fear, indignation, or satisfaction), the more you'll contact the deep, resourceful life energy that's constantly moving through you and undergirds all of life.

However, emotions and moods are typically resistant to being addressed simply on a rational level—in truth, it's biologically impossible. What we label as emotion is constructed from elemental sensory experiences that we "interpret" to make sense of our experiences. When we intellectually neglect, dismiss, or denigrate our emotions and moods as irrelevant, the predominant stance since Descartes's injunction "I think, therefore I am," we run a risk of incongruence between what we say, how we say it, and how we behave. Mixed messages confuse people, which is not great for a leader. Yet in feeling more vis-à-vis sensation, not only do you have greater access to emotion information critical for decision-making and next steps, but you also increase your coherence, tap more of your intelligence, and increase your power—a phenomenon called emotional fortitude.[8] It's a kind of readiness to stand true to your concerns.[9] It's also the skill to remain clearheaded while exploring your emotional reactions under stress. The good news is that emotional fortitude can be cultivated. Reflecting on your own sensing experiences, noting how those give rise to your thoughts and feelings, and acknowledging your concerns and the concerns of the moment—including others' emotional inputs—as essential aspects of the decision-making process, which is critically important when complexity is ratcheted up, you'll deepen your emotional fortitude, or resilience.

Mark Melson, president and CEO of Gladney Center for Adoption, knows the power of self-awareness and the impact of sending mixed messages: "Throughout my career, I've had the mentality that if I outworked or outpaced everybody around me, I'd be successful. Yet, I wasn't fully listening." Rather than having to have all the answers or to quickly come to a decision on his own, a reflection of his own early winning strategy, Mark learned to use a pause to create the space to hold these inherent tensions within himself so that a new, emerging response would show up. "Beginning to pause and shift into a learning mindset has helped me realize I don't necessarily have to know all the answers."

Learning to slow his pace, Mark attuned to: 1) his automatic tendency to action; 2) his energy—he energetically blew past the sweet spot with little renewal; and 3) his beliefs about what would occur should he slow down, for example, "Maybe they'll realize they made a mistake in hiring me." Feeling himself more deeply via the pause made a world of difference to Mark personally but also in his leadership. He created space for others to give him feedback, which is often sorely lacking as leaders rise in the ranks. Tapping into his people for more input, a process known as outsourcing, helped him clarify his thinking, feelings, and even helped him make sense of the constant flow of sensations occurring within.

As Mark began feeling himself more, catching himself being himself, and, in his case, being aware of his competitive need to prove himself, he has become more able to feel others (empathy) and their concerns as well (empathic concern). As he says, he's more able to "make a better assessment before I react. I was built on the mode of reacting. Let me solve problems. Let me get through this and go."

Ultimately, feeling *more* makes conscious leadership possible. Emotions, and their energy levels, tell us what we care about. When we disconnect from our feeling self, as so many of us have been trained to do in our professional lives, our natural energies can become further disconnected, and our most heartfelt concerns go unaddressed. Think of the community leader keen to improve child health, who is praised and rewarded at the office yet barely knows her own children. Or the environmental leader who is deeply committed to mitigating environmental degradation but looks the other way as supply chain managers downplay sketchy practices with broad, negative impacts. Last, think of the entrepreneur who constantly drives the business yet can't tell you why it matters to her beyond the bottom line.

Today there's too much at stake to shut off, ignore, devalue, or minimize the wisdom of your sensing and energetic feeling self. Leaders are called to a greater ethic of care and responsibility in the twenty-first century. As Doug Silsbee explains in his book *Presence-Based Coaching,* "Our world is composed of what we sense and our interpretation of what we sense. Since that interpretation is a result of our unique conditioning, my world is distinctly different from yours."[10] Skillfully noting internal feeling states—in order to read your own internal energetic signals and respond to them appropriately—grows your emotional literacy and will result in more skillful external actions.

Moods

Moods are somatic, linguistic mind-body phenomena that provide a layer of texture to our experiences in the world, coloring and shaping what we "see" and how we "listen" to the world. Moods are an intricate strand in the braid of our inner experience, largely influenced by our shifting energies. Though typically outside of our awareness, moods nonetheless influence how we interpret just about everything in our day-to-day lives, including in leadership. Some would say[11] that moods are experiences that we fall into or that seem to come over us like a cloud, predisposing us toward certain possibilities and away from others. Just as we're essentially thrown into our first families (I didn't know I'd be welcomed into my family as a fourth-generation German!), we're hurled headfirst into the predominant mood of that family—and our relationships, in turn, are shaped by our ongoing interactions, upbringing, culture, and geography.

Moods serve as a backdrop to our day-to-day emotions and reveal our embodied orientation to life. Feelings and emotions have an immediacy that respond to particular situations and last for a much shorter duration than the enduring mood. Neuroscientist and researcher Lisa Feldman Barrett shares that "an emotion is your brain's creation of what your bodily sensations mean," relative to your surrounding context.[12] Research points out that our biological, sensory experiences of perception—sensations, feelings, and thoughts, like that uprush of agitation you experienced when your colleague was late—last only 60–90 seconds before they dissipate.[13] It's in the construction of our interpretation that we may come face-to-face with our predominant mood and our unique experience of the world.

That's because your mood will determine what emotions and feelings are even available to you to be expressed. Sometimes we fall into unproductive moods, which don't serve us unless we can learn to navigate our way through them. If your mood is one of resentment, you may become irritable and suspicious of your colleague. If, however, your mood is one of wonder, you may simply become curious about the reason for the delay. Our language reflects what we're capable of and is directly related to who and how we are somatically, in our bodies. We all know how tricky it is to express excitement when we're in a blue or despairing mood. It's safe to say that moods color our emotional palette. We don't so much have a mood, nor are we in a mood—we *are* a mood. By paying attention to our moods, we can learn to observe and work with our predisposed view of life and our subsequent strategies for engaging it.

Language of Sensation

What makes this work of pausing so essential can be found in the language of sensation. Language is embodied, developed as we grow up. Many parents today hang up those colorful emotion charts, the ones that depict a variety of facial expressions, so that kids can learn to identify emotion words—angry, happy, and sad—to match their inner sensing experience. Yet if those are the only emotion words available in your vocabulary, it'd be nearly impossible to sort out the subtle nuances between one's enthusiasm and curiosity, or one's experience of resentment or resignation.

As with kids, by tuning in to your own felt experience and expanding your vocabulary for sensation, you'll unlock worlds previously unknown to you. Language arises as much from our guts and hearts as from our thick-skulled cranium. You'll begin to notice the energetic subtleties of body movements and how certain words take up residence in your tissue, a process called "interoceptive learning."[14] By learning to first sense and then identify and label your internal experiences, you can begin to connect the dots between your sensing experience and the pattern of events you run up against in the world. By describing moods, sensations, and emotions while you're in action in the world, your ability to access and interact with them will become commonplace. You'll learn to track your reactions while fully participating in relationships, holding conversations, making decisions, taking direct actions, and putting your learning to the test in real-life situations.

Presence is a function of focused attention. By way of expanding your awareness 360 degrees, you can create right action in language. By allowing more energy to move through you, you can align and relax into your physical body, centering on what you care about and attending to both yourself and others at the same time. The more fully embodied you are, the more present you will be.

Relevance for Leaders

Whatever difference you want to make in this work will happen through resonance . . . Help people embody the principles and develop their sensitivity to naturally vibrate with the change that is theirs to make.

—GINNY WHITELAW, AUTHOR OF *RESONATE*, BIOPHYSICIST, AND FOUNDER & CEO OF THE INSTITUTE FOR ZEN LEADERSHIP

As leaders in the Western world, we're attached to getting things done, producing, making things happen, and creating something new, novel, or newsworthy. We're eager to get into action and produce results. This only makes sense since our natural state is one of movement and energy—we're designed to move. Energy exchange is an aspect of social resonance and learning, moving beyond simple survival to connect with others in our tribe. It's an embodied, relational process in which we share and direct energy and the flow of information.

Yet so often, especially under intense pressure, we push through, not listening to the subtle energetic shifts within ourselves and thus failing to recognize their power. Instead, our energies can become jammed up, literally armored within our body's physical patterning and therefore inaccessible to us. James Joyce, in the novel *Dubliners*, found that "Mr. Duffy lived a short distance from his body"—his natural energies dampened, his feelings muted, and his impact truncated. He was cut off from his life's purpose and his vitality.

Leaders, of course, are trained to observe the world, collect data, and base decisions on that data. It's crucial for leaders to recognize the dynamics of complexity that make up the current context of volatility, ambiguity, and uncertainty, so they can learn to identify where their energy is going and not truncate their life energy—often a by-product of today's complexities.

However, if we focus our attention exclusively on what's happening out in the world, "out there," we'll miss essential information about our internal state "in here." Leaders who can sense and feel themselves and the vitality of life moving through them also experience greater cognitive and affective empathy for others. They consistently stay connected to what's important to them and are more congruent and in integrity with who they want to be.[15] They're more purposeful, consistent, and trustworthy in both their professional leadership and in their personal lives.

• • •

Tracking Sensations

Tracking your sensations gives you access to your intuition, the power skill so many conscious leaders tap into. This practice builds by noticing your own *interoceptive learning*. In short, instead of defaulting to deliberation and analysis, interoceptive learning involves paying attention to your own sensations first, and only later drawing your own connection between what you've felt and the pattern of events that you encounter each day as a leader. For this journaling practice, find a quiet space for reflection, or consider taking a walk.

First re-center yourself in the moment and in your body. Then bring to mind a decision you're facing. In a journal, draw out three columns—the first to record what you're facing into and the second to record a detailed account of your own internal sensations and potential options for the decision. In the third column, track what decision you did make along with any other sensations that arise. It might look like this:

What you're facing	Internal sensations and potential options	Decisions and any other sensations
_____	_____	_____
_____	_____	_____
_____	_____	_____
_____	_____	_____
_____	_____	_____
_____	_____	_____

Over time, the process of pausing to raise your awareness of sensation is invaluable to honing your intuition. Research suggests that those leaders who do so make smarter decisions, tapping into the wisdom of their own experience.[16]

• • •

Skillful Leadership

> Your first and foremost job as a leader is to take charge
> of your own energy and then to help orchestrate
> the energy of those around you.

—PETER DRUCKER, AUTHOR OF *THE ESSENTIAL DRUCKER*
AND WORLD'S FOREMOST PIONEER OF MANAGEMENT THEORY

Skillful leadership has this kind of attunement. Presence can unite. Presence can build relatedness and connection. Instead of the traditional model of a leader acting *on* the world and intentionally shaping it, we begin to experience leadership as a deeper process of interacting *with* the world.

In short, our internal state is a significant factor in the dynamics of the VUCA complexity we experience all around us. Remember, one of my own strategies was to hang back, get small, and squelch my voice when the situation at hand required fierceness. That strategy had worked growing up yet had outworn its usefulness.

Similarly, any problematic strategy a leader encounters was acquired previously in conditions that no longer exist. But because these strategies did work at one time, they've became embodied as tendencies that emerge under pressure and stress—even decades later. By not leveraging our attention, or minding our minds, we risk having our precious energies scatter like confetti, flying around at the mercy of both internal and external distractions.

Anxious, driven, and overfocused leaders reinforce teams and organizations that are themselves anxious, driven, and overfocused. However, when we begin to embody states that are congruent with what we care about, our attention and energies begin to sync up. The result? Settled, open, and optimistic leaders who foster the same traits in other humans around them.

We can harness the mechanisms of neuroplasticity and embodied learning to develop and integrate new congruent states that are organized around our values, commitments, and the future of our own choosing. When we practice in this way, we deepen our own emotional and social learning, cultivating useful and resilient states that are available to us both now and in the future.

The more resourceful and congruent we become, the more our energy and presence begin to shape the interpersonal relational field in which we're interacting. Our presence, the organizing principle that we embody, then becomes an organizing principle in the larger system, opening the spigot of the natural flow of energy moving through us, invigorating our lives, thinking, feeling, and sensing, and, as Strozzi-Heckler says, "weaving the tapestry of who we are—bodily, emotionally, psychologically and spiritually."[17]

Self-Awareness: Key to Emotional Intelligence

The more emotionally demanding the work,
the more empathic and supportive the leader needs to be.

—DANIEL GOLEMAN, AUTHOR OF *PRIMAL LEADERSHIP*
AND SCIENCE JOURNALIST

Emotional intelligence is your ability to be self-aware: to recognize your own emotions and feelings, their energy, and those of others around you; to discern emotional subtleties and to name them (name them to tame them); and to then use the wisdom of that emotional input to inform and guide you by integrating these feelings into your thinking, decision-making, and action. Taken together, they expand your ability to be nimble and adaptive in the myriad of environments and conditions of today's VUCA landscape.

If you're connecting the dots back to cultivating presence, you're in your learning groove. Presence is a function of attention and full 360-degree awareness, which includes being aware of your own embodied experience and that of others, as well as awareness of the environment you're in at the moment. It begins by noting sensations in your body—your feelings and thoughts. When emotions are activated, they're accompanied by changes in bodily functions such as breathing rate, muscle tension, heart rate or interoception, and the perception of internal signals.

Research from the Korn Ferry Hay Group suggests that leaders with higher EQ are more innovative—92% have teams with high energy and high performance, and they have higher job satisfaction than those with lower EQ, who create negative cultural climates 78% of the time.[18] They're also more confident, and they tend to be adaptable and able to make better decisions in shifting circumstances. Due to holding a more positive outlook, they build stronger relationships, are kinder, and—because they're in tune with others—end up dealing well with conflict and communicating more effectively. And, like in aikido as aikidokas' energies blend and meld together, emotionally intelligent leaders can effectively direct their energy to positive ends.

In a 2018 study by psychologist and best-selling author Tasha Eurich, she found that "though most people believe they are self-aware, self-awareness is a truly rare quality: We estimate that only 10%–15% of the people we studied actually fit the criteria." Without a sense of knowing who you are, what drives you, and, more importantly, what you care deeply about, emotional intelligence skills will be strained. Research shows that those with higher EQ are: better workers who secure more promotions; more highly effective leaders who have more satisfied employees and more highly profitable companies; and less likely to lie, cheat, or steal.[19]

By tapping into one or more of the pause practices for support, here are four best practices to cultivate self-awareness:

1. Self-Observation

2. Self-Acceptance

3. Self-Correction

4. Self-Generation

Self-Observation

Attention practices are essential to growing self-awareness. We must learn to sense the energy of the current context and how it is affecting the situation. By choosing to observe yourself in action, emotional information becomes quickly available—with immediacy and clarity—within the rich tapestry of sensation-based information contained within your body. It's not merely cognitive, analytic head knowledge or based on someone's external admonition about what *should be* the case. Rather, it's revealed in the unfolding, ever-present moment at hand—in yourself.

Practicing self-observation will help you see your direct, in-the-moment experience with fresh eyes and less interference from your mindset and past successful strategies. Feeling more and presencing yourself in this moment will enable you to avoid automatically shutting down, cutting off, or squeezing out any aspect of your own lived experience.

The natural result? A stronger, more compelling presence that draws others to you.

Self-Acceptance

From a foundation of awareness, we can move to accept what is most true and congruent in our lives rather than living life out of an old strategy or another's agenda. Do I know my limitations and strengths? The conscious, embodied leadership skill of lingering longer at the edges of our experience to expand our self-acceptance is what has allowed us as a species to transform the minute, atomic firings of neurons into trips to the moon and Mars, rich and lasting relationships, voluminous tomes of wisdom, financial successes, and humanitarian and environmental justice around the globe.

Self-Correction

In the moment, self-correction is about regulating your emotional response. When you're triggered and able to catch yourself, re-center, and return to the moment with what one Zen teacher calls an "appropriate response": you're regulating your emotions based on what you care about. We build that capacity to cultivate inner conditions of our own choosing based on our core values and how we behave in congruence with them or not. We can shift to these values when we find we're off course. Holding the focus of what we care deeply about is not simply a matter of creating a mental picture of what it could look like or coming up with a set of words to describe what is important to us. It does include both, but it's more. It's a matter of experiencing these as a felt, inner state and as an organizing principle in our lives.

Self-Generation

We can learn to lead in complex and dangerous times by intentionally playing and practicing with the elements of SCOPE. This will allow you to embody greater creativity, resourcefulness, and ingenuity in the wide-open spaces of innovation and positive energy. By doing so, you'll become internally congruent with a value, a cause, or a destination that matters to you, further reinforcing what you take a stand for. When we embody a stand and become present to it—as Ray Anderson did at Interface Floor—we organize ourselves to *become that person*, committed to that particular cause, through a set of distinctions and practices.

● ● ●

TOUCH AND GO: PAUSING TO SELF-CORRECT

By pausing, we can self-correct, downshift our pace, and rejigger our energy to move more effectively through our lives.

For this moment, bring your attention to your breath and follow your next three inhalations, extending the length of your outbreaths and settling your nervous system.

Then pause and summon one of your triggers and the underlying belief that supports it. Listed below are a few common triggering beliefs.

○ I need to be "right."

○ What's the right way to do [X]?

○ I can't afford to lose face.

○ I'll be "found out" if I speak up.

○ I'll be hurt if I say anything.

○ Something bad will happen, or I'll lose something or someone important.

○ Add your own.

Do the beliefs seem to register in a particular place in your body? When and where do they show up most frequently? Do they have a texture? A color? A vibe?

On purpose, allow yourself to touch the rising energy of the trigger with your attention and to let it go, dissipating as surely as your outbreath. You're rewiring your nervous system by learning from your triggers. Reflect on what you're learning.

• • •

Paul's Story

> Vulnerability sounds like truth and feels like courage.
> Truth and courage aren't always comfortable,
> but they're never weakness.

—BRENÉ BROWN, AUTHOR OF *DARING GREATLY* AND RESEARCHER

The impacts of early developmental trauma, difficult childhood experiences, or simply typical upbringing can influence the growth of neural integration in the brain. Or, as Dan Siegel writes, "Where attention goes, neural firing flows, and neural connection grows."[20]

Earlier, we met Paul, the booming-voiced leader who couldn't understand why his team wouldn't listen to him. Before starting his own business, Paul had gone through a lot: a childhood of neglect, the travails of war as a young man, testy relationships, and unwise decisions that later landed him in legal hot water.

Yet, he persevered. He finished school after his military stint and went on, after some fits and starts, to start a business (out of his garage!). Paul had grown the business successfully over the past bunch of years, yet it had plateaued and he was beginning to panic. And his health was suffering too.

At the recommendation of his therapist, Paul sought me out to participate in an upcoming mindfulness course I was teaching. Since his stint in Vietnam, Paul had not slept soundly through the night—a common symptom of post-traumatic stress disorder. He'd tried everything he knew to do: meds, short naps, working out. Yet nothing seemed to work. This lack of sleep for some thirty-plus years had taken a huge toll on his physical health, his clarity of thinking, and his relationships. He was desperate to find something to help him literally get rest.

At our initial interview, he wanted to know if mindfulness could help and whether my class would be worth the investment of his time and energy. Of course, I couldn't promise him anything, except to say that those who take on the practice of becoming present to *what is* in the moment can cease fighting themselves and learn to work their central nervous system instead.

Paul soon realized that he had more than daily stresses fueling his body's reactivity; his early life strategies were breaking down. He was falling apart and energetically maxed out. On top of his overcompensating behaviors, he felt ill-equipped to handle any new stresses, of which there were many. All in all, he was game for something new.

Over the eight weeks of the mindfulness course, he participated fully in class. On Week Three, he choked up as he told his classmates that he'd actually been sleeping through the night the past week. Miracle of miracles!

With such an impactful experience at his back and a fledgling mindfulness practice in tow, he brought this offer to his team too. In those next few months, Paul began to turn his life and his business around. The three biggest experiences Paul reportedly took away were practices: *to pause* in the moment, *to stay*—even when he didn't want to and linger longer with his discomfort, and *to commit* to training his attention on a regular basis.

Paul had started to listen to *his* still, small voice—the voice of his Core Presence. He began to play with loosening up his tendency to push away from discomfort and avoid unpleasantness in order to please some invisible other. He learned that it was pointless to try to stop an emotional reaction or a thought he didn't understand from occurring, and he started to welcome what came his way. He began to be a bit kinder as he made sense of himself, his choices, and his future. An energetic shift was underway, making his life's energies more accessible to him.

Emotional Revelations of Pause

Pausing mindfully can reveal emotional states that then inform one's decision-making and purpose. Like Paul and Rand, whose emotional states were buried underneath their own stories, the pause provided turning points to help each of them zero in on what was most important—their purpose—more clearly. Ultimately, the same tricky emotions allowed them, with awareness, to choose differently and make decisions, not out of automaticity but out of authentic reflection about what mattered most to each of them. What did Paul or Rand do to get clarity? Each turned into the winds of personal complexity and old strategies to face himself.

A Vendor Story—What Not to Do with Your Emotions

On a phone call with a vendor—attempting to articulate a situation gone south and deep in the details—I was interrupted midstream with a torrent of words, imagined hands waving in my face.

"I can't believe what you're telling me! This isn't what we agreed to! It's inaccurate, not to mention unfair! What we need is . . . ! And what you need to do is . . . !"

If you've ever found yourself on the receiving end of a rant, you know the kind of experience I was having that afternoon.

Stunned. Agitated. Outraged. Someone was yelling at me—*at work, no less*!

And, like me, you may have reacted.

I felt attacked. My heart rate increased; my jaw tightened. I felt defensive and thought, *What the @#%*?* while the adrenaline in my body had me primed to act.

In fact, I was straining to contain the words ready to pop out of my mouth:

"*How could you?*"

"You don't understand at all!"

"I'm done!"

"We had an agreement!"

"Doesn't he get it?"

When we're distressed by an external event or comment, we react. It's how we're biologically wired.

We may feel triggered by something outside ourselves.

We might become defensive or expressive with an obvious outburst of feeling.

We can find ourselves in a defensive dance of excuses or blaming.

We likely notice we're shutting down, distancing from the experience with stony silence or resentful resolve.

Or, we may simply think, *Get me outta here!*

Believe it or not, your reaction—an Obvious Outburst, perhaps paired in a Defensiveness Dance or Get-Me-Out Gladys! or Super Silence or Resentful Resolve—can open a secret doorway into your own internal mindset about the situation and provide the key to handling it well.

When I react, however, the results can leave me in a bit of a mood. Or maybe a lot of a mood. Moods that aren't necessarily effective in offering an appropriate response.

Resigned. Resentful. Revengeful.

When I react from those moods, does it work in the moment to clarify the joint concerns? To move the situation forward? To stay in the conversation?

Not so much.

In fact, chances are good that none of these typical reactions work super well, despite the fact they're actually hardwired by design in all of us—first and foremost to keep us safe and out of harm's way. When we feel unsafe, we can't think clearly and our emotional brains are on high alert. We compromise our concerns, settling for less and tolerating more. Feeling unsafe, we avoid conversations that are necessary to move work forward and to be an effective team member. We can react in kind, dismissing and blaming the other.

When we simply react in situations that are difficult, we suffer. Moreover, the conversation—and ultimately the relationship—will suffer too. The words we speak in haste will become the house we live in, our word-out-of-mouth ratio the building blocks.

So if your reactions don't work as well as you'd like, what will?

It's likely that you already have some great ideas about what to do differently. Maybe bits of wisdom gleaned from some wise elder in your life like:

1. Count to ten.

2. Take a deep breath . . . or two, or three.

3.　Walk it off.

4.　Laugh it off, kiddo (my dad's favorite)!

Research reveals that minding our own emotional reactions is key to our emotional health and well-being, even if we'd really rather yell and stomp our feet. Minding our word-out-of-mouth ratio is essential to responding to stress, and to rants by others.

That said, to do so, we have to be aware enough to tune in to our own experience, which is hard to do when you feel like you've been hit by a Mack truck of nasty energy coming at you. It can take your breath away!

So, first off, pause to notice which reaction seems to be your typical one—the Obvious Outburst, Super Silence, Defensiveness Dance, Resentful Resolve, or Get-Me-Out Gladys! (We all have typical tendencies under stress, by the way, so don't sweat it. It'll help you to know your own first reaction so you can choose to shift it up).

Then take that deep breath (recent research indicates it takes about six seconds to shift gears from reacting to responding), because breath will help your rational mind kick into gear after it was hijacked only moments before.[21] Feel your feet on the ground as you walk it off.

As you're settling, ask yourself a few clarifying questions: What actually happened here? What most irritated you? The tone? A promise broken? What can I learn from this situation? Writing out what occurred and asking a trusted other to listen to the situation can help you gain the clarity for an appropriate response.

Then, be bold. Choose to let your reaction go, on purpose. Request a conversation with the ranter. Listen. Mind your word-out-of-mouth ratio. Notice what house you're living in.

RECAP

- We are energy bodies

- Feelings, moods, and the language of sensation = emotional fortitude

- Conscious leadership is a deeper process of interacting with the world

- Embodied intelligence is emotional intelligence

- Leadership best practices for cultivating self-awareness

  · Self-observation
  · Self-acceptance
  · Self-correction
  · Self-generation

SCOPE: SPACE, CONNECTION, OPENNESS, PACE, ENERGY

S – Between today and next week, how many open slots do you have in your calendar?

C – How often do you feel life is happening "out there" vs. "in here"?

O – When was the last time you admitted a weakness at work? Or were open to feedback or support?

P – Do you know your own best speed limit?

E – What are the warning signs you're running on empty?

CHAPTER 8

Purpose: What Do You Love?

What in your life is calling you?
When all the noise is silenced,
the meetings adjourned,
the lists laid aside,
and the wild iris blooms by itself
in the dark forest,
what still pulls on your soul?
In the silence between your heartbeats hides a summons,
do you hear it?

—RUMI, THIRTEENTH-CENTURY PERSIAN POET

Honey, you can do or be anything
you want to be in this world.

—PATTY K, MY MOM

was lucky enough to have been raised on a Midwestern gentleman's farm. My sister and I had plenty of fresh air, trees to climb, and stars to gaze upon in the black night sky. My parents—a building contractor and his whip-smart partner—had built an extraordinary home, nestled in a verdant valley a quarter mile off the main road. A strong German Lutheran work ethic circled the perimeter of our lives not unlike the dilapidated barbed-wire fences that cordoned off the farm.

As kids, we had the freedom to wander outside all day and discover new universes each evening. Living in the country, with the big, open sky, opened up all kinds of possibilities to dream about the future. Perhaps like you, I wanted to "be" a lot of things when I grew up.

You'd often find my sister and me playing in the creek that snaked through our property. Depending upon precipitation through the year—from spring rains, winter snowstorms, etc.—the creek beds would either be dry, exposing all the limestone slates jutting up, or the water would be high, with greenish-blue moss growing on that same limestone, and minnows darting to-and-fro in the icy cold water. Sometimes we'd find interesting rocks, even arrowheads, in the streambeds. I used to love exploring in the creek barefoot, looking for interesting objects, watching the animals, and splashing my sister. *It's amazing what secrets will emerge from the earth if we explore it.*

Finding Direction

Earth Day was declared in 1970 after a big oil explosion occurred in Santa Barbara the year before, spewing over three million gallons of slick, black oil across eight hundred square miles of water and killing more than ten thousand dolphins, sea lions, and seabirds. Thousands of university students, along with twenty million others, came out to declare environmental rights, celebrate, and protect the earth.

I heard about Earth Day at school. Though I didn't fully comprehend its impact, I knew that if something had damaged my little corner of natural beauty, it would've felt personally devastating. I loved climbing trees and exploring the woods. I knew in my bones that I wanted to be a forest ranger to protect our earth.

On bad weather days, we'd be inside with games and library books spread out. Sometimes I'd copy beloved quotes into my notebook. Since I loved words, reading, and big ideas, I wanted to become a writer to explore them all.

Reading Nancy Drew fueled my fascination with the mystery of people: what makes them tick, what makes them fight, and what generates love. For a time, I fancied becoming multilingual and working at the UN as a translator. It seemed to me that translating was what we all needed to get along better with people and to be able to listen through our differences.

The Morning

The Way It Is
There's a thread you follow. It goes among
things that change. But it doesn't change.
People wonder about what you are pursuing.
You have to explain about the thread.
But it is hard for others to see.
While you hold it you can't get lost.
Tragedies happen; people get hurt
or die; and you suffer and get old.
Nothing you do can stop time's unfolding.
You don't ever let go of the thread.

—WILLIAM STAFFORD, AMERICAN POET, APPOINTED
CONSULTANT IN POETRY AT THE LIBRARY OF CONGRESS

The big burr oak that sits at the end of a long, winding driveway is well over two hundred years old, its acorns topped with bristly husks like rough woolen ski caps. It provided shelter from the gusty winter winds and shade for the muggy dog days of August in the Midwest. It was my constant companion growing up. Waiting for the bus, I'd follow the grooves of the deeply textured, grayish bark, and feel into the livingness of this tree I long ago claimed as my own. One morning it seemed to be sitting there as if witnessing my private thoughts, unsurprised at my jolt of clarity.

That's when I first came to know the Thread, the one that has continued to weave and work its way into the fabric of each aspect of my life. I would become a psychologist to help kids and their families get along. I'd work to protect the life and beauty of the natural world. I'd share my insights about how we're all connected to God—who at that time was the only one I shared bits of my heart with, and then only late at night as I sang myself to sleep.

You see, while the country was a terrific place to grow up, home life was not always terrific. My parents missed the memo on how to carry on great conversations, at least with each other. Given the tension and lack of harmony in my childhood household, it's no surprise that I found solace in nature and in spirit, or that I wanted to help people to get along better and to love each other.

As I got older, my parents' arguing was intermittent and intense. I hated the fighting. I was convinced there was a better way. By then I had realized that simply translating their intentions to one another, however, wouldn't be enough at all. I needed to know *why* they fought so I could make sense of *my* feelings. Inklings of inner tension had begun surfacing in me. I wanted to explore, shine, and be myself. Yet a core belief, unknown and buried deeply, was that I must take care of them *first*. The belief gnawed within me, though at the time I had no words for it.

This intuitive "knowing" as an eleven-year-old, odd as it seemed to me even then, was influenced by our dysfunctional family dynamics. They fueled my interest in making sense of it all. I'd pore over encyclopedia pages, desperate for answers to life's questions in the detailed description of the lives and works of Freud, Jung, and Adler.

The "thread" in William Stafford's poem has woven its way through my life in the flowing form of questions: How do we deal with difference, especially if it's hard? When do we need to listen more deeply? Is it possible to love more deeply—what is it to really love someone anyway? Could something good come out of the conflicts people have with one another? How do we care for the earth? Where does respect come in—is it offered or earned? When do we need to act? Isn't it all about love?

This circulating tension has played out in my life: What *is* the bigger picture, and how do I help others while being myself? Will relationships suffer if I don't step in? What if I shine too much? Can I really listen to and trust my own intuition? Can I simply be me, no apologies? Who *is* that anyway, I wondered? Forest ranger, linguist, writer, or psychologist? (Of course, race car driver and jazz singer were up there too when I discovered the thrill of speed and became entranced with Nina Simone.)

As in the last line of Stafford's poem, I've never let go of the Thread. The current iteration of my personal purpose statement is "To extend embodied leadership to innovators creating the future." Writing this book is a step forward for me to fulfill living my purpose, a purpose that doesn't change.

And I share all of this because the seeds of my leadership path, my purpose, took shape way back then, unbeknownst to me. And, likely, so did yours.

Passion

> Don't ask what the world needs. Ask what makes
> you come alive, and go do it. Because what the world
> needs is people who have come alive.

—HOWARD THURMAN, PHILOSOPHER, CIVIL RIGHTS LEADER,
AND FIRST DEAN OF RANKIN CHAPEL AT HOWARD UNIVERSITY

We're born into the positive energy of life with a personalized gift to offer to the world. It's our work to come to terms with what that gift is, to learn about it, and create space for it to grow and flourish.

Our early life experiences, coupled with our unique interests, are foundational building blocks for where our life's energies will be played out. We're born into, grow up with, and are socialized in our first family. A natural outcome includes learning, adopting, and embodying beliefs and values of our first family, and later those of our community. While we can't *not* do this, the process of our own inner listening can become faint: we can forget who we are.

It's rare that people take the time to step back and reflect on their personal values or their purpose in life. In fact, many of us live our entire lives with the "borrowed" set of standards, beliefs, and values that we inherited—and are invisible to us—until we begin to get curious about what matters most to us.

Our early life shaping either dulls or animates our energy, setting us on a path toward finding and living into our unique purpose or not. The great teacher Krishnamurti wrote, "Without passion life becomes empty, shallow, and without much meaning."[1] He understood that we're drawn to what impassions us. Experiencing our own inner spark of life can transform our raw experience to provide the light of awareness we need to see our path to purpose with clarity.

Consider those activities in your life that you absolutely love to do. What sort of things put you into flow and make you lose track of time? What activities energize you the most?

As kids, we're naturally drawn to activities that engage and excite us. A kid's job is to play and play—using their imagination, exploring, and learning in the process. They dream up many different futures: one day it's being a baseball player, the next it's a doctor, fireman, teacher, or scientist. The lure of the woods, where my sister and I clomped through the creek, and the discovery of things like tiny irises by the side of a path next to the morels growing under the crumbling wood heap—all of it excited and moved me, revealing the amazing wonders of nature. To allow the excitement of *what is* to shape us is what grows our passion.

To keep learning requires intentional deep listening, at multiple levels, for what makes *you* feel most alive, energized, and impassioned. Passion is the juicy combination of what you love, what you're drawn to, and what you deeply care about. Passion is what puts you into flow and energizes you.

Storying a Life

It was early one Saturday afternoon when I first heard a soft, muffled knock on a window while clearing out the bed of irises in our front yard. Occasionally, my husband, Brian, will knock on our window and smile at me or maybe signal that I have a phone call from Mom.

Yet today, Brian was nowhere to be seen. So, I resumed cutting back the late summer foliage—prepping for next spring's passionately purple display of beauty. I heard the knock again. I looked up and still didn't see my husband. *What the heck?* I thought.

Curiously, my gaze scanned across to our next-door neighbor's yard.

Aha! I saw young Levi, age three, knocking on the front window of his house and grinning broadly. Delight crossed his face as our eyes (*finally*) met. We both smiled in giddy acknowledgment of one another.

A few minutes later, there was another knock. I looked up, my eyes met Levi's, and we both smiled again. As I continued with garden tending, Levi and his parents were leaving home for an afternoon at the park, with their baseball gear ready to go.

Levi excitedly told me he'd seen me and that "I wanted to say hello," so he knocked on the window to get my attention. I thanked him, though he now looked shyly away, tightly holding his mom's hand. His dad went on to say, "He gets really bummed when he knocks at people passing by and, for whatever reason, they don't respond. He gets really sad when they don't see him."

Like Levi, we all have moments when we want to connect—when we want to be seen—if not for some specific reason, then for the sheer pleasure of it.

As young children, we don't "know" we're creating our life's stories with such simple actions, yet it's in the seeds of our early experiences that our personal stories begin to grow. Ultimately, those early stories filter our incoming experiences and become the future stories we tell ourselves.

It's an invisible process, this "storying" of a life.

Our stories become embodied with time and repetition—living in our bodies as well as in our minds. And, of course, we don't have just one story but multiple stories that we craft and rejigger over time. It's in the telling of stories that we not only texture our lives with an understanding of the social context—the intentions, instructions, and collaborations involved in living with others in a particular place, time, and culture—but *we also learn about ourselves.*

In fact, Jonathon Gottschall, author of *The Storytelling Animal*, says that "story—sacred and profane—is perhaps the main cohering force in human life. A society is composed of fractious people with different personalities, goals, and agendas. What connects us beyond our kinship ties? Story. Story is the counter-force to social disorder, the tendency of things to fall apart. Story is the center without which the rest cannot hold."[2] Stories hold us together, and stories can change our behavior. They can influence our perceptions, bookending our lives with meaning. Leading American theologian Brian McLaren tells us that story "gives people direction, values, vision, and inspiration by providing a framework for their lives. It tells them who they are, where they come from, where they are, what's going on, where things are going, and what they should do."[3] This "framing story" textures our general beliefs of the culture, nation, religion, and even humanity as a whole. Our stories also may have the potential to, quite literally, change history.

Meaning

> The individual needs the return to spiritual values,
> for he can survive in the present human situation only
> by reaffirming that man is not just a biological and
> psychological being but also a spiritual being.
>
> —PETER DRUCKER, AUTHOR OF *LANDMARKS OF TOMORROW*,
> PHILOSOPHER, AND MANAGEMENT CONSULTANT

Of course, not all passions are equal. Many are born of challenge and suffering in the face of intense conflict, divorce, or trauma in our family of origin. Workplace violence, economic fragility and inequity, and environmental degradation with cascading impacts can all provoke intense passions that inform your purpose, and your story too.

Viktor Frankl wrote his seminal work, *Man's Search for Meaning*, in 1946 in the aftermath of his experiences during World War II. In spite of the horrific conditions in the Auschwitz concentration camps, Frankl—an Austrian Jewish psychiatrist charged with tending to those living in the camps—found that by focusing on a positive purpose rather than the bleak, inhumane conditions of the camps, some prisoners found a way to survive them. He posited that we don't just seek to understand but to make meaning from life's experiences—including deep suffering.

Of course, Frankl wasn't the first to address the quest for meaning. That search is as old as humanity. In his book *A New Earth*, Eckhart Tolle says that everyone's purpose is to bring the power of presence into the world. More recently, Simon Sinek writes in *Start with Why* that his why is to support each of us to change the world, in whatever way we can, for the better.

Purpose itself is at the core of who we are. It goes back to that tiny seed of light, your Core Presence. Learning to follow that light and stay connected to it, like the Thread, is the journey of following your path toward purpose.

Birdsong

A bird doesn't sing because it has an answer,
it sings because it has a song.

—MAYA ANGELOU, AUTHOR OF *I KNOW WHY THE CAGED BIRD SINGS*,
POET, AND CIVIL RIGHTS ACTIVIST

We each have a distinctive song. What is yours? Can you allow it to be sung?

Everyone's purpose will be different, like so many fingerprints, and your job is to move toward uncovering and exploring it. Get curious about how your contribution to the world—which is uniquely your own—shows up in your actions, the way you carry yourself, and how you engage with the world. You might be surprised.

Pausing into presence can help you listen for the call of your purpose. The bridge between where you are today and deeply knowing your purpose is essential in your life as a conscious, purpose-driven leader.

Whether you realize it or not, your purpose is likely evident to others, though it may be invisible to you. It shows up in just about every project, activity, conversation, or relationship you've ever had—even since you were very young. When you're living and acting on purpose, you can situate yourself for the most useful impact while being more personally fulfilled.

Simply put, purpose answers the question of existence: Why are *you* here? What are you meant to do in your life? Who are you meant to be? What moves you to do what you do? These perennial questions compel a response.

Your purpose is fundamental, sacred even—and fully discoverable.

Purpose is certainly not off the shelf. It's *not* about generating a list of competencies or skills to learn to become like another leader you admire, though you might. It *is* about pausing to reflect and open up space for personal inquiry so that you *discover* your unique purpose, the one that reflects the authenticity of your life path, distinct from others.

Discovering your purpose involves a turning over of your earlier life strategies to explore and mine, through rigorous self-inquiry, your values and experiences to discern your uniquely personal answers to these life questions. By listening and *feeling into* your experiences, your purpose will gradually come into view, though it may take some time—purpose discovery can't be rushed. Circling in and landing on your purpose, you'll likely tap in to what impassions you and move toward your next steps on your leadership path. As leadership experts Nick Craig and Scott Snook say, "Leadership purpose springs from one's identity, it's the essence of who you are."[4]

Conscious leaders have a responsibility to pause and listen deeply to the instinct of their purpose inside the larger context of life: what and how will my life's choices impact others? Ultimately, *purpose is a definitive statement about the difference you are trying to make in the world*. Only *you* develop your personal purpose.

If you lived your purpose and were making the difference that you aspire to make, what would that look like in one year? Three years? Five years?

Core Values

> Today you are you, that is truer than true.
> There is no one alive who is you-er than you.

—DR. SEUSS, CHILDREN'S AUTHOR AND CARTOONIST

Alice asks the Cheshire Cat in *Alice in Wonderland*, "Which way ought I go from here?" The Cheshire Cat replies, "That depends a good deal on where you want to get to." "I don't much care where—" says Alice. "Well [says the crafty cat], then it doesn't matter which way you go, you'll get somewhere . . . if you only walk long enough."[5] Many people go through life without ever identifying what they want, where they want to go, or who they want to become. It's only later that they wonder why they feel frustrated, off-kilter, and unsatisfied at not achieving anything of significance in their life.

A great starting place for purpose hunting is to investigate your core values. We look for value in our purchases, our trips and hobbies, and in our work and relationships. Why not within ourselves? Clarifying our values steers us in the directional path of purpose. Core values answer the question, "What is most enduringly important to me?" Values are deeply embedded perceptual filters that anchor our identity, and influence what we see, whom we choose to interact with, and how we behave. Many values are invisible, yet their impact is obvious in the actions we take each day.

Rooted in our biology, values equip us to quickly size up a situation to determine if it resonates, or if it violates one or more of our values. Thanks to our implicit memory, this ability gives us a nearly instant read on people, their behavior, the context and circumstances, and the available choices. We're quickly attracted to, motivated by, or even inspired by certain people, without having to stop and evaluate each detail. Conversely, we may feel put off, irritated by, or even repelled just as quickly, all without consciously thinking or evaluating the details.

While it's true that we're not likely to believe in values that aren't truly our own, when we make choices and take actions out of sync with our values, we become uncomfortable. Like my client Tom. Asked by another leader to engage in unethical behavior that not only ran counter to the company's values but his own values too, his discomfort opened the door for new, and necessary, conversations at his company.

Because core values determine what we pay attention to and how we act on our purpose, it's essential that we're clear what our core values are. When our core values ignore an essential dimension of life (e.g., relationships, ethics, or personal growth), then we'll have a blind spot that will adversely affect how we live and work. If we violate our own core values, we may feel guilty, disappointed, or let down. Yet when our actions align with our core values, we feel pride and can work with a clear conscience.

Consciously understood and cultivated, values provide a foundation for wisdom, good decisions, and performance on the way to living our purpose. It's in the time we set aside to listen deeply—whether on a walk, in the elongated pauses of heartfelt conversations, or in quiet reflective moments—that we can discern what's most important and move toward it with clarity. It's in those moments that we're able to affirm what we care about and shift out of our tried-and-true strategies to craft a new framing narrative for our future. Living congruently with our own values provides deep satisfaction and reward.

● ● ●

PAUSE FOR VALUES

Our values cluster together in buckets, with similar values grouping together. Over time, the prominence of our values may shift depending upon our current circumstance and life stage.

Set aside 15–20 minutes to pause and reflect on your values, using the following questions:

○ What core values do I bring to my work?

○ What are the core values I would tell my family that I live by in my day-to-day work?

○ If I were to begin a new business tomorrow morning, what core values would I want to build into my new company?

○ What values do I want to live into as a leader?

Now, test each of your final core values against the following criteria:

○ Is this value a currently lived value or an aspirational one?

○ Is this a value that I would adhere to even if it were to disadvantage me, my family, or my business?

○ If I awoke in the morning with enough money to retire, is this a value that I would continue to hold dear?

• • •

Joyful Journey

"Know thyself" was the inscription over the Oracle at Delphi.
And it is still the most difficult task any of us faces.

—WARREN BENNIS, AUTHOR OF *ON BECOMING A LEADER*
AND ORGANIZATIONAL LEADERSHIP SCHOLAR

Ron and I started working together when he found himself at a crossroads. He's the CEO of Continental Sales "Lots 4 Less," which is Chicago's premier closeout retailer. At the time he contacted me, the state of the fifty-five-year-old family business was in flux, and so was he.

In the previous five years, Ron had been dealing with issues common in family businesses: strained familial relationships and roles, particularly around who holds power and controls decision-making; separating business concerns from family issues; and addressing conflicts. The tensions that had been brewing between Ron and his father impacted not only productivity but also potential growth for the business.

Ron's dad, who had started the business back in 1965, was the de facto CEO, though compromised health prevented him from performing the day-to-day work of the business. That had fallen to Ron.

Ron's crossroads involved nothing less than coming to terms with himself. This kind of deep work is comparable to the geological forces deep beneath the earth's crust that create powerful pressure so intense that even the tiniest nugget of hard coal can be transformed into a beautiful diamond. Such personal power points provide a possibility for transformation and for growth. Ron was at one of these points as his go-to strategies were collapsing.

On vacation with his wife, Ron realized, "Looking back on it all, I was emotionally drained: I had become numb to all of it. I'd emotionally checked out of the business. On the outside, everything looked good for the most part, but I was torn up on the inside." Ron's body was quite literally taking the hit. On average he'd been sick five or six months of each of the past five years. His doctor had declared a diagnosis: excessive stress.

By the time we started with executive coaching, he'd already taken a few steps forward. He committed to himself to "make my health a priority and start tapping into my heart, then acting from that place." He shared his initial goals:

- Put my health first

- Respond from a place of resilience; don't just react under stress

- Feel myself again

- Regain my confidence + own my power

- Get support to transition to CEO

Early Life Influence

Ron's early home life included intermittent moments of "extreme anger and violence" fueled by alcohol. Not recalling much from those early years, he did his "best to keep it all together as I got older." Though he was a good student, his self-confidence slowly waned until he reached junior high school. Switching from a Catholic school to a public school, he blossomed, earning recognition for his academic work as well as his athleticism.

By his senior year in high school, one of Ron's key strategies for coping was in full swing. In true competitive spirit, he worked hard, very hard. He was captain of the football and baseball teams, student council president, and a national honor society member. He stopped playing basketball—his beloved sport—to take a more practical route of focusing on baseball, with his goal being to play for a Division I college.

Training hard the summer before his first year of Division 1 baseball, Ron stretched and honed his skills. His coach told him to "start fielding like the Latino you are." The offhand comment clicked for Ron—"He wanted me to stop being robotic and let my body do what it was built to do. By the end of that summer, I was like a new player. For the first time, I felt I had a chance to make it to the Big Leagues. It wasn't just a fantasy." Unfortunately, a herniated disc later that same season took him out of play, dashing his base-ball dreams.

Ron, he was later to discover, had developed a few strategies to get by in the world, strategies that worked well—until they didn't. They continued to trip him up not only in his baseball aspirations but later when he joined the family business. For example:

- Competition is what counts. Work hard, really hard.

- Forgo what you want, be practical, and figure it out.

- Don't feel yourself or your emotions.

- Live life carefully—stay small and invisible.

"Over the next few years, work got more challenging as we hit a growth plateau," Ron said. "I knew at that point I needed more support, but it was very challenging with my dad. It went on for almost five years. I was struggling."

Ron's wife shared a book with him—*Turning the Mind into an Ally* by Buddhist teacher Sakyong Mipham.[6] Intrigued by the title, since figuring it out hadn't worked so well, he read it. Then he googled the author and found that he was hosting a four-day workshop in "the middle of nowhere in Colorado." Feeling a keen resonance with the event, he signed up. "I'd never done anything like this in my life. I didn't know if I'd be with a bunch of hippies smoking pot or joining a cult, but I went. It changed my life. It was the first time I was gentle with myself."

Our Work

Building on his Colorado experience, we set to work. Ron had participated in a mindfulness-based stress-reduction class I'd taught a few years before, and later he had taken courses at the Meditation Center, so he was already engaged in a daily mindfulness sitting practice. With the excessive stresses he was under, he'd become disconnected from his sensing, feeling self. His attempts to hold it together were costing him precious life energy. I encouraged him to begin a centering practice, with focused attention on feeling the sensations in his body.

Centering isn't a static technique but a living process of self-organization. It increases our capacity to self-observe, self-correct for healing, and to self-generate in our lives. "To center ourselves is to shape ourselves in a particular way to life."[7] When centered, our energies and actions are in congruent alignment with what we care about. From such a centered place, Ron would discover what was most true for him on this journey.

In taking planned pauses to reflect and write out his Emotional Autobiography, Ron gained perspective, voice, and a little compassion for the experiences he'd gone through in his life. In the quiet of the early mornings, he began to see the ways he'd typically handled pressure in his life: "At times, I would suppress what I was feeling and power through in my pitch to get stuff done. But I learned that when I pause, become aware, that's when I can observe that the pressure is actually an opportunity to overcome my past habitual fear-based strategies."

Within a few months, building on his growing understanding and leveraging his coach's comment from a few years ago ("Start fielding like the Latino you are"), we explored his embodied shape. The body is the shape of our experience—the emotional, intellectual, and spiritual shape, as well as the physical. Thus, as Richard Strozzi-Heckler says in his book *The Leadership Dojo*, "The self that we are is indistinguishable from the body."[8]

To work through the body is to access the wisdom of feeling, intuition, and compassion. Ron's powering through had cost him; he lost connection with his own inner longings. He needed to rediscover his own natural energetic rhythms to deeply connect with his heart. Directing keen attention to his body's sensations, he learned where he was holding his tension and stress. He practiced interrupting and investigating his old strategies and releasing them on purpose. New energy and a sense of life began to emerge and flow through him. By engaging with his practices, he was able to reflect on his life, his strategies, and his deep concerns. Ron had begun to reconnect more deeply with his purpose.

He had known he wanted to grow the business before, a desire not shared by his father, yet clarity continued to shine forth.

A few short months after we began our work, Ron's father died. With this stress, his old strategies kicked up once again, pushing him into yet another set of business and personal decisions that would need to be made. Yet Ron stayed true to his commitment to himself and continued the work we'd started.

In addition to his centering practice, which resonated in his baseball body (he knew how to hit from center), I taught him a thirty-one-count jo kata practice from aikido. Nearly everyone who picks up the wooden staff and learns thirty-one-count form loves it. Ron was no exception. His natural athleticism kicked in as he diligently learned and practiced the moves. He loved it too. Moving through a kata increases the awareness that we live inside of bodies, that our life energy is designed to flow—a kind of pausing-in-action—and that we can extend energy and influence beyond our physical body.

Like me back in chapter four, Ron quickly noticed his impatience and need to "get it right," as I slowly taught him the moves in the ensuing months. He learned the purposeful pacing of "1 is 1, 2 doesn't exist until 1 is complete."[9]

I invited Ron to verbalize his purpose statement in the form of a declaration, saying it aloud as we began each iteration of the kata. In this way, sensing into how his body related to his commitment reinforced the individual moves and generated more energy to be the declaration, with his whole being. He deepened the power of his voice as we ended together, blending our voices with a *kiai*, or spirit sound, generated from our shared center. Practicing kata builds confidence by accessing our innate power—the power of embodied presence.

The Future

Consciously practicing pause during his workday never came easily to Ron, but it has been instrumental for him because he's on the move now to create the future. Ron and his team are on a new path. He's realized that he doesn't want to let some old scars, those impressions from the past, dictate his life going forward. As he says, "A lot of the things that I wanted to do, in the past, came from this deep pain that was there." We are transitioning from that moment to what the current moment is calling us to do.

"I think it would be fair to say, in retrospect, that I couldn't handle the pressure of running and trying to grow the business, yet not feeling supported," Ron says. "Dad knew what he wanted, he just didn't want what I wanted. The pressure with my father was one of the things that I had a hard time doing a very conscious pause about. There was too much emotion, and the biggest thing was that I couldn't let go of it all until the very end."

Today, pausing helps him align with his intention of cultivating a culture of growth and kindness in the business. As he says, "There's a human being in front of me I need to listen to. We want to create a joyful journey for all our stakeholders—our team, customers, vendors, and the community—and treat them authentically."

• • •

PAUSING TO EXPLORE PURPOSE

Pause supports the process of digesting, settling, and feeling into what actually matters to us, including values, people, and activities. What factors shaped you and set you on your path? Who you've become? Consider going on a walk as you contemplate your responses to the following questions.

○ What activities do you absolutely love? What sort of things put you into flow and make you lose track of time?

○ When have your values been most severely tested? How did you respond?

continued

○ What values are most difficult for you to maintain? Why is that?

○ What practices, structures, and relationships do you have in place to support you in maintaining your values?

○ What contribution will you make on your short sojourn on the planet?

• • •

Extending Leadership Purpose

The way to do is to be.

—LAO-TZU, CHINESE PHILOSOPHER AND FOUNDER OF TAOISM

When leaders connect with core values and clarify personal purpose, then bring them to their teams and organizations, their influence cannot help but grow. Though discovering purpose is a subjective process, it's not a solitary one. Organizations built on purpose and trust tend to gather like-minded people together. Collectively they work to create a shared purpose, multiplying their impact well beyond current constituents, and extending it out into the larger community. Executive coach Tim Kelley writes that "this kind of leadership does not require a gifted person, but simply a person willing to put their gifts to the service of collective purpose."[10]

Shared core values lie at the foundation in purpose-oriented businesses and permeate nearly everything that happens, blending in the stew of workplace culture. By personally sharing their own purpose and listening as others tune in to their personal purpose, these leaders become mirrors supporting others in living with purpose too.

To embody one's purpose is to increase congruency between one's values, philosophy, and actions, and results in a robust stand for human dignity. It's through the practice of making particular distinctions that we begin to embody a stand.

When we simply *take a stand*, like a stand to increase pay for the minimum wage, it's often in a particular organization, at a specific point in time. However, when we *embody a stand*, as Ray Anderson did when he committed Interface to climbing Mt. Sustainability, we move to become that person, committed to that particular cause, through a set of distinctions and practices we make over a longer horizon of time—typically our lifetimes. "When we embody a stand, we are the stand. It is not a thing, issue, or project apart from us," says Richard Strozzi-Heckler. "Our very identity is the stand. An embodied stand becomes the trajectory of purpose."[11]

Make. Awesome. Work.

> Walking our own true path is finding our way
> toward wholeness: the unity of body, mind,
> spirit and the everything of the universe.
>
> —WENDY PALMER, AUTHOR OF *THE INTUITIVE BODY*
> AND AIKIDO INSTRUCTOR

A recovering people-pleaser and self-identified perfectionist—a "Type A cubed"—Nancy Pautsch has done a lot of work to identify her default strategies in her leadership to align with a larger purpose. Currently the Chief Evangelist of Stakeholder Value—aka president—at Envision IT, a technology optimization firm, Nancy's story began several years ago with her longtime business partner, Bill.

Working together at a previous tech company, she and Bill, her "rock," were under tremendous pressure in the churn-and-burn industry to grow the business, which they did. The company was later acquired by private equity, and with the technology space being pretty rough-and-tumble, the new owners continued to pile on additional responsibilities atop new objectives, and, Nancy says, "We both just kept taking it all on."

The mounting stress prompted Nancy to begin questioning her commitments and alignment within this "new" organization. About that time, Bill, who tended to absorb and internalize his stress, walked through her door one afternoon with a textbook case of stress-related Bell's palsy. She was stunned. "His face was contorted, paralyzed in place; he was in immense pain." Triggered by her care for Bill, she vowed, "That was the day I said, never, ever, ever again! We're going to find a different way!"

Within a few short months, two events occurred that shifted Nancy's direction. First, the book *Firms of Endearment* by Raj Sisodia, the co-founder of the Conscious Capitalism movement, crossed her desk. "That book was really my inspiration. That was the intersecting point of my career and the personal growth journey I'd already been on for the past few years," says Nancy. "I started asking myself these big questions. What's my purpose? Why am I here? I began to awaken and see the toxicity of the business that I was in. I was leading but not owning."

She continued reading, fascinated by Sisodia's description of the historic social transformation of capitalism that's underway. Capitalism has long been regarded as an economic concept without a soul; it's all about business, markets, and the bottom line. Firms of Endearment, or FoEs, are companies that believe in the transformative power of capitalism to elevate humanity and better the world.

The search for meaning is changing expectations in the marketplace and in the workplace, and, as Sisodia said, "We believe it is changing the very soul of capitalism." FoEs have extended their purpose beyond simply maximizing *shareholder* profits to align the interests of all *stakeholders* to share in the gains of doing good while doing well. Those firms that pay attention to creating value for all their stakeholders perform better. Over a ten-year horizon, the thirteen FoEs outperformed the companies featured in Jim Collins's classic book *Good to Great*—1,026% to 331%—and the S&P 500, by

122%. Finishing the book, Nancy thought, "OMG, this *is* the better way!" and shared her excitement with Bill.

Then, just weeks later, the second event occurred. Nancy met a young man named Beau Smithback, the founder of Envision IT. Kindred spirits from the start, having met to discuss potential partnering for a client project, they naturally began to share their mutual interest in business with a capital B. On reading Raj's book, and giddy with enthusiasm, Nancy gave Beau the book, saying, "This is what I want to build and lead," to which he replied, "That's what I want Envision IT to become. Let's do this!" Shortly after, Nancy and Bill joined Beau and got to work.

The rest is history. To hear Nancy tell it, technology companies aren't trying to do what Harvard lecturer Rebecca Henderson articulates in *Reimagining Capitalism in a World on Fire*—"embracing the idea that while firms must be profitable if they are to thrive, their purpose must be not only to make money but also to build prosperity and freedom in the context of a livable planet and a healthy society."[12] Instead, Nancy's take is that in technology "everyone's trying to flip the business. So, our first commitment was to be in this for the long term."

Since that early decision, Nancy and Envision IT's leadership team have re-architected the company and operationalized the business based on the four tenets of Conscious Capitalism: Conscious Leadership, Purpose, Stakeholder Orientation, and Conscious Culture. As Nancy says, "We've certainly set our purpose right, we've operationalized our entire business around it. Our Why is 'to enrich the lives of all our stakeholders.' Up and down the halls at Envision IT, everyone knows how they're contributing to that shared mission, and that inspired alignment helps Envision deliver on their promise to clients, which is to *Make. Awesome. Work.*

To take a stand as a purpose-driven business requires a quality of courage and an unwillingness to make moral compromises. To embody that stand by aligning values with purpose and to rejigger the bar for what it means to "do good business by doing good" can only be defined as dignity, an embodiment of care.

Besides leading strategy to make sure they're executing on their purpose, a big part of Nancy's job today "is to work on conscious leadership," which fulfills her personal purpose, too: to live an enriched life and inspire others to do the same.

A short story captures the essence of what happens when a leader, like Nancy, commits to being conscious and leading on purpose. As she tells it, "Envision IT is a unicorn in our industry as a conscious business. Our purpose-driven foundation, long-term vision, and people-first approach makes us an anomaly among our peer technologists, along with the fact that we're woman-led."

Nancy was to speak on behalf of one of Envision IT's business partners (and a key stakeholder), Citrix Systems, at their technology analyst meeting in Silicon Valley. All the major industry analysts would be present. It was the first time Citrix had invited partners to participate as panelists. Their moderate-sized group of one hundred or so analysts in the audience was nonetheless influential since an analyst's perspective operates as a key influencer of client behavior for the upcoming year.

Nancy sat backstage among other speakers and Citrix leaders, listening while a presentation kicked off the day. As the time of their panel discussion drew closer, she felt her anxiety begin to kick in. Her jitters were stoking doubt: "Our story is so different—would anybody get it? I'll be on stage, a four-foot-ten-inch woman along with a male moderator and three other male panelists. These guys will introduce themselves and their organizations in the traditional way: length of time in business, technology focus areas, annual revenues, etc. I'll introduce Envision as a group of curious and compassionate people growing a soulful company. Is that crazy? Would they agree? Or, should I just fall in line?"

The significance of the event and their nontraditional story sparked her nervous system with a quickened heart rate and muscle tension. That's when she knew to mindfully ground herself as she was waiting. "I slowed my breath and planted my feet solidly on the ground. I placed my hands on top of my thighs intentionally to feel my palms connecting to the strongest muscles in my legs. Soon I felt my body start to ease, and I shifted my focus to my thoughts, which were racing."

Nancy grounded herself, pausing purposefully to allow her mind to slow and enabling her intentions to come into focus. "I chose to think about our intention and our purpose for being in business: to enrich the lives of our stakeholders," she said. With that, she could see "our family of Envision-ers. I felt a sense of warmth and care continue to calm my mind. My mind-body grew calmer and more focused, I chose to think about our path, and I began to smile." This was an opportunity to shine a light on their differentiated conscious-business model. Nancy was hopeful the analysts would welcome a fresh, purpose-driven, and people-centric approach to technology implementation. At the very least, she knew she'd speak authentically, from her heart, about Envision IT's truth.

Seated in the third chair in the panelist lineup, she figured she'd have more time to reflect on questions. As they took the stage, the first panelist opened just as she'd predicted: "I'm John Doe, president of ABC company, founded in YEAR. We have annual revenues of $X and we sell a LONG LIST of technologies." The second panelist followed suit, and by the end of the second introduction, Nancy noticed the audience was heads-down, buried in their laptops.

"Panelist number three..." She was up. "Hello, I'm Nancy Pautsch, Chief Evangelist of Stakeholder Value with Envision IT. We're a group of curious and compassionate people growing a soulful company." Eyes glanced upward and several people sat back smiling widely as laptops slowly began to close. Nancy shared Envision IT's story, their business and leadership practices, and their purpose to enrich the lives of their stakeholders and how they *Make. Awesome. Work.* "It was an exhilarating session," Nancy said. "The following year, they invited us back to the analyst event, this time to co-present with Citrix."

A responsive focus for leaders today is to articulate concisely *what you stand for, not against*, which is what Nancy expressed on the panel. Rather than being viewed as overemotional, heavy-handed, or arrogant, for the leader with a clear purpose, embodying a stand becomes an invitation and produces meaning that inspires others to want to follow you and join in your purpose. And, like Nancy discovered, it's less important that others agree with you than the fact that they find you credible, congruent, trustworthy, and committed.

• • •

YOUR NEW STORY

Our early stories are the seeds we water to craft our lives; to live in a coherent story shapes our identity. Over time, our stories become embodied with time and repetition—living in our bodies and emotions as well as in our thinking minds.

And through repetition in telling our stories (to ourselves and others), we become who we are. Our stories color what we see, how we feel, and what we believe is possible. In short, our stories shape our behavior, influence our perceptions, and drive our actions.

As we get older, it's useful to review what stories we've been telling ourselves, because sometimes a story becomes old and outdated. If that happens, we can begin to feel boxed in or stuck in our lives.

Take some time—say, maybe 20–30 minutes—to pause and reflect on the story you've been telling yourself. Record your reflections for later.

○ Is it an old, worn-out story, or does it still serve you well and
   enrich your life?

○ Does it keep you in a certain mood? Does it allow new moods to surface?

○ Does your story tell the truth of who you are, or of a journey on the road
   to who you're living into?

○ What's the new story you'd like to create in your life?

○ What do you need to release to allow your new story to unfold?

○ Then, what do you know you need to allow for your new story to emerge?

Last, fast-forward a year from now. Based on your reflections here, what are three obvious changes you've made over the course of the year that have you living into a new story?

Allow yourself the time to craft your new story. Consider where you are, what you'll be doing, who you'll be doing it with, and why it's important. Allow yourself to access the faculty of your imagination, and let your new story unfold.

● ● ●

RECAP

- Purpose is what you're made for—follow your Thread

- Passion drives purpose

- It's an invisible process, this "storying" of a life

- Core values can reveal your purpose

- Your purpose extends beyond you

- What's your new story?

SCOPE: SPACE, CONNECTION, OPENNESS, PACE, ENERGY

S – How often do you walk in nature? Notice the blue sky?

C – What is your Thread?

O – Do you ever ask yourself *What's possible?* instead of *What's practical?*

P – When was the last time you operated at 25% capacity on purpose?

E – What makes you feel alive?

CHAPTER 9

Perspective: Let Go of What You Think You Know

As human beings, our greatness lies not so much in being able to remake the world as in being able to remake ourselves.

—MAHATMA GANDHI, INDIAN LAWYER AND NONVIOLENT ACTIVIST

My husband found out about a local two-day Blues and Heritage fest over the Labor Day weekend with a terrific musical lineup: Buddy Guy, Mavis Staples, Laith Al-Saadi of *The Voice* fame, and Coco Montoya. We were thrilled. We purchased tickets and enjoyed the first night singing "Respect Yourself" with Mavis Staples, swaying in sync with the crowd.

The second day, the weather was perfect, and our early arrival found us, again, in choice lawn seats, sipping tasty lemonade. Then it started.

We were sitting on the lawn, midway back on the green, and enjoying the afternoon listening to fabulous music. Immediately in front of us was a small space just big enough to squeeze in a couple of lawn chairs. Sure enough, right before the evening show, two women arrived—chairs in one hand and cigarettes in the other—only to finagle not two but four chairs into that small space!

Soon they were joined by others . . . popping open beers, talking loudly over the music, and dancing—that is, if public pole-dancing constitutes dancing in any way. Clearly, *they* were enjoying the concert.

Agitation came my way about twenty minutes into the new set, capturing my attention and darkening my mood. I was *not* enjoying the concert at this point.

Who are these people—thinking they can home in on our neighborhood? I thought as I moved their multiple chairs literally off our feet.

Nobody's smoking out here—they should know better! I thought as I fanned away the drifting smoke.

How rude is that! Can you believe it? Go get a room! I thought but didn't say as the couple next to us proceeded to grope one another to the sweet sound of the blues.

You get the idea. I was in a twist.

As the evening wore on, agitation now completely settled in. I knew I needed to shift my perspective gears if I had any hope of enjoying the remainder of the concert.

I got up. I took a walk, because moving my body always helps me shift my mind. I slowed my breathing. And I realized a few things.

First, observing signs of our own internal distress can reveal that a value or belief has been crossed, challenged, or threatened. I was distressed by a lack of concert etiquette and the boisterous intrusions into *my* concert experience!

Then, as I walked around, pausing to reflect on exactly what I was feeling, I became acutely aware of physical tension in my jaw and neck, followed quickly by immediate judgments. Both were driven by my emotional reactions. I needed to step back, gather my wits, and sort through these judgments with an eye to the bigger picture. Otherwise, I'd simply be driven by them, stay annoyed, and not enjoy the concert.

Pausing this way allowed me the space I needed for self-reflection. It allowed me to "see" the "what is" that was right in front of me instead of staying caught in my head about what my "already knowing" mind believed.

My beliefs:

- People should be courteous at public events.

- The behavior of the women in front of us was not courteous.

- Stepping on others' feet, flinging cigarettes, and get-a-room groping—even at a concert—were over the top by anyone's standards.

- Wasn't it obvious that they were being rude?

You can hear the tension in my strained inner dialogue:

It's a free country, they can sit wherever they like . . . yet, can't I too?

This *is* a public concert, Chris (I always use my first name when trying to reason through these kinds of emotional reactions; it helps), *so get over it!* . . .

But I don't want to get over it!

They're just having a good time . . . at the expense of the rest of us trying to enjoy the concert?

Continuing to walk, possibilities came next. Should I say something? What would happen if I did? What could I say that would get me what I wanted (an enjoyable evening of music)? The right conversation conducted in the wrong mood is the wrong conversation. Yet I actually rehearsed what I thought was an appropriate response: "You're enjoying the concert, right? Great, we'd love to as well." Which might've worked, except it was a bit prickly, and by then they were drunk—very drunk.

Other possibilities included moving to a new seat, leaving altogether, and choosing to do nothing (though that option felt like caving in to poor behavior to me). I'd gotten triggered, hooked on what I thought of as correct concert etiquette, but—truth be told—I simply lost my perspective of the bigger picture.

The bigger picture here involved these facts: 1) it was indeed a public concert, 2) those folks had paid for the privilege of listening too, and 3) the belief I was holding, that I thought was *right*, was simply my belief—not the truth.

My annoyance and agitation had, upon reflection, helped me to clarify my own standards: treat others at concerts as I would like to be treated, assume good intent, and take the action necessary to defuse tense situations.

I could either hold to these standards rigidly and continue to be irritated, with a tense set to my jaw, or hold to them lightly and tune in to what *was* working (beautiful day, great music) in an otherwise personally tense situation. By the time I'd circled the park grounds, I'd chosen to re-center and shift my self-talk, this time with a more helpful tone: *Breathe. Refocus your attention, tune in to the music.* Though I didn't *love* the outcome, by shifting my perspective, I didn't feel like I was caving—and I was able to enjoy the rest of the concert.

When we're not able to catch ourselves and use the power of the pause to review, gain perspective, and resolve a situation, we're at the mercy of our old default habits, strategies, and stories. And, because we all live inside our stories as a way for our lives to hang together and make sense, we're likely to reinforce stories that may not be accurate or true. In effect, we can easily let ourselves off the hook.

Here's the rub—we all do this. It's part of making sense of our lives, and it's biologically driven—we cannot not do it. Yet it's possible to develop the skill to work it all out differently.

● ● ●

PAUSE PRACTICES FOR PERSPECTIVE

○ Make it your habit to ask for multiple perspectives in any conversation. Allow generous time to listen.

○ Be a curious social detective, not a judge.

○ Provide openings and opportunities for feedback. We learn to read others' perspectives by giving and receiving feedback.

• • •

The Ladder of Inference

My Blues Fest story played out in what business leader Chris Argyris calls the Ladder of Inference.[1] Triggered, we sprint up the proverbial ladder, as I'd done, and this well-worn mental pathway becomes littered with abstractions that lead to misguided conclusions, reinforced beliefs, and subsequent behaviors.

Our old stories and strategies, including those we've adopted unawares, are anchored in place by beliefs that have taken on a life of their own, quite literally in our very tissues. If left untested, or until something triggers us and compels us to turn toward it for examination, our self-reinforcing beliefs remain buried and inaccessible to us, yet still subtly influencing our actions. The outcomes we're looking for (I had in mind a courteous lot to share music with on a summer's evening) can easily be eroded because of what we hold to be so:

- Our beliefs are the truth.

- The truth is obvious.

- Our beliefs are based on real data.

- The data we select are the *real* data.

In a workplace example, see if the following trek up the Ladder of Inference sounds at all familiar to you.

Imagine that I'm making a presentation to a leadership team at an off-site. To a person, everyone's alert and engaged. That is, except for Phil—one of our hypothetical team members. He looks bored, yawns often, and has been typing on his phone the entire meeting. He's quiet, asks no questions, and makes no comments, except at the end of the hour when he says, "We'll need a full written report."

By the time I get back to my office, I've concluded that Phil was indeed bored and clearly thinks I'm incompetent, though I'm convinced my ideas could help his team. Come to think of it, I don't think he's ever liked my ideas. He's obtuse and distant—a jerk by any estimation. I shift to making my decision: nothing of importance to Phil will go in my report because I *know* he won't read it anyway. Worse, he could use it against me somehow.

My lickety-split decision process started with the observable data we could all see: Phil's lack of engagement or comment.

Then I selected some details about Phil's behavior: yawning and typing on his phone.

I moved quickly then to assume Phil was bored.

I added my own meaning—this organization expects too much—based on my experience of the culture (it's dog-eat-dog).

I further conclude that Phil thinks I'm incompetent. He's somehow a danger to me. I can feel it.

As I reach the top of the ladder, I'm now actively plotting to thwart him.

Seems so reasonable, right? It happens so quickly, unconsciously, that I'm not even aware I'm doing it. Worst of all, my perceptions at each rung of the ladder, with the exception of data visible to others at the bottom rung (he's yawning and typing), only take place in my head. The rest of my trip up is invisible, intense, unquestioned, and abstract. Leaps like mine, up the ladder, are oft called "leaps of abstraction," though I call them "making s%*#t up!"

The more I choose to believe that Phil is obtuse, distant, and a jerk, the more I reinforce my own tendency to notice these behaviors of his in the future. Over time, as I act on my erroneous beliefs, I become unpleasant and antagonistic myself, with Phil likely picking up the vibes and doing the same. Before long, we're trapped in a mutual, bitter "reflexive loop."

After years of inferential leaps, you might find yourself saying things like, "Muslims/Catholics are so-and-so," "liberals/conservatives are so-and-so," "millennials/baby boomers are so-and-so." In succumbing to these inferences you're at a remove from the moment at hand, like I was with Phil. Input buried or long since lost from memory fuels this inferential leap up the ladder, providing an explanation for the disconnection between our immediate reactions and their historical genesis. Instead of "I'll believe it when I see it," it's more accurate, though counterintuitive, to think, "I'll see it when I believe it."

Getting Off the Ladder

> Imagine that every person in the world is
> enlightened but you. They are all your teachers,
> each doing just the right things to help you learn perfect
> patience, perfect wisdom, perfect compassion.
>
> —JACK KORNFIELD, AMERICAN AUTHOR OF *BUDDHA'S LITTLE
> INSTRUCTION BOOK* AND TEACHER IN THERAVADA BUDDHISM

Though none of us can live outside of our stories (e.g., fish don't know they're swimming), we can learn to skillfully check our own inferences and assessments to test them for accuracy. Upon catching ourselves in a story, we can employ a pause (walking, sitting to reflect, journaling, etc.) to walk our way back down the Ladder of Inference and gain a new perspective. Here are some other strategies you can use:

- *Pause* to notice and *name* the triggers you experience as they occur (self-awareness).

- *Become aware* of the impact of triggers on your thinking and reasoning, and on your emotions (reflection).

- *Share* your experiences—including feelings, thinking, and reasoning—and make them more visible to others (advocacy).

- *Inquire* about others' experiences, thinking, and reasoning; and listen (inquiry).

- *Flip the script* by switching roles and warming up to another perspective by predisposing yourself to new data versus the "real data."[2]

By making our emotional and thinking processes visible to ourselves and others, via considered reflection of our full-bodied experiences, we're able to see both differences and commonalities in our perceptions. Whether others agree or disagree, like Nancy's experience at the conference, they'll see what informs your reasoning, and you'll see their viewpoint too.

It's true that our assessments and conclusions are tricky to test. They just seem like common sense to us, so why would I risk being vulnerable to check them out? Certainly I could pull Phil aside and ask, "Phil, do you think I'm incompetent?" But would he answer me honestly? Would I believe him? Likely not.

However, if I acknowledge my own triggers—e.g., *I'm irritated that Phil looks bored and my neck is tight; maybe that means I'm boring or my idea is boring*—I can then go on to test my assessments by asking, "Phil, are you bored?"

I can go further and simply ask for his perspective in an open-ended way: "Phil, what was your reaction to my presentation?"

Or I could offer the observable data: "You've been quiet, Phil." To which he might reply: "Yeah, I've been taking notes on my phone to share with my direct reports; I love this stuff."

Quite a different story.

Perspective-Taking and Empathy

As young children, we learn early to notice a parent's or teacher's shifts in energy and mood—from irritated to excited to angry—to anticipate their behaviors. Perspective-taking is an innate human capacity, and this ability to notice and "read" or "feel" other people provides us a compass to navigate our social world. To attune this way and feel into another person's emotions and experience is to have empathy, even to the point of feeling their experiences in our own body too.

Pausing to purposefully step into another's shoes allows us to infer and interpret the motivations and behaviors of our friends, neighbors, and colleagues (like Phil) in order to see situations from the point of view of strangers and understand and appreciate values and beliefs quite different from our own. Without perspective-taking, we can't empathize, engage in moral reasoning, extend love, or even hold a healthy conversation.

As leaders, it's important to create relationships of trust in which we can minimize potential blind spots (yes, we all have them) and reduce the mischief caused when we believe our stories without verification. This involves the attentive work of entering each other's world to get to know what we each mean about the same experience in order to broaden our perspectives. You heard my struggle with my concertgoing point of view and witnessed how I ultimately decided to stop trying to convince the Blues Fest concertgoers that they were "wrong" and I was "right." Yet, did I convey how much energy it cost me that evening?

Our lives are a web of interactions that occur over time in every conceivable relationship. Doesn't it make sense to learn how to understand this dynamic? To learn how to come down the ladder to reverse previously untested, often faulty conclusions and clarify new ones? This is the openness that provides the candor required for trust.

Yet, perspective-taking is complex; it's tricky as we struggle to stay present to experiences that we create in reactivity (my reaction to Phil) or to those that aren't our own. (How *did* the women at the concert understand "concertgoing" anyway?) Perspective-taking involves opening to a new view or outlook, one that you don't share or perhaps never considered, and staying open despite difference or challenge. It involves viewing the world through another's eyes to see how life appears from their vantage point. Of course, one doesn't literally take another's place or look through their eyes . . . except perhaps on the aikido mat.

Tenkan

Tenkan is the act of turning, pivoting to take in the full panorama of action on the aikido mat—including your partner's energy as he moves in for the attack. Ideally this involves *blending with*, instead of *resisting*, a partner's energy. At our dojo, the sensei would often yell, "More tenkan, more ten-kan," because only in the turning can we see what is so, open up space for new moves to appear, and lead into the next moment.

When a fellow aikidoka comes, full force, with a grab to my wrist, if I tenkan from center just before contact is made, I can lead him and set the pace. If I don't tenkan from center, my energy will be sluggish or stiff. I'll be out of sync with my partner, working at cross-purposes, and making the moves harder, not easier. Moving from the hara, or the energy center, is the secret key. My friend Renee, a poet and fellow aikidoka, knows the power of moving from center. She calls it "belly knowing," where you can *know* the other person's next move because you feel it in your body, belly to belly. By turning from center, I can feel and see my partner's perspective more clearly, while not compromising my own.[3]

As a leader, being able to shift perspective is especially important in these VUCA times when you're required to pivot quickly in moments of challenge and complexity. Your willingness to turn, imagine, and not only see what's on the mat but also what's required in your day-to-day life, is to grasp another's perspective. Not a childish imagination of make-believe, but rather a quality of imagining that's adventurous, curious to see what might happen, and willing to linger longer in a pause—without leaping up any ladders—to allow space for an unexpected answer or wildly different point of view to surface.

Pausing-in-action with a two-step (an off-the-mat name for tenkan) can support you in your leadership by helping you shift from one conversation to another or from one part of your day to the next. Two-stepping is useful to practice, to embody an ability to turn, for when you need to quickly respond to all the incoming data and want to have a clear head. Training your body in the two-step will allow you to two-step mentally, shifting perspectives by being curious about a conversation, a project, or, as Ron stated, the person right in front of you. By two-stepping you can train in a more centered, alive presence—the one necessity to perspective-taking.

• • •

BODY-BASED MOVEMENT PRACTICE—TWO-STEPPING

Two-stepping is centering in motion. Two-stepping will allow you to notice when you're centered and when you're thrown off balance. And it's a great way to build centering-in-action into your body-self. It may seem awkward or unnecessary, yet I'd encourage you to get outside your comfort zone and try it out! Read this practice first, then try it out.

Begin by centering yourself.

Allow yourself to feel centered—settled, present to yourself and your surroundings, and connected and open to what wants to come into form. Feel the soles of your feet.

As you move into the two-step, start with curiosity, and ask how you're showing up. What expectations are being jarred open? What do you notice about how you sense your body in space? What's your mood?

Begin by putting your left foot in front of your right at a comfortable distance, one that allows you to feel solidly placed on the earth. Bend your knees slightly as you face forward; square your hips to align with where you're facing. Settle in by taking a few breaths from your center, breathing up from the soles of your feet to the crown of your head.

Next, step forward with your right foot and then pivot on the ball of your right foot, turning your body 180 degrees as you bring your left foot behind you. You're now facing the opposite direction from where you began and your right foot is in front.

Step-turn again—left foot comes forward, pivot on it, and turn and bring your right foot behind. Continue practicing this move until you don't have to think about it.

Two-stepping builds the muscle to pivot in the moment in your body, which can translate to greater agility in your conversations. You can think of two-stepping with a partner as a conversation in which two people, both of whom have important concerns and wish to be heard, are centering with a goal of gaining perspective and coordinating action together.

• • •

What's Your Story: Distinctions You Can Use

Listen first, speak last.[4]

—PETER DRUCKER, MANAGEMENT CONSULTANT

Remember Paul, the business owner who couldn't understand why his people didn't simply "just listen" to him?

He was caught up in his story. I challenged him to step back, pause, and observe his situation from another angle—a current view rather than the one that drove his story and took him in a flying leap up the Ladder of Inference. A second step involved *seeking perspective* from those who worked for him. His team had great contributions to make to both Paul and the business, but without stepping into their shoes, effectively turning toward them to gain their perspective, such contributions would be lost. Paul needed a new set of distinctions from which to craft a new story.

Distinctions are rooted in actual experiences and acquired over a lifetime. It's our distinctions that finely filter how we make sense of the world. We all operate from a large body of distinctions, whether we're aware of them or not, and they influence our day-to-day common sense. And we add distinctions in an ever-expanding list over the course of our lifetimes, layering and refining new learning as we go.

Distinctions refer to conceptual limits or boundaries. Can you distinguish red from green? For someone who is red-green colorblind from birth, like my husband, the words red and green possess little distinction when selecting a shirt to wear for the next day.

Distinctions drive competence. You can only become competent in the areas in which you possess distinctions. Let's say you're a business owner and it's the beginning of March. You're reviewing your year-end numbers. Suddenly, it seems, you find you're not feeling very well. You get a glass of water or take a nap (or both), yet the feeling persists—so long, in fact, that you decide to consult the experts. Your doctor and your accountant will listen in different ways to your account of not feeling well.

"I have a twisting pain in my gut that kind of burns, then I feel a bit nauseous."

Your doctor listens and says, "It could be irritable bowel syndrome that requires medication and shifting your diet" or "It could be a hernia, so let's check it out."

She's listening to you through the distinctions she's learned in her medical training.

On the other hand, should you consult with your accountant, he'll have an entirely different perspective based on a different set of distinctions, one that's less refined in the terrain of what's going on with your body. His listening will result in a response more like this, "It's spring, tax season. It's obvious that you're stressed. I'm guessing you likely have heartburn. Want a Tums?"

Perspective comes through listening to others' distinctions, observing their subsequent actions in a specific domain, then choosing the best next action. In the preceding case, after receiving another's perspective—the doctor or the accountant—you'll either schedule a battery of tests or pick up a package of Tums. Distinctions also include more than words: swinging a golf club, performing a classical guitar score, and making an incision with a scalpel are all embodied distinctions that live in a particular domain.

A lack of distinction can limit your options or even impair your decision-making. For example, you'd never want to seek advice from me on tax issues because I have no domain expertise there—though on the personal development front, I'd have you covered.

Listening through Distinctions

The point of listening is to develop a shared disclosive space,
to develop a new relationship.

—FERNANDO FLORES, CO-AUTHOR OF *BUILDING TRUST:
IN BUSINESS, POLITICS, RELATIONSHIPS, AND LIFE*

In today's VUCA workplace, with high intensity and constant chaos and churn, there's a strong attraction to certainty. In seeking certainty, we feel like we're taking action. It can seem soothing. In fact, tracking for *certainty* has become a distinctive lens that filters, then sharpens our attention to specific data (remember, I focused on Phil's yawning, typing on his phone, and lack of comment) that can skew our understanding. It's from that data that we move to make sense of what we see; our interpretations are often incomplete.

We're *certain* we know what the other person is going to say, *certain* he or she is a genius, an ass, or simply boring, *certain* that we like or dislike what someone is saying. Paul *certainly* knew his team should be listening to him, because he was *certain* he had all the answers and details about running his business.

Another commonplace lens today is *pretense*. *Pretense* is, of course, about pretending. *Pretending* that we're not racing up the ladder with one of our own internal conversations, and pretending our erroneous conclusions are the real ones. Or we simply smile, *pretending* to agree or not care, and ending conversations because we don't want to contradict, annoy, or stir up the proverbial pot of conflict. Or we have a boss who, like Paul, barks directives instead of listening, so we *pretend* to respect him so the barking will stop.

Neither certainty nor pretense are useful to perspective.

Rather, it's in the spirit of a purposeful pause that discovery of perspective comes about. Listening, learning to ask great questions, and then listening again is the place to begin.

Discovery is the practice of listening for what's possible in a conversation. It's where we can share of ourselves, disclose what's important, and listen. Of course, we don't just listen with our ears, we listen with our entire body. Our capacity for embodied self-awareness opens space to *feel into* another's experience and their concerns—that belly-to-belly sense of connection. It's called "limbic resonance," and it describes the neural processes that occur as two people's emotional states sync up in energy rhythms that deepen connection.[5] It's in that state of *discovery* that one is willing to be open and curious, to explore and to literally discover what the other person brings to the table—*their perspective.*

Discovery opens new worlds. In our day-to-day business lives, the old, prevailing distinctions of funneling information, knowing all the right answers, "managing" talent, and allocating resources are no longer effective, nor enough. Through distinctions we can open to possibilities that reveal others' ideas, concerns, and skills that would never be clear through the lens of certainty or pretense.

Paul's New Story

The power to question is the basis of all human progress.

—INDIRA GANDHI, FORMER PRIME MINISTER OF INDIA

Stories are explanations, accounts of causes and effects, and personal narratives from which we construct meaning from our experiences. To better understand another's way of making sense of the world, learn how to listen to their stories and the distinctions embedded in them.

Of course, Paul was no different than the rest of us in his tendency to run up the ladder. Yet his current set of distinctions, his common sense, wasn't serving him at all. Paul's prevailing distinctions were born out of his experience in Vietnam: funneling necessary information, being the "expert" with all the "right answers," and directing action with minimal conversation. Despite having been useful, and even necessary, in wartime, his distinctions were no longer effective for his leadership team or employees.

Paul's biggest challenge initially involved addressing his own strategy for leading, which he described using three Ds: "As an entrepreneur I'm driven, determined, and demanding." When he opened up his team meetings for comments and no one responded, he'd "push and push and push. I don't know when to stop." He expected that they should "go along with me and have some faith," because in his heart of hearts he cared about what they thought. Yet his hard-driving style, suitable for addressing troops, only produced an unwillingness to learn and a heap of mistrust. *How long before the next thing goes wrong?* This thought reinforced his conclusion, a core distinction in his own mind—he'd have to do it all himself.

Triggered by what he thought of as his team's lack of listening, his façade of toughing it out cracked. "I've lived most of my life with intense fear and shame. Can I do this? Do I have the knowledge to pull it off?" Yet he knew, in spite of his own self-doubt, that something more was possible.

I reminded Paul of what he'd learned in the mindfulness class: he could center himself in the moment, let the doubt and difficult feelings pass through, and settle in himself. Then I asked for his commitment to practice pause, centering himself at first in his body and then in what he cared about in the upcoming weeks. Once he settled himself, then he was to ask clarifying questions and listen to his team members about their concerns.

To his credit, he took on this challenge. He paused. He asked questions. In a leadership meeting that proved to be a watershed, Paul turned to his operations director, Joe, surprising everyone, and simply asked, "Can you tell me your opinion about how the process on the floor is working?"

That simple question opened a robust conversation (Joe, the ops guy, had a very different set of distinctions than Paul) that ultimately led to positive outcomes. His question was a "wow moment" for his team. By engaging them around *their* experience, expertise, and perspective, a mood of openness was created.

No longer focused solely on what was going wrong in the company, his team went on to improve their processes, cut delivery times, and reduce turnover to near zero (in a highly regulated market), which saved on costs of hiring and training. Employees across the business started to report feeling like valued members of the company. All of this resulted in happier employees, satisfied customers, and a boss who exclaimed, "It's so much nicer, so much more fun and gratifying to look in their eyes and see the expressions on their faces." Over time, with a commitment to pausing and practicing and perspective-taking, trust within the leadership team began to grow. Paul had begun to learn when to step back, how to allow and even welcome conflict, and to support his team.

Paul credits his progress to mindfulness—"It's a constant part of my life now. I've learned to stop, pause to breathe, listen, and ask questions. I question myself, too. 'What's going on? What am I feeling?' And instead of just reacting to things, I feel less like I have to have all the answers. You know, it's made a big difference."

Dialogue: The Ultimate Interpersonal Pause

Suppose that we were able to share meanings freely
without a compulsive urge to impose our own view or to
conform to those of others and without distortion and
self-deception. Would this not constitute a real revolution
in culture and therefore eventually in society?

—DAVID BOHM, AUTHOR OF *CHANGING CONSCIOUSNESS* AND
PIONEER IN THEORETICAL PHYSICS AND QUANTUM THEORY

As conversation moves along the continuum from debate to discussion and on, we become more attuned to the possibility of a shared meaning of reality, or we might call a "shared common sense."

Debate tends toward being combative. It's about winning an argument and being victorious. *Discussion* might be described as debate "playing nice." Much like debate, *polite discussion* involves advocating its viewpoints and challenging those of others. The etymology of the word "discuss" means the "breaking apart" of issues, concerns, or situations to gain agreement. For our purposes here, we might call it "everyday conversation."

Because decisions do need to be made, plans worked, and work processes followed, you'll find—somewhere midway between polite discussion and dialogue—the *skillful discussion*. Skillful discussions are always focused on a real task at hand, involving many elements of dialogue yet with a difference of intention. They allow teams to make their thought processes transparent, to surface and challenge assumptions, and to look more closely at sources of disagreement instead of shying away from conflict. Skillful discussion tends toward a sort of convergence and closure: an agreement, a decision, or a shared agreement of standards or benchmarks or protocol.

Dialogue, however, takes an additional step: one suspends one's own assumptions, or assessments, to understand a bigger picture of reality than one's own. Dialogue signifies a "flow of meaning." The intention in dialogue is to surface ideas, explore perceptions, and discover insights to improve *the quality of collective thinking and interacting*, resulting in the emergence of a new disclosive space of shared reality, a greater sense of connection, and an ability to act in collaboration toward innovation.[6]

Dialogue involves pausing to listen with an open spirit and a beginner's mind. The word dialogue comes from the Greek root words *dia* and *logos*, roughly translated as "meaning passing between." It's a way of discovering the shared meaning moving among and through a group of people. It's shared meaning that forms the basis of culture. Dialogue involves exploring the thinking, feelings, and formulated conclusions that underlie a group's culture or way of being with each other.

Although a newcomer to modern-day leadership and organizational practices, dialogue has been around a long time. It can be traced to the works of ancient Greece (for example, the Dialogues of Plato and works of Socrates), seen in Native American council processes, found in Quaker meetings, observed in counseling models like that of Carl Rogers, in Eastern meditation practices, and in the philosophical works of Martin Buber.[7]

Dialogue occurs, says William Issacs, CEO of dialogos and senior lecturer at MIT's Sloan School of Management, "when you explore the uncertainties and questions that no one has answers to. In this way you begin to think together—not simply report out old thoughts. In dialogue people learn to use the energy of their differences to enhance their collective wisdom."[8]

Dialogue seeks to find a shared connection. The playing field of conversation is equalized by setting aside differences in roles or status, allowing each person equal opportunity to speak. People speak one at a time. The pace of conversation is likely slower, maybe including moments of silence. People are encouraged to speak to their own experience, to speak into the center of the group, and to speak from the heart—to what matters most.

It requires a special kind of listening and speaking in which we suspend judgment to explore different perspectives, beliefs, and assessments at a deeper level. Its goals are to explore, discover, and perhaps uncover something completely new in what Fernando Flores calls the "shared disclosive space" between conversational partners.[9]

When a comment triggers an emotional reaction, and this will undoubtedly occur, the expectation in dialogue is that you will internally settle yourself and then identify and share the assessment or belief you hold that's being challenged. Understanding and perspective-taking grow with increasing awareness and the use of skillful interpersonal pauses in conversations.

Perspective Potluck

Dialogue is a bit like going to a potluck. Think about it. At a potluck, everyone brings a different dish. In a dialogue, everyone brings different assessments, beliefs, and strategies. At a potluck, you *could* eat only the green beans you brought, or you could try the cauliflower salad and maybe the chicken dish, too.

The same is true in dialogue. You could simply hold on to your perspective (you're not asked to give up your own beliefs), though you have an opportunity to sample a rich feast of different perspectives and worldviews.

As a result, in dialogue it's not about convincing or winning or losing at all, but rather about aspiring to listen deeply and build a shared understanding. When conflict and tensions arise, it's dialogue that guides the conversation back to a renewed sense of connection and respect, despite differing opinions. Dialogue is generative. It points to *what could be* rather than fixing *what is*.

Dialogue creates the space for safe, fully engaged conversations or interpersonal pauses. Dialogue allows participants to craft their own experience and opinions over the course of the conversation, not requiring one to "know" at the outset.

Dialogue is about creating an environment that builds trust, encourages communication with respect, honors and values diversity as essential, and seeks a level of awareness that promotes the creation of shared meaning (culture) that supports individual and collective well-being. Dialogue informs and builds alignment without the need to pursue a specific outcome.

Elements of Dialogue

We live in the world our questions create.

—DAVID COOPERRIDER, FOUNDER OF APPRECIATIVE INQUIRY[10]

Key elements in the process of dialogue include:

- Mindfully suspending judgment
- Exploring and checking assumptions all around
- Listening beyond one's own opinion or view
- Inquiring, reflecting, and seeking to understand

When we temporarily suspend our judgment, we open our capacity to engage as listeners. In doing so, we create sacred space through conversations. Greater inquiry into others' viewpoints helps us better understand the mindset of others and allows for new ways of thinking and innovation.

When we explore assumptions, our own or others', we'll encounter unchallenged ideas, unchecked biases, and patterns of thought—or mindsets—that will reflect the level of consistency between our words and our actions. It will be uncomfortable at times, yet we'll have an opportunity to be more aligned in our minds and actions. And we may learn that others have more effective methods for approaching situations than we do.

Questions

- "What do you think?" (general interpretation)
- "What leads you to think what you think?" (facts and reasoning)
- "What would you like to accomplish?" (goal)
- "What is the most important thing to you?" (concern)
- "What do you suggest we do?" (proposal for concrete actions)

Blocks to Dialogue

Blocks thwart real dialogue and strain the process of real connection in conversations. Passivity, dismissing, redefining, and overdetailing are four big blocks on the way to successful dialogue.

Passivity occurs when a person uses the language of withdrawal or a strategy of being nonresponsive in behavior, while *dismissing* occurs when someone discounts himself or others in the conversation. *Redefining* changes the focus of the conversation to deflect or avoid, while *overdetailing* involves providing so many details that the point gets lost in the barrage of information.

Being overly rational, too emotional, overgeneralizing, indirect, or dishonest also blocks conversations. Awareness of one's own blocks enables the ability to stay in the conversation, returning to dialogue.

Relevance for Leaders: Letting Go

Effective leaders know when to speak, when to listen, and when to be silent. It requires a kind of letting go of one's own perspective to move into the deeper connection and conversation that today's environment requires.

In dialogue, as in aikido when the body falls to the ground, there's a power in the letting go. "There is a weightlessness to the experience. What occurs has come from a place of such utter trust, with such an openness of heart and spirit, that the 'fall,' the surrendering, has a power to it that one could not possibly sense otherwise."[11]

Leaders who engage in dialogue consistently uncover the hidden creative potential in any situation. They have the ability to evoke people's genuine voices, to listen deeply, and to hold space for one another's views as legitimate and rich, thereby broadening awareness and perspective.

Leo and the Internet

Jean Pitzo has a daily practice, one that sets her up well to practice perspective-taking. She's in the office by six fifteen a.m. and starts her day with a bit of reading and focusing her intentions. Only then does she begin her daily "fun stroll" around the shop floor, what I'd call a pause-in-motion. Jean is CEO of Ace Metal Crafts, a sixty-year-old manufacturer of stainless steel components used in a variety of industries from medical to pharmaceutical to environmental to food processing. Their shop is full of welders, machinists, and fabricators. Her daily stroll allows her to check in with her team members "to get a pulse on the morale and mood of our team."

It was on one of her morning jaunts that Jean's eyes were opened. To hear her tell it, "The other day, I was doing my stroll in the plant. I was in Leo's welding booth, saying hello to him, checking in, and I happened to pick up a different vibe. I just thought, *What is it I just picked up?*"

She loves this part of her morning, saying, "On occasion a team member takes this time to make a request, share a problem, ask for a favor, or offer advice. This is when I practice a pause. I'd been listening intently to Leo, but on hearing, 'I'm fine. Everything's fine,' I turned to go. Yet, I couldn't shake the vibe I felt, so I turned around and said to him, 'You look very, very out of sorts and stressed. Are you sure you're okay?' I was thinking COVID might be on his mind. Then he just let it out, 'My third-grader . . . we don't have internet at our house for school. Our girls are upset about it, their teachers are on them . . .' Could you imagine the stress? So of course, I went into fix-it mode. But if I hadn't paused, I wouldn't have picked up the vibe."

Jean had picked up something that didn't quite feel right in what was a typical, daily interaction with Leo:

"His face looked different somehow. He normally has this really big smile when I visit with him. That morning, he just didn't have it. It made me want to inquire more deeply. I learned that because they live out in the country, they've little access to internet; the likes of AT&T don't have cable that goes that far out to their house!

"I thought of the pain he must've had going home every day, only to hear his daughters cry because the teachers were getting mad because his third-grader kept getting kicked off Zoom.

"I never would have dreamed somebody didn't have internet. The school district, by law, has to educate that third-grader, and they should've fixed it. But they didn't do their job. And someone like Leo would never ask them to do their job, would never expect that."

Jean goes on to tell the ending to the story. She ushered him into the front office, over his objections, saying, "We have internet here; you could bring the girls to work with you."

She brought in Ace's IT guys and explained, "Leo doesn't have internet at his house out in the country. He's been trying to use a cell-phone hotspot, but with two people on Zoom and all the lessons for school, the girls are getting dropped off their classes. And now the teacher's mad at the third-grader; a third-grader is in tears! You guys, we can't have this third-grader flunk; no one can fail third grade. We've got to figure this out."

Within an hour, IT had ordered a gadget with "weird things sticking out of it," and when it came in a couple days later, the IT guys taught Leo how to set it up.

Part of what distinguishes Jean as a conscious leader is that she used her emotional antenna, listened, and took the right action. Our ability to read others supports one of our primary drives as human beings, the drive to relate to others and form social bonds. Jean's ability to empathize and take Leo's perspective, called *empathic concern,* allowed her to identify with his concerns and to step outside the constraints of her own immediate, biased frame of reference to connect the dots to a solution that worked.

Jean shared that "to pause that morning was amazing—it allowed me to listen and notice a subtle vibe, a difference in Leo. A few days later, his daughters begged him to FaceTime with me. He obliged them. His little girls' faces were so happy. They said, 'Thank you, thank you, Mrs. Pitzo.'"

Developing Perspectives—Practice

Consider what happens when you meet someone, whether a new acquaintance, or an old colleague, or even a distant family member. The process of leaping up the Ladder of Inference shifts into high gear, lickety-split in a matter of nanoseconds, leaving us with opinions and beliefs that are often inaccurate and, worse, contribute to harm.

Like Jean and Leo, recent research indicates that we gain understanding about someone only when we acquire new information from them, a kind of *perspective-getting*. Attempting to understand the experience of another person—a stranger, your spouse, a direct report, or your customer—is unlikely to provide broad benefits by simply imagining yourself in that person's shoes, though that is helpful, or by simply guessing what he or she feels or wants. Accurate understanding requires getting perspective vis-à-vis asking questions, making distinctions, and listening.

When we take on this practice, like Jean did with her daily strolls, we become more skillful at pausing to listen, asking the best right question in the moment, and thereby gaining perspective. We're less likely to stereotype others or to react aggressively when provoked.[12] As we saw with Leo, and as Strozzi-Heckler writes in *The Anatomy of Change*, "The way someone is tells us more about them than what they say or profess."[13] To seek perspective is to be interested in the qualities, capacity, and rhythm of their energy—the feel of them. This skill enables us to develop more positive relationships with those whose beliefs differ from our own.[14]

This is a critically important factor in intergroup conflict, as perspective-taking not only seems to be a necessary condition in reducing stereotypes and prejudices that interfere with successful conversations but may actually empower good relationships and positive solutions in strained work cultures.

Findings suggest that improving this one core capability can generate ripple effects across many of the other aspects of our social-emotional learning. Overall results suggest a key conclusion: perspective-taking and empathic concern have powerful effects on work-related outcomes.[15]

• • •

LET THE PENDULUM SWING—TENSION TO RELEASE

Our bodies learn, and they hold all kinds of tension and stress, including traumatic stress. This five-step practice involves pausing for moments to feel your sensations, then toggling between states of negative tension and positive release. Doing so will allow your body to rewire body-based memories of your tense, negative experiences.

○ Find a place in your body where you're holding tension around a recent negative, unpleasant event, or even a traumatic one. Notice your physical sensations—tightening of the jaw, churning of the stomach, or tight shoulders.

○ Now locate a place in your body where you don't currently register any distress at all—a big toe, elbow, or pinky finger. Notice sensations in these areas too: a calm, ease, relaxation in them, maybe even a sense of safety. If you're feeling at all charged up now, this window might be small, yet focus your attention on the calm place in your body and welcome the ease there.

○ Now, on purpose, toggle between the physical sensations of pleasantness in the nonstressed areas of your body and the unpleasant sensations in your body where you might be holding stress and trauma.

○ Allow yourself to stay with the sensations in each area for 30–60 seconds before shifting. If the unpleasant seems "too much," trust yourself to shift when it feels right for you.

continued

○ Toggle back and forth between pleasant and unpleasant for a few rounds, gradually increasing the amount of time you spend focusing on the pleasant experience. Notice how the unpleasant sensations shift or fade.

When the intensity of the unpleasant shifts or fades a bit, pause to reflect on your entire experience.

By practicing this kind of pendulum toggling, you're increasing your ability to be with difficult, unpleasant sensations and building resilience simply through your body sensations alone (no story required), broadening your perspective-taking skills.

In this practice, by focusing your attention, you're allowing your brain to relax so that your nervous system can reset itself back into equilibrium.

Perspective-Taking and a Life of Choice

Grecian Delight is a forty-five-plus-year-old family business whose core business is selling Mediterranean food products. Peter Parthenis's father started the business as a young immigrant in the United States. Appreciation for his parents' choices and sacrifices was evident in Peter's voice. "They came with nothing, no family, and no money in their pockets, yet my dad worked his way first as a busboy, then as a waiter, to earn a living for us and to get himself into school. Once he got his degree, he went on to start two companies, always with a vision of this Greek food business, even way back in 1974."

His dad had a big vision, too—one that he followed in creating Grecian Delight, and the business grew steadily. When Peter took over, about twelve years ago and around the same time he stepped onto the path of conscious leadership, Grecian Delight had already far exceeded expectations: from an enterprise value of wealth creation to an influencer around Greek food and culture around the world. Yet one of Peter's biggest, deepest desires as he stepped into the role of CEO was the challenge of "buying and merging with a competitor who never wanted to sell to us." Peter and I discussed this within a few weeks after his long-held vision had come to pass, and I wanted to know how the impact of pausing on his path of conscious leadership had informed his decision.

He said, "I pause to remind myself that all of life is laughable at a distance, meaning, you know, to put life into perspective. Pausing is a way for me to shed day-to-day stress and allow me to open up more creativity to find the opportunities through adversity. It's hard to do that if you don't open up your mind and hold it all a little more lightly."

Realizing that his own risk tolerance was far greater than the others in this family business, Peter knew "that the only way we would be able to make this move was to bring on another, outside-the-family, partner. And everybody—both my parents, my sisters—had to be comfortable with that."

Together they set out over two years of the kind of deep conversations that can only be had in an extended pause—to reflect, explore, and disclose their respective needs—to come to an understanding around the business, family, career, and financial well-being. Theirs was a process or prolonged pausing to gain perspective, "to find a way to meet everybody's needs and wants around those different verticals, if you will, to create a win for everyone."

To make such a big decision "would require us all to let go of controls so we could learn and grow with a new equity partner." They ultimately agreed to take the risk and move into action on the M&A, because everyone's needs had been addressed in the process of listening, gaining perspective, and learning.

Today, Grecian Delight's valuation is six times what it was when Peter took over as CEO. His personal goal has been achieved, allowing him to create what he calls "a life of choice, not obligation."

RECAP

- Stories, strategies, and the Ladder of Inference
- Getting off the Ladder of Inference
- Perspective-taking and empathy for conscious leaders
- Tenkan—how in turning we can see—pausing in motion
- Distinctions you can use
- Dialogue: the key to perspective-taking

SCOPE: SPACE, CONNECTION, OPENNESS, PACE, ENERGY

S – What happens to you when someone moves into your space?

C – How do you stay connected to yourself and others in challenging situations?

O – Are you open to engaging with difficult people?

P – Can you control your speed when the world seems to be spinning too fast?

E – Can you catch yourself midstream before making a snap decision and leaking your energy?

CHAPTER 10

Step into the Stream:
Purposeful Practice

Practice
Be soft in your practice.
Think of the method as a
Fine silvery stream, not a raging waterfall
Follow the stream, have faith in its course.
It will go its own way, meandering here, trickling there.
It will find the grooves, the cracks, the crevices.
Just follow it. Never let it out of your sight.
It will take you.

—SHENG-YEN, BUDDHIST SCHOLAR, POET, AND
FOUNDER OF DHARMA DRUM MOUNTAIN ORGANIZATION

T oday's VUCA whitewater requires that leaders be skillful in responding
to what's emerging in the environment of constant churn and change.
Business-as-usual practices, of necessity, will be displaced by practices
that make way for the future. We need leaders who are conscious: *mindful* of

themselves and the world around them; *embodying* an ethic of care, courage, and skillful action; and *generative* in creating the future rather than simply reacting to the complexities out of fear.

Since our lives are made up of the practices we engage in from moment to moment, *we literally become what we practice.* I often ask my clients, "What are you practicing these days?" or "How are your practices going?" If practice makes perfect (as so many of our grade-school teachers said) or if practice makes better (as my aikido sensei teaches) or if practice simply makes possible—it only makes good sense to know what we're practicing.

Only when we pause to notice our day-to-day actions and interactions can we make adjustments, sync up our behaviors with what we care about, and choose to practice embodying behaviors that will make our leadership more effective and our lives more meaningful. We can move toward our higher purpose instead of merely reacting out of unconscious strategies and habits.

Habit or Practice? A Word

Much has been written of late about habits, how they develop, how we shape them, and how we're at their mercy if we're not tending to them. The beauty of a habit, or the string of habits known as a routine, is that once set in motion, our brains can stop working so hard. The brain can divert necessary energy resources to other behaviors instead (like focused analytical or creative work), and over time, our habits and routines become invisible to us.

To take on a practice signifies the conscious intention to create actions specific to a situation. For example, Paul took on the specific practice of asking questions of his staff and stepping back to listen. Over time his practice became embodied; instead of being the type of leader who wanted people to listen to him, by shifting up his practices he became the type of leader who people wanted to listen to.

Other practices are considered *generative* because practicing them is useful in organizing one's life across multiple situations. These include body-based practices like centering and other mindfulness practices or movement practices. Consider the simple micropause that Rand took on:

before automatically answering his phone on the first ring, he adopted the mantra to "pause, ground, center" before answering. In practicing this simple micropause before picking up the call, he brought himself fully present to the moment and his conversation partner.

As a leader, taking on a conscious practice is to *choose* to stay on the leadership path and to act in ways that become embodied in us. In short, we become that commitment. As Strozzi-Heckler says, "The leadership path of self-cultivation is concerned with developing leaders who embody the ethics of individual responsibility, social commitment, and a moral and spiritual vision."[1] Literally, the leadership practices we take on will shape who we are and the leader we will be.

While leaders have many important responsibilities, three stand out: *directing attention* to pursuing a common vision; *harnessing and cultivating their own energy* and working with others' energies—like the orchestra conductor who coordinates the moves of the entire cast of musicians to create a beautiful symphony; and *engaging skillfully in generative conversations* around common values to create the future. All begin with a simple pause and conclude with continued commitment to deliberate practice.

Attention as a Gate

Focus is the superpower of the 21ˢᵗ century.

—ERIC BARKER, BUSINESS WRITER

Amazing as it may seem, what you focus your attention on literally grows and shapes the various regions of your brain over time through the process of neuroplasticity. It's impossible to take in every sight, sound, smell, and sensory stimulus all at once. To manage this sensory overload, attention functions like a gate, allowing some information in and editing some out. Unless attention is focused on it, incoming sensory information doesn't register in the mind. As you focus your attention on reading this—now, for example—you automatically tune out many of the background sounds, white noise fading into the background.

When we repeatedly focus attention on a new thought or action, the electrical and chemical connections between the involved brain cells strengthen. In this way, frequently trafficked ideas and behaviors are reinforced until they ultimately become an intrinsic part of both your behavioral and biological identity: who you are, how you perceive the world, the actions you take, and quite literally the structure and function of your brain. Long-held beliefs, expectations, and behavioral strategies take on a physiological shape and become embodied so that the very structure of our brains reflects the lives we have led up to this point.

By the time an action has been repeated hundreds or thousands of times, the neural connections are strong enough to make the action easy, effortless, and automatic. Aristotle got it right when he said: "We are what we repeatedly do. Excellence, then, is not an act, but a habit." He may not have had the benefit of high-tech brain scans, but even without medical technology it's not difficult to see: *what we practice, we become.* Where we focus attention and what we repeatedly do shapes our entire nervous system, substantially influencing the actions we're capable of taking.

This is good news, because it makes it possible to do complex tasks efficiently and frees up cognitive load to make space for other endeavors. That's useful in a complex, fast-moving world where we don't have time to stop and consciously consider our every move, a world where a pivot is often required. However, it does make grappling with our own strategies and changing our own behavior more complex and challenging.

The most developed and reinforced neural pathways (think old tried-and-true strategies) tend to act like ruts, sucking you back into old behaviors again and again, despite your best efforts. If you're like many, you've gone the willpower route with only minimal success. That's because it's not about willpower or effort at all but because we default to our level of training. That's why habits are hard to break. You need more than just a good idea—you literally need to change the physiology of your brain to adopt and then embody new behaviors, including leadership behaviors.

This brings us back to that new idea that you learned in a recent leadership training and why, even though you know "what to do," you're not doing it. This typical type of training focuses on *teaching people what to do* through ideas and models (like taking an assessment to discern your "type") instead of *developing who they are* (as if you could be reduced to a small box). Logic would suggest that this teaching in *what to do* might be just the right purpose for training—and for some arenas it is. Yet with respect to developing the very personal and interpersonal qualities of leadership, it's a mistake to overlook the impact of neurobiology in learning. Distinct from what you can do, leadership is about *who you are* and what's possible for you and your leadership.

The early strategies you developed to find your way in the world shaped your identity, including your leadership identity, and are securely held in place by well-worn neural pathways long ago laid down in your nervous system. "Identity" is originally derived from the Latin words *essentias* or "being," and *identidem*, meaning "repeatedly." Your identity is literally your "repeated beingness," or *the way you show up* as observed by your habits, strategies, and practices.[2]

Stretching the behavioral skills of leadership and expanding your self-identity as a leader will require you to surface and loosen the invisible neurological boundaries of your current identity so you can shift to become the best version of yourself. Given the depth of those early pathways, and despite your conscious interest in shifting, you can unwittingly create unconscious resistance to change, with your new actions now posing a threat to your sense of identity. Herein lies the difficulty in shifting habits.

So, though there is a place for training in what to do, especially in more technical domains, such training alone is insufficient for people to develop the deeply embodied leadership capacity required to bring about a better future, given all of the unexpected surprises that we're each subject to every day.

The best, most reliable lasting change occurs when we practice over time in low-risk, low-stakes situations. This kind of training in a safe environment gives people the opportunity to try, fail, and try again without putting their job, their relationships, or their business on the line. *They can develop who they are as leaders.* At the very least, this requires a coach or mentor who has experience in what you want to learn and who can offer focused feedback, along with a community of fellow practitioners who are on the path with you.

Putting yourself into new leadership practices, instead of sitting in a conference room absorbing new data, facilitates insight with just enough discomfort to combat the cultural overemphasis on cognitive learning that has atrophied our natural somatic, or body-based, intelligence. You develop mastery through *consistent practice over time*, not by taking a class or reading a book, making it possible to experience new insights and to take new, more effective actions.

Instead of creating resistance, internally generated insights release a pleasurable chemical rush throughout the brain and body. That's the feeling of new neural pathways being laid down, literally; it reinforces new learning on a deep and lasting level. This kind of low-stakes training builds new neural pathways that will prepare you for the high-pressure situations that inevitably arise in business and in life.

This kind of intentional, deliberate training allows people to truly learn and embody their learning. Leaders can lead from within, regardless of the gravity of the situation they're faced with in any moment. Rather than believing that "knowledge is power," it's more accurate to say that *practice is power*.

So the question then arises: what and how are we to practice to develop leadership mastery?

Choosing Deliberate Practices

> This is a fundamental truth about any sort of practice:
> If you never push yourself beyond your comfort zone,
> you will never improve.
>
> —K. ANDERS ERICSSON, AUTHOR OF *PEAK*, SWEDISH
> PSYCHOLOGIST, AND INTERNATIONALLY RECOGNIZED
> RESEARCHER ON HUMAN PERFORMANCE

We've all heard stories about people shifting their habits and practices after receiving a scary medical diagnosis or encountering a sudden shift in life circumstances or work—not unlike what occurred for many as a result of the 2020 global pandemic. It's decidedly not, however, a typical notion that we change our leadership through intentional, pragmatic practices. The process, however, is not so different: facing the situation, accepting the reality, assessing resources, prioritizing and choosing next steps, and leaning into action.

As Anders Ericsson says in "The Making of an Expert," "The journey to truly superior performance is neither for the faint of heart nor for the impatient. The development of genuine expertise requires struggle, sacrifice, and honest, often painful self-assessment. There are no shortcuts."[3] Ericsson should know; he spent his career studying what constitutes excellent performance. In addition to setting clear goals with a focus on technique, be it for golf or piano or the hula hoop, receiving qualified feedback and adjusting it with deliberate practice—that's what develops expertise in any arena.

With regular practice, like going out for a walk each evening, we can maintain our current fitness level, though that evening stroll won't prepare you for the upcoming 10K in your neighborhood and certainly not for a twenty-six-mile marathon. However, deliberate practice, unlike regular day-to-day practice, is all about focusing at the other side of your current skill level and at the edge of your comfort zone to stretch into the next level. While it could be in a sport like aikido or golf or swimming, or in music like the violin or piano, leading well into the future will require deliberate practice too. That's because deliberate, body-based practice allows you to contact your deepest values, including presence, that will move you along the path of excellence, support you to overcome the plateaus that will inevitably arise, and improve your skills most quickly. The real key to deliberate practice, however, is that it be done with the right approach; it's not only the reps, but also the quality of the reps involved.

As with aikido, you'll need to get clear about what you'd like to learn and improve upon: a plan for training; a coach to give feedback, point out errors for improvement, challenge you, and offer vital motivation to keep moving despite the plateaus you'll inevitably encounter; and a community of practice partners to not only track your success but to also get the best results. Besides, celebrating wins supports everyone's learning.

The reason my executive coaching clients undertake specific practices is the same reason that Steph Curry of the Golden State Warriors, arguably the best shooter in NBA history, routinely puts up three hundred shots *after* formal practice during the regular season. He's committed to an amazing outcome. This particular deliberate practice of his enables him to pull off his amazing "spot-up" three-pointers. By the way, did you know that professional athletes practice three times more than they play, and this ratio is higher for other performing artists?

That's also why Yo-Yo Ma begins his practice each day with thirty minutes playing basic scales on his cello. "Practicing is about quality, not quantity. Some days I practice for hours; other days it will be just a few minutes. Practicing is not only playing your instrument, either by yourself or rehearsing with others—it also includes imagining yourself practicing."[4]

Curry and Ma are both practicing to *incorporate new distinctions into their bodies*—distinctions that result in peak performance. The new deliberate practice for leaders? Committing to practice pause for the sake of cultivating your leadership presence and to perform with high-level mastery as a conscious leader is to embody the ethic of care, radical responsibility, social engagement in the world, all within a moral and spiritual vision. Bottom line? Becoming the best version of yourself as a conscious leader will require your commitment to deliberately practice the pause.

Since the body is the source of all experience—even conceptual understanding has a sensorimotor basis—and learns through contrast and exaggeration, it's important to play with pause in the body in all its elements—space/sensation, connection, openness, pace, and energy. With awareness, yoga, martial arts, dancing, mindful walking, or hiking all become vehicles to embody deeper leadership presence. Because only by intentionally working through your body will you interrupt your old strategies and learn what's required in the moment versus getting caught up in your old, automatic strategies. Athletes know this. Musicians know this. Martial artists know this.

Deliberate Conscious Leadership

> Too often, our lives cease working because we cease working
> at life, because we are unwilling to take responsibility for
> things as they are, and to work with our difficulties.
> We don't understand that it is actually possible to attain
> clarity, understanding, and transformation right in the middle
> of what is here and now, however problematic it may be.
>
> —JON KABAT-ZINN, AUTHOR OF *WHEREVER YOU GO,
> THERE YOU ARE* AND FOUNDER OF THE CENTER FOR
> MINDFULNESS, MEDICINE, HEALTHCARE, AND SOCIETY

To up your conscious leadership game by taking on the deliberate practice of pausing, you must abandon business as usual or leadership as usual. Your commitment will take you out of your comfort zone, and, as George Leonard spoke to mastery earlier, it will require you to stay on the mat, despite your discomfort.

The deliberate practice of pausing is what's called an *irimi* move in aikido, a move right into the heart of an attack. Here, it's to enter into the heart of what matters most to you as a leader, to take up the courage of your convictions and practice to embody them.

On the mat, we enter to blend with the energy of our opponent, to move in and up close to resolve the attack in a nonviolent manner by redirecting his energy. Here, the irimi move is to blend with and extend our attention to form new relationships with ourselves, our colleagues, the community, and world.

Adopting the pause, making it your own, and practicing in this hands-on way, you'll stretch and shift out of old strategies that keep you at arm's length from your vision; you'll move into a new way of being to bring your vision to life. By tuning in to your body's wisdom, you'll tap your intuition for valuable information about the world, tolerate strong sensations that increase your ability to respond and choose, increase your own emotional regulation, and connect with your deeply felt concerns and match them up to current actions. You'll learn to listen into others' nonverbal and verbal communications to engage with them, and use all of this in service of creating high-performing, feedback-seeking teams as aspects of a new business as usual.

It's true, of course, that leaders are in different situations than athletes or artists. Often, they're so busy they don't feel as though they can take the time out to practice the new skills essential for their work: teamwork, strategizing, selling, etc.

But what happens when we don't have low-stakes opportunities to learn? When staying engaged is tricky, even risky? Deliberately stimulating challenges that stretch yet don't overwhelm existing skills, while lingering at the edges of one's comfort zone, provide the greatest sense of satisfaction.

Love of the Game

> Who you are, what you think, feel, and do,
> what you love—is the sum of what you focus on.
>
> —WINIFRED GALLAGHER, AUTHOR OF *RAPT* AND CANCER SURVIVOR

Mihaly Csikszentmihalyi is a well-known psychologist, peak performance researcher, and the author of the landmark book *Flow*. When interviewing professionals across industries, he discovered that their "love of the game" and their experiences of "effortless flow" proved to be the ultimate reward for the countless hours of drudgery they invested in deliberate practice. It seems that passion helps us to stay energized and engaged, especially when practicing feels tedious and redundant. Further, to stay highly engaged, a learner must strike an optimal balance between how hard it is to do something and how good she is at doing it. Too difficult, and it becomes impossible to establish any momentum. Too easy, and there's not enough challenge to hold her interest.

Your passion and how it syncs up with your purpose will provide the necessary energy to achieve exceptional levels of ability and leadership. Early practice is rewarded with greater increasing automaticity, or new embodied behavior. Cited in Anders Ericsson's article "The Making of an Expert," violinist Nathan Milstein asked his mentor, Professor Auer, how many hours he should be practicing. Professor Auer responded by saying, "It doesn't really matter how long. If you practice with your fingers, no amount is enough. If you practice with your head, two hours is plenty."[5] In fact, most highly accomplished experts practice no more than a few hours with high concentration and deliberate practice. They keep working their edges. Golf champion Sam Snead, who held the record for winning the most PGA Tours—and is also famous for his beautiful swings—cited the key to his success, "Practice puts brains in your muscles."

In his book *Deep Work*, Cal Newport describes deliberate practice, or as he calls it, "deep work," as those "professional activities performed in a state of distraction-free concentration that push your cognitive capabilities to their limit. These efforts create new value, improve your skill, and are hard to replicate."[6] He goes on to elucidate that deep work is invaluable in today's complex work environments because leaders are required to master complicated, ever-changing skills in order to be effective. Additionally, today's workplace requires value that can only be created from a place of depth cultivated by deliberate practice.

The reason deep work works has everything to do with our biology and the fatty myelin that wraps around our brain's neurons, effectively insulating them for increased speed. Brain circuits pick up speed and outperform with less effort and greater ease. "To be great at something is to be well myelinated," according to Newport.[7] With repeated, focused practice, the firing of circuits wires neural pathways, deepening learning and embodiment of new skills. By bringing deliberate practice to work, leaders also model a cultural norm of practicing together. This could include new skills of speaking, presenting, giving and receiving constructive feedback, coordinating on projects, and strategizing for the future. And it builds trust.

Will You Choose Full Engagement?

Not everything that is faced can be changed;
but nothing can be changed until it is faced.

—JAMES BALDWIN, AMERICAN NOVELIST, POET, AND ACTIVIST

Engaged in the creative process we feel more alive than ever,
because we are making something and not merely consuming,
masters of the small reality we create. In doing this work,
we are in fact creating ourselves.

—ROBERT GREENE, AUTHOR OF *MASTERY*

There's a lot to face in today's VUCA world: environmental degradation and consequential immigration, globalization at a grand scale, the acceleration of technological change, a rise in economic inequality.

More is required of today's leaders, so leaders are required to train differently. Acquiring more knowledge will not prepare you to lead in the future of tomorrow. Not at all. To face what the world is asking you to face—within yourself and outside—is to echo a comment of a teacher of mine: "What the heck else do you have to do with your lifetime than see it all the way through?"

Ericsson's research demonstrated that not all practice makes perfect. Practice simply makes permanent. If you're unaware and practicing but in the wrong direction, you're headed in the wrong direction. Only deliberate practice develops new ways of being and the ability to take new action, performing at one's optimal best.

Only deliberate practice makes possible.

Truly effective leadership taps into our somatic intelligence and those certain qualities of being that enable you to get things done in cooperation with others. Qualities like empathy, integrity, and the ability to inspire. Qualities like vision, steadfast commitment, and the responsible use of authority and power. Qualities like courage, accountability, and presence.

As a conscious leader, will you accept the challenge and possibility suggested by deliberate practice?

Why choose full engagement? Because it matters, and you care.

It starts with the simple pause, the linchpin in the flywheel of attention.

With the determination to take on any new practice, there's a story about why we're choosing this practice to commit to that will become part of us too. What's your story as a leader who longs to make a difference? As a conscious leader, what keeps you from practicing deliberately?

Can you risk your success today in order to take on new learning? Are you willing to commit to that competitive risk? What could you accomplish if you devoted yourself to two hours a day of concentrated practice?

Getting good at anything, including leadership, inevitably comes with mistakes and failures. You should expect it. This is where developing a tolerance for discomfort, and practicing for the sake of practice, comes in handy. Learning itself, particularly embodied learning, is the way to developing potential, not reaching it.

What will keep you going on your journey? What matters most to you? What kind of legacy do you care to leave? Impact that you wish to make?

Are you willing to be a beginner?

Being a Beginner—Getting Uncomfortable

Being a beginner involves stumbling around a bit in attempts to learn something new, even though you've already learned a lot. To learn something new, or to create a new habit or practice is challenging. If you've ever set out a New Year's resolution, you'll know how hard this can be to do.

Why is it hard?

It might be that you're not really committed—well-intentioned, perhaps, but not committed.

Or maybe you're not pausing to be *fully in* the new commitment. Life's busyness and activity roster have your dance card full.

Or maybe you're simply not pausing to give yourself enough time or space or energy and patience to develop yourself, what I'd call "letting the practice work on you."

We're so often in a hurry to see results that we sabotage ourselves. We tell ourselves, "I don't have enough time" or "It shouldn't take this long" or "I should already know this."

Or maybe you opt out of practicing because you're tired or think you've done enough and deserve a break, dismissing your inner longing out of exhaustion and fear of what it will take to move forward.

We do not rise to the level of our goals or aspirations. Under stress, especially the stress of today's VUCA world with intense uncertainty, we fall to the level of our training. There are no handholds for this ride, unlike on the whitewater raft. The only handholds live within—the direction of your attention and energy is what matters.

Deliberate Daily Practices

JEAN PITZO, CEO OF ACE METAL CRAFT

"Two deliberate practices sustain me and have provided for breakthrough innovations we've seen at ACE. The first is a 'clarity break' that we've incorporated on our leadership team. It's done weekly, out of the office. It's a time when we work 'on' the business, not 'in' the business. And, it's got a decidedly meditative feel for me. I journal during my clarity breaks. This is typically when I get my best thoughts for breakthrough innovation."

The new addition of a clarity break rests atop Jean's decade-long practice, in which she's worked on her business on peaceful Sunday mornings. She says, "I take a few hours to reflect on the past week and think about what's possible. I'm positive this has enabled me to get ahead of the curve and thrive."

RON ROJAS, CEO OF CONTINENTAL SALES

"Pause was never natural for me. I'd just keep punching through. Yet consciously practicing a pause during the day, which I do with the help of my phone, helps me to be aware of my breath and of what's going on around me. Just doing that breaks up my nonstop doing that's unconscious. It's been instrumental to coming back to align with my intention of creating a culture of growth and kindness."

PETER PARTHENIS, CEO OF GRECIAN DELIGHT

"I take time every morning when I get up before I exercise. I spend about twenty minutes to thirty minutes, as I'm drinking my coffee alone, to pause, presence myself, and make sure that I'm in integrity with the life that I choose. I'm always reflecting on it, looking back in life, to ask, *Where did I say I wanted to go, and am I making progress?*"

AMY FELIX-REESE, SVP CLIENT SERVICES AT FULL CIRCLE GROUP

"I'm a trail runner, and on my daily runs, I'm pausing to connect with nature and connecting to my breath as I run. Even the sound of my shoes on the trail, it's like a metronome. If you think of running as the pause, my pace as my foot hits the ground reminds me of how fast or slow I'm going, and if it feels like the 'right pace.'"

NANCY PAUTSCH, PRESIDENT OF ENVISION IT

"I won't get in the office before nine, and people may wonder, 'She's late.' No, I've been up since five a.m. doing my own work. I go to bed early, I rise early. I'll get my coffee, have my little dog, Gus, sit beside me while I read some inspirational or spiritual book, and then I'll meditate for 15–30 minutes. Then, I walk my dog, Gus, no matter the weather, even here in Wisconsin. We're out about thirty minutes. So my day starts with reading and reflecting, meditating, and walking out in nature."

NICK SARILLO, FOUNDER AND CEO OF TRUST AND TRACK INSTITUTE

"Deliberate practice, it didn't come easy to me at all. Growing up the way I grew up, traditional Italian Catholic, Chicago kid . . . we don't do anything soft. It's all about needing to fight through and push to get people out of the way. I started sitting to meditate each day, though that doesn't just happen; now I meditate two times a day and I do yoga, too. This journey of self-awareness takes time, and you've gotta be just totally fine with it."

Shugyo

> Life itself is always a trial. In training, you must
> test and polish yourself in order to face the great
> challenges of life. Transcend the realm of life and death,
> and then you will be able to make your way calmly and
> safely through any crisis that confronts you.
>
> —MORIHEI UESHIBA, FOUNDER OF AIKIDO

Discipline, rigor, passion, and training toward excellence—these reflect *shugyo*. Shugyo literally means to "master a practice," represented by two Chinese characters, "to master" and a "practice." Or, as O Sensei said, "to tighten the slack, toughen the body, and polish the spirit."

In our everyday language, we can understand shugyo as a process of self-cultivation via physical practices. Shugyo is at once an intensive period of training and, simultaneously, the ongoing daily practice of sincerely committing to a discipline of rigor in order to listen to the voice of your inner essence or Core Presence. This intensive training isn't for one's self, either; rather it's for the sake of something bigger. As sixth-degree aikido black belt Wendy Palmer explains in her book *The Practice of Freedom*, "It involves the totality of a person's being: the body, the mind, and the spirit. It can be understood as the manifestation of the intention to embody a state of virtue."[9]

As we train in this deep listening, the body is relaxed, the mind is free of thoughts of success or failure, and one's energy flows freely. Cultivating *one point*, that balance point that exists between grasping and pushing away, promotes right action to address any situation at hand, regardless of how stressful. The results of this body-mind integration include pragmatic wisdom, skillful action, and grounded compassion.

Black Belt

To say that training for any of my black belt tests was hard and challenging would be an understatement. I learned, again, of the strength of my self-criticism, how hard I am on myself, and that my impatience requires constant polishing. I learned how my early life strategy showed up in me: I'd embodied being small (not dainty!) as a way to protect myself, even though it no longer served the life I'm called to live into the future. I learned that, with the right conditions, the discipline of being "big" can be grown just like that burr oak tree at the end of the drive where I grew up.

In the midst of throwing and being thrown, I experienced how deeply I long to be met by and connect with others. I felt the lifetimes of space that exist as I entered into moments of contact with partners, and that trust lives there in the space between us. I learned that conflict is body-based and can be generative—fun, even—and that yelling can be a sign of love, not merely of hatefulness.

I learned anew the importance of centering in each moment and with the breath. I learned that I love a challenge, and that shihonage can shape me to rise to meet the unseen, 360-degree challenges of the future. I learned that strength lives in the moment as it unfolds, revealing contours of choice—not in brute force or attitude.

I learned that it's imperative to hold a settled stance and to take up space—no lazy-ass tai sabaki! And I learned to decline those feelings that swell and belittle me (e.g., *You know nothing!*) while simply acknowledging what I do well. I learned that *it's not about knowing more, it's about being more*—present, open, connected. I've deepened in my purpose and now experience a fierceness that's an embodied stance to fight for life for all, with no exceptions.

Family members and friends who never quite understood why I was drawn to this practice—this discipline, this art—have voiced wonder. I've had to explain.

It's not simply training for black belt that stirred my heart (though it certainly brought my heart to a near stop more than a few times), but rather feeling the pulse of life itself more—knowing that I am cultivating a deep, embodied listening to Spirit that allows me to further extend my gifts to the world.

In short, it's in the tenkan back to the Thread, to what I've "known" in some way since childhood, back to a flow of life's questions woven into the texture and tapestry of my life's story that aikido, and shugyo in particular, trains us for. I can't get lost if I hold on to the Thread. In continuing to train, rigorously, and to hold on to the Thread, despite the fact that . . .

"Tragedies happen; people get hurt
or die; and you suffer and get old.
Nothing you do can stop time's unfolding."

• • •

I can learn about fully living life each moment.

What Will You Choose?

More is required of you as a leader today than ever before. *The Leadership Pause*—the call to take on the simple practice of a pause—will open the door to possibilities to create your future and potentially the future of the planet.

Without the simple pause, we're swept up into the violent waves to whitewater, thrashing and adrift. Our lives unmoored.

I leave you with a quote from Jack Kornfield. Pause a moment here to let the questions work on you.

"In the end, these things matter most:
How well did you love?
How fully did you live?
How deeply did you let go?"

RECAP

- We become what we practice

- Specific practices, generative practices

- Attention is a gate

- Deliberate practice can create new distinctions and shape your identity

- Deliberate practice is the secret to peak performance

- To be a conscious leader is to be a beginner

SCOPE: SPACE, CONNECTION, OPENNESS, PACE, ENERGY

S – How much space do you take up practicing being, not simply doing?

C – How can you connect with and move your team's energy?

O – What behaviors do you need to let go of to create new practices?

P – Will you give yourself permission for deliberate practice?

E – Can you tenkan with the energy of those around you to change your point of view?

Recommended Reading

1. Barrett, Lisa Feldman. "The Theory of Constructed Emotion: An Active Inference Account of Interoception and Categorization." *Social Cognitive and Affective Neurosciences* (2017), 1–23.

2. Beard, Alison. "Mindfulness in the Age of Complexity." *Harvard Business Review*, March 2014.

3. Begley, Sharon. *Train Your Mind, Change Your Brain*. New York: Ballantine Books, 2007.

4. Blake, Amanda. *Your Body Is Your Brain: Leverage Your Somatic Intelligence to Find Purpose, Build Resilience, Deepen Relationships, and Lead More Powerfully*. California: Trokay Press, 2018.

5. Blakeslee, Sandra and Matthew Blakeslee. *The Body Has a Mind of its Own*. New York: Random House, 2008.

6. Brewer, Judson, Patrick Worhunsky, Jeremy Gray, Yi-Yuan Tang, Jochen Weber, and Hedy Kober. "Mediation Experience Is Associated with Differences in Default Mode Network Activity and Connectivity." *PNAS* 108, no. 50 (2001).

7. Bruch, Heike and Sumantra Ghoshal. "Beware the Busy Manager." *Harvard Business Review*, February 2002.

8. Damasio, Antonio. *The Feeling of What Happens*. San Diego: Houghton Mifflin Harcourt, 2000.

9. Davidson, Richard and Antoine Lutz. "Buddha's Brain." *IEEE: Signal Process Magazine,* 25, no. 1 (2008): 174–176.

10. Doidge, Norma. *The Brain that Changes Itself.* New York: Viking, 2007.

11. Edmonson, Amy and Tomas Chamorro-Premuzic. "Today's Leaders Need Vulnerability, Not Bravado," *Harvard Business Review*, October 2020.

12. Finzi, Benjamin, Mark Lipton, Kathy Lu, and Vincent Firth. "Emotional Fortitude: The Inner Work of the CEO," *Deloitte Insights* (blog), 2020. https://www2.deloitte.com/us/en/insights/topics/leadership/ceo-decision-making-emotional-fortitude.html.

13. Fogel, Alan. *The Psychophysiology of Self-Awareness*. New York: W.W. Norton, 2009.

14. Goleman, Daniel and Richard Davidson. *Altered Traits*. New York: Penguin, 2017.

15. Hallowell, Edward. "Overloaded Circuits: Why Smart People Underperform." *Harvard Business Review*, January 2005.

16. Hanson, Rick. *Buddha's Brain*. Oakland: New Harbinger, 2009.

17. Hawkins, David. *Power vs. Force*. Carlsbad, CA: Hay House, 2002.

18. Issacs, William. *Dialogue and the Art of Thinking Together*. New York: Random House, 1999.

19. Kabat-Zinn, Jon. *Wherever You Go There You Are*. New York: Hyperion, 1994.

20. Kornfield, Jack. *The Wise Heart*. New York: Bantam, 2009.

21. Kramer, Annette. "10 Principles for Leadership Presence," *Strategy+Business*, December 2019.

22. Leonard, George. *The Silent Pulse*. Layton, UT: Gibbs Smith, 2006.

23. Levitin, Daniel. *The Organized Mind*. New York: Viking, 2015.

24. Lewis, Thomas, Fari Amini, and Richard Lannon. *A General Theory of Love*. New York: Vintage, 2001.

25. Mackey, John, Steve McIntosh, and Carter Phipps. *Conscious Leadership*. New York: Random House, 2020.

26. Mann, Jeffrey. *When Buddhists Attack*. North Clarendon, VT: Tuttle, 2012.

27. Mehl-Madrona, Lewis with Barbara Mainguy. *Remapping Your Brain*. Rochester, NY: Bear & Company, 2015.

28. Palmer, Wendy and Janet Crawford. *Leadership Embodiment*. San Rafael, CA: The Embodiment Foundation, 2013.

29. Paul, Annie Murphy. *The Extended Mind*. New York: Houghton Mifflin Harcourt, 2021.

30. Pert, Candace. *Molecules of Emotion*. New York: Scribner, 2003.

31. Ryskin, Rachel, Aaron Benjamin, Jonathan Tullis, and Sarah Brown-Schmidt. "Perspective-Taking in Comprehension, Production, and Memory: An Individual Differences Approach." *Journal of Experimental Psychology: General* 144, no. 5 (2015): 898–915.

32. Silsbee, Doug. *Presence Based Leadership*. Asheville, NC: Yes!Global, 2018.

33. Sisodia, Raj, Jag Sheth, and David Wolfe. *Firms of Endearment*. Upper Saddle River, NY: Pearson Education, [2007] 2014.

34. Sisodia, Raj and Michael Gelb. *The Healing Organization*. New York: HarperCollins, 2019.

35. Siegel, Daniel. *The Developing Mind*. New York: Guilford, 1999.

36. Siegel, Daniel. *Mindsight*. New York: Bantam Books, 2010.

37. Solomon, Robert and Fernando Flores. *Building Trust*. New York: Oxford University Press, 2001.

38. Spinosa, Charles, Fernando Flores, and Hubert Dreyfus. *Disclosing New Worlds*. Cambridge: MIT Press, 1997.

39. Taggart, Lynne. *The Field*. New York: HarperCollins, 2002.

40. TenHouten, Warren. "Embodied Feeling and Reason in Decision-Making: Assessing the Somatic-Marker Hypothesis," *Cuerpos, Emociones Y Sociedad, Cordoba* 8, no. 20 (2016): 87–97.

41. Van Boven, Leaf, George Loewenstein, David Dunning, and Loran Nordgren. "Changing Places: A Dual Judgment Model of Empathy Gaps in Emotional Perspective Taking." *Advances in Experimental Social Psychology* 48 (2013): 117–171.

42. Van der Kolk, Bessel. *The Body Keeps the Score*. New York: Penguin Books, 2015.

43. Whitelaw, Ginny. *Move to Greatness*. Boston: Nicholas Brealey, 2008.

44. Whitelaw, Ginny. *Resonate*. Virginia Beach, VA: Koehler Books, 2020.

45. Williams, Michele. "Thinking About You: Perspective Taking, Perceived Restraint, and Performance." *Leading Through Conflict: Into the Fray* (Palgrave Macmillan/Springer Nature, 2016): 85–108.

46. Zorn, Justin and Leigh Marz. "The Busier You Are, the More You Need Quiet Time." *Harvard Business Review*, March 2017.

Notes

INTRODUCTION

1. National Ocean and Atmospheric Administration, *Assessing the Global Climate in 2019*, January 15, 2020, https://www.ncei.noaa.gov/news/global-climate-201912.

2. Intergovernmental Panel on Climate Change, *Special Report on the Ocean and Cryosphere in a Changing Climate*, September 24, 2019, https://www.ipcc.ch/srocc/.

3. Fiona McKay, "US Income Inequality Statistics to Know in 2021," *SPENDMENOT*, May 19, 2021, https://spendmenot.com/blog/us-income-inequality-statistics/.

4. Katherine Schaeffer, "6 Facts about Economic Inequality in the U.S.," *Pew Research Center*, February 7, 2020, https://www.pewresearch.org/fact-tank/2020/02/07/6-facts-about-economic-inequality-in-the-u-s/.

5. McKay, "US Income Inequality Statistics to Know in 2021."

6. Rachel Cautero, "Are You in the Top 1%?" *smartasset,* March 4, 2021, https://smartasset.com/financial-advisor/are-you-in-the-top-1-percent.

7. Schaeffer, "6 Facts about Economic Inequality in the U.S."

8. Federal Reserve, "Distribution of Household Wealth in the U.S. since 1989" (chart), June 21, 2021, https://www.federalreserve.gov/releases/z1/dataviz/dfa/distribute/chart/#quarter:122;series:Net%20worth;demographic:race;population:all;units:shares;range:1989.3,2020.1.

9. CDC, "Health Equity Considerations and Racial and Ethnic Minority Groups," April 4, 2021, https://www.cdc.gov/coronavirus/2019-ncov/community/health-equity/race-ethnicity.html#fn19.

10. Jon Hilsenrath, "Homicide Spike Hits Most Large Cities," *Wall Street Journal*, August 2, 2020, https://www.wsj.com/articles/homicide-spike-cities-chicago-newyork-detroit-us-crime-police-lockdown-coronavirus-protests-11596395181.

11. Alex Pattakos, *Prisoners of Our Thoughts: Viktor Frankl's Principles for Discovering Meaning in Life and Work* (San Francisco: Berrett-Koehler Publishers, Inc., 2008).

12. Dawna Markova, *Spot of Grace* (Novato: New World Library, 2008), 5–6.

CHAPTER 1

1. American Psychological Association, "Stress in America 2020," press release, October 2020, https://www.apa.org/news/press/releases/stress/2020/report-october.

2. David Cheng and Carys Chan, "5 Ways to Be a Better Leader," *Business Insider*, Sept. 11, 2017, https://www.businessinsider.com.au/how-to-be-a-better-leader-2017-9.

3. David Ross, Julie Exposito, and Tom Kennedy, "Stress and Its Relationship to Leadership and a Healthy Workplace," in *Occupational Stress: Breakthroughs in Research and Practice* (Hershey, PA: IGI Global, 2020), 3.

4. Richard Alleyne, "Welcome to the Information Age," *Telegraph*, February 11, 2011, https://www.telegraph.co.uk/news/science/science-news/8316534/Welcome-to-the-information-age-174-newspapers-a-day.html.

5. Peter M. J. Gross, "Daniel J. Levitin: Multi-Tasking Doesn't Work," *Enterprising Investor* (blog), May 15, 2019, https://blogs.cfainstitute.org/investor/2019/05/15/daniel-j-levitin-multi-tasking-doesnt-work; Christine Rosen, "The Myth of Multitasking," *New Atlantis*, Spring 2008, https://www.thenewatlantis.com/publications/the-myth-of-multitasking; See also: Clive Thompson, "Meet the Life Hackers," *New York Times Magazine*, October 16, 2005, https://www.nytimes.com/2005/10/16/magazine/meet-the-life-hackers.html.

6. James Van Doren, "Project Management Is for Everyone," Weatherhead School of Management at Case Western Reserve, March 8, 2012, https://weatherhead.case.edu/news/2012/03/08/project-management-is-for-everyone.

7. Steven Applebaum, Adam Marchionni, and Arturo Fernandez, "The Multi-Tasking Paradox," *Management Decision* 46, no. 9, October 17, 2008, https://interruptions.net/literature/Appelbaum-ManagementDecision08.pdf. See also: Gloria Mark, Justin Harris, and Victor Gonzalez, "No Task Left Behind?" (paper presented at SIGCHI Conference on Human Factors in Computing, Portland, OR, April 2–7, 2005, 321–330).

8. Olivia Goldhill, "Neuroscientists Say Multitasking Literally Drains the Energy Reserves of Your Brain," *Quartz*, July 3, 2016, https://qz.com/722661/neuroscientists-say-multitasking-literally-drains-the-energy-reserves-of-your-brain/.

9. Gloria Mark, Laura Dabbish, and Victor Gonzalez, "Why DO I Keep Interrupting Myself?" (paper presented at SIGCHI Conference on Human Factors in Computing Systems, Vancouver, BC, Canada, May 7-12, 2011); Gloria Mark et al., "Focused, Aroused but Distractible," (paper presented at the 18th ACM Conference on Computer Supported Cooperative Work & Social Computing, Portland, OR, March 14–18, 2015).

10. Steve Lohr, "Slow Down, Brave Multitasker, and Don't Read This in Traffic," *New York Times*, March 25, 2007, https://www.nytimes.com/2007/03/25/business/25multi.html.

11. Laura Scroggs, "The Pomodoro Technique: Beat Procrastination and Improve Your Focus One Pomodoro at a Time," *todoist*, https://todoist.com/productivity-methods/pomodoro-technique.

12. Lillian Cunningham, "Exhaustion Is Not a Status Symbol," *Washington Post*, October 3, 2012, https://www.washingtonpost.com/national/exhaustion-is-not-a-status-symbol/2012/10/02/19d27aa8-0cba-11e2-bb5e-492c0d30bff6_story.html.

13. Thomas Merton, *Conjectures of a Guilty Bystander* (Garden City, NY: Image Books, [1965] 2014), 81.

14. Sherry Turkle, *Reclaiming Conversation* (New York: Penguin Random House, 2015), 21.

15. Linda Stone, "Beyond Simple Multi-Tasking: Continuous Partial Attention," *Linda Stone* (blog), November 30, 2009, https://lindastone.net/2009/11/30/beyond-simple-multi-tasking-continuous-partial-attention.

16. Andy Campbell, "Talking to Our Computers Is Changing Who We Are," *Huffington Post*, May 20, 2016, https://www.huffpost.com/entry/tech-artificial-intelligence-human-brain_n_573f063ee4b00e09e89eb7c8.

17. Thomas Davenport, *The Attention Economy* (Boston: Harvard Business Review Press, 2001), 3.

18. Martin Heidegger, *Discourse on Thinking*, trans. John Anderson and E. Hans Freund (New York: Harper and Row, 1966), 44–46; See also: Heidegger, *The Question Concerning Technology, and Other Essays*, trans. William Lovitt (New York: Garland Publishing, 1977), 27.

19. Nick Petrie, *Future Trends in Leadership Development*, Center for Creative Leadership, Greensboro, NC, 2014.

20. IBM, *Capitalizing on Complexity: Insights from the Global Chief Executive Officer Study*, Somers, NY, 2010.

21. Margaret Wheatley, *Who Do We Choose to Be?* (Oakland: Berrett-Koehler, 2017), 46.

22. Bob Johansen, *The New Leadership Literacies* (Oakland: Berrett-Koehler, 2017), 33–34.

23. Richard Boyatzis and Annie McKee, *Resonant Leadership* (Boston: Harvard Business School Press, 2005), 28.

24. Ray Anderson, *Confessions of a Radical Industrialist* (New York: Random House, 2011).

25. Paul Hawken, *The Ecology of Commerce*, rev. ed (New York: Harper Business, 2010).

26. Mikhail Davis, "20 Years Later, Interface Looks Back on Ray Anderson's Legacy," *Greenbiz*, September 3, 2014, https://www.greenbiz.com/article/20-years-later-interface-looks-back-ray-andersons-legacy.

27. Bob Johansen, *Leaders Make the Future* (Oakland: Berrett-Koehler, 2012), 7.

28. Pema Chödrön, *Taking the Leap* (Boston: Shambhala, 2009), 33.

29. William James, *The Principles of Psychology* (Pantianos Classics, [1890] 1918), 175.

CHAPTER 2

1. Boyatzis and McKee, *Resonant Leadership*, 6.

2. Daniel Goleman, *Focus*, (New York: HarperCollins, 2013), 3.

3. Emma Seppälä et al., "Research: Why Breathing Is So Effective at Reducing Stress," *Harvard Business Review*, September 2020, https://hbr.org/2020/09/research-why-breathing-is-so-effective-at-reducing-stress.

4. Goleman, *Focus*, 65.

5. Antonio Damasio, *Descartes' Error* (New York: Penguin, 1994), 177.

6. Ibid.

7. Timothy Egan, "The Eight-Second Attention Span," *New York Times*, January 2016, https://www.nytimes.com/2016/01/22/opinion/the-eight-second-attention-span.html.

8. Microsoft Attention Spans Research Report, Scribd.com, Spring 2015, https://www.scribd.com/document/265348695/Microsoft-Attention-Spans-Research-Report.

9. Chödrön, *Taking the Leap*, 17–18.

10. Goleman, *Focus*, 4.

11. Goleman, *Focus*, 211.

12. Jon Kabat-Zinn, *Full Catastrophe Living* (New York: Bantam Books, [1990] 2013), xxvii.

13. Barry Boyce, ed., *The Mindfulness Revolution* (Boston: Shambhala, 2011).

14. Veronique Taylor et al., "Impact of Meditation Training on the Default Mode Network during a Restful State," *Social Cognitive and Affective Neuroscience* (March 2012).; Marcus Raichle et al., "A Default Mode of Brain Function," *Proceedings of the National Academy of Sciences* (January 2001).

15. For more information, see: Daniel Kahneman, *Thinking, Fast and Slow* (New York: Farrar, Straus and Giroux, 2011); Jim Taylor, "Cognitive Biases Are Bad for Business," *Psychology Today: The Power of Prime* (blog), May 20, 2013, https://www.psychologytoday.com/us/blog/the-power-prime/201305/cognitive-biases-are-bad-business.

16. Jon Kabat-Zinn, *Coming to Our Senses* (New York: Hyperion, 2005), 162–164.

17. Kabat-Zinn, *Coming to Our Senses*.

18. Ray Harvey, "What Is the Difference Between a Cynic and a Skeptic?" *The Journal Pulp*, February 9, 2012, https://journalpulp.com/2012/02/09/what-is-the-difference-between-a-cynic-and-a-skeptic/.

CHAPTER 3

1. For more information on burnout, see: Hans Selye, *The Stress of Life*, (New York: McGraw Hill, 1956); Monique Valquor, "Steps to Take When You Start Feeling Burned Out," *Harvard Business Review*, June 20, 2016, https://hbr.org/2016/06/steps-to-take-when-youre-starting-to-feel-burned-out.

2. Selye, *The Stress of Life*, 66.

3. American Psychological Association, "Stress in America 2020."

4. Humberto Maturana and Francisco Varela, *The Tree of Knowledge* (Boston: Shambhala, 1987), 27.

5. Jon Kabat-Zinn, *Full Catastrophe Living* (New York: Random House, 1990).

6. Fernando Flores, "Biology and Dasein on Emotional Fortitude and Three Dimensions of the Self," unpublished notes (Pluralistic Networks, 2019).

CHAPTER 4

1. Kevin Cashman, *The Pause Principle* (Oakland: Berrett-Koehler, 2012), 12.

2. Warren Bennis, *On Becoming a Leader* (New York: Basic Books, 1989), 105.

3. Amanda Blake, personal communication.

4. Amanda Blake, *Your Body Is Your Brain* (CA: Trokay Press, 2018), 44–62.

5. Amanda Blake and Chris Johnson, "Leadership and Somatic Intelligence" (unpublished manuscript, 2010).

6. George Leonard, *Mastery: The Keys to Success and Long-Term Fulfillment* (New York: Penguin Books, 1992).

7. Leonard, *Mastery*, 120.

8. Leonard, *Mastery*, 39.

9. Leonard, *Mastery*, 96.

10. Stephen Porges, *The Pocket Guide to Polyvagal Theory* (New York: W.W. Norton, 2017), 43.

11. Kelly McGonigal, *The Upside of Stress* (New York: Random House, 2015), 112.

12. Amanda Blake, *Your Body Is Your Brain* (CA: Trokay Press, 2018), 59.

13. McGonigal, *The Upside of Stress*, 112.

14. McGonigal, *The Upside of Stress*, 54.

15. McGonigal, *The Upside of Stress*, 52.

16. Amanda Blake, "Developing Somatic Intelligence" (unpublished manuscript, 2009).

17. Goleman, *Focus*, 223.

18. McGonigal, *The Upside of Stress*, xii.

19. McGonigal, *The Upside of Stress*, 50.

CHAPTER 5

1. Carol Dweck, *Mindset* (New York: Ballantine Books, 2007).

2. A. J. Crum et al., "Mind over Milkshakes," *Health Psychology* 30, no. 4 (May 2011): 424–429.

3. HBR editors, "How Companies Can Profit from a 'Growth Mindset,'" *Harvard Business Review*, November 2014, https://hbr.org/2014/11/how-companies-can-profit-from-a-growth-mindset.

4. A. J. Crum and Ellen Langer, "Mind-Set Matters," *Psychological Science* 18, no 2 (February 2007): 165–171; Also see: A. J. Crum et al,. "Mind over Milkshakes."

5. A. J. Crum, Peter Salovey, and Shawn Achor, "Rethinking Stress," *Journal of Personality and Social Psychology* 104, no. 4 (February 2013): 716–733.

6. Daniel Siegel, *The Developing Mind* (New York: Guilford Press, 1999), 253.

7. Jamil Zaki, "Kindness Contagion," *Scientific American*, July 26, 2016, https://www.scientificamerican.com/article/kindness-contagion/.

CHAPTER 6

1. Sally Helgesen, "What's the Secret to Leadership Presence?" *Strategy+Business*, June 30, 2014, https://www.strategy-business.com/blog/Whats-the-Secret-to-Leadership-Presence.

2. Peter Senge et al., *Presence* (New York: Doubleday, 2008), 10–103.

3. Daniel Siegel, *Aware* (New York: Tarcher Perigee, 2018), 57–58.

4. Doug Silsbee, "Presence in Complexity Series #1: Reading Our Context," *Presence-Based Coaching* (blog), November 4, 2016, https://presencebasedcoaching.com/blog/presence-in-complexity-series-1-reading-our-context.

5. Stephen Gawtry, "Where Are You Now? An Interview with Eckhart Tolle," *Watkins MIND BODY SPIRIT Magazine*, Summer 2013, https://www.watkinsmagazine.com/where-are-you-now-an-interview-with-eckhart-tolle.

6. Marshall Goldsmith, *What Got You Here Won't Get You There* (New York: Hachette Books, 2007), 16.

7. James Hollis, "The Goal of Life Is Meaning Not Happiness," interview with Tami Simon. *Sounds True* (blog), June 9, 2020, https://resources.soundstrue.com/podcast/james-hollisthe-goal-of-life-is-meaning-not-happiness/.

8. Amanda Blake, Body + Brain course, 2015.

9. William James, *Essays in Radical Empiricism* (Cambridge: Harvard University Press, [1912] 1976), 86.

10. Gay Hendricks, *The Big Leap* (New York: Harper One, 2009), 113.

11. Terry Hershey, *The Power of Pause* (Chicago: Loyola Press, 2009), xix.

12. Kevin Cashman, *Leadership from the Inside Out* (Oakland: Berrett-Koehler, 1998), 20.

CHAPTER 7

1. Siegel, *Aware*, 9–10.

2. Shohaku Okumura, "What Is Kokoro?" *Lion's Roar* (blog), December 10, 2018, https://www.lionsroar.com/dharma-dictionary-kokoro/.

3. Earl Conway and Paul Batelden, "Like Magic? ('Every System Is Perfectly Designed . . .')," *Institute for Healthcare Improvement—Improvement Blog* (blog), August 21, 2015, http://www.ihi.org/communities/blogs/origin-of-every-system-is-perfectly-designed-quote.

4. Bruce Schneider, *Energy Leadership* (New Jersey: John Wiley & Sons), 75.

5. The Yerkes-Dodson Law reveals that the optimal level of arousal involves "the relation of strength of stimulus to rapidity of habit formation." "The Yerkes-Dodson Law: Performance and Arousal—Exploring Your Mind," ExploringYourMind.com, accessed October 5, 2021, https://exploringyourmind.com/yerkes-dodson-law-performance-arousal/.

6. Jim Loehr and Tony Schwartz, *The Power of Full Engagement* (New York: Free Press, 2005), 11.

7. Christine Comaford, "Emotions Have Energy. What Energy Are You Sending?" *Forbes*, June 2, 2018, https://www.forbes.com/sites/christinecomaford/2018/06/02/emotions-have-energy-what-energy-are-you-sending/?sh=55f525ef2545.

8. Benjamin Finzi et al., "Emotional Fortitude: The Inner Work of the CEO," *Deloitte Insights*, July 9, 2020, https://www2.deloitte.com/us/en/insights/topics/leadership/ceo-decision-making-emotional-fortitude.html.

9. Flores, "Biology and Dasein."

10. Doug Silsbee, *Presence-Based Coaching* (San Francisco: Jossey-Bass, 2008), 74.

11. Gloria Flores, *Learning to Learn and the Navigation of Moods* (San Francisco: Pluralistic Networks Publishing, 2016), 23.

12. Lisa Feldman Barrett, *How Emotions Are Made* (Boston: Mariner Books, 2018), 30.

13. Jill Bolte, *My Stroke of Insight* (New York: Penguin, 2009), 146.

14. Lisa Feldman Barrett, *How Emotions Are Made* (Boston: Mariner Books, 2018), 30.

15. Jill Bolte, *My Stroke of Insight* (New York: Penguin, 2009), 146.

16. Sahib Khalsa et al., "Interception and Mental Health: A Roadmap," *Biological Psychiatry: Cognitive Neuroscience and Neuroimaging* 3 (June 2018): 501–13.

17. Nick Craig and Scott Snook, "From Purpose to Impact," *Harvard Business Review*, May 2014, https://hbr.org/2014/05/from-purpose-to-impact.

18. Mark Fenton-O'Creevy et al., "Emotion Regulation and Trader Expertise," *Journal of Neuroscience, Psychology, and Economics* 5 (November 2021): 227–37.

19. Richard Strozzi-Heckler, *The Anatomy of Change* (Berkeley: North Atlantic Books, 1997), 59.

20. Daniel Goleman, "What Is Emotional Self-Awareness?" *Korn Ferry—This Week in Leadership* (blog), https://www.kornferry.com/insights/this-week-in-leadership/what-is-emotional-self-awareness.

21. Tasha Eurich, "Working with People Who Are Not Self-Aware," *Harvard Business Review*, October 19, 2018, https://hbr.org/2018/10/working-with-people-who-arent-self-aware; Eurich, "What Self-Awareness Really Is (and How to Cultivate It)," *Harvard Business Review*, January 4, 2018, https://hbr.org/2018/01/what-self-awareness-really-is-and-how-to-cultivate-it.

22. Daniel Siegel, *Aware*, 19.

23. Emma Seppälä et al., "Research: Why Breathing Is So Effective at Reducing Stress."

CHAPTER 8

1. J. Krishnamurti, "Public Talk 4 Madras (Chennai) (Chennai), India—22 January 1964," accessed October 5, 2021, https://jkrishnamurti.org/content/public-talk-4-madras-chennai-chennai-india-22-january-1964.

2. Jonathan Gottschall, *The Storytelling Animal* (New York: Mariner Books, 2012), 138.

1. J. Krishnamurti, "Public Talk 4 Madras (Chennai) (Chennai), India—22 January 1964," accessed October 5, 2021, https://jkrishnamurti.org/content/public-talk-4-madras-chennai-chennai-india-22-january-1964.

2. Jonathan Gottschall, *The Storytelling Animal* (New York: Mariner Books, 2012), 138.

3. Brian McLaren, *Everything Must Change* (Nashville: Thomas Nelson, 2007), 5–6.

4. Craig and Snook, "From Purpose to Impact."

5. Lewis Carroll, *The Annotated Alice: The Definitive Edition* (New York: W.W. Norton, 2021), 65.

6. Sakyong Mipham, *Turning the Mind into an Ally* (New York: Riverhead, 2003).

7. Richard Strozzi-Heckler, *Holding the Center* (Berkeley: Frog Ltd, 1997), 96.

8. Richard Strozzi-Heckler, *The Leadership Dojo*, (Berkeley: Frog Ltd, 2007), 21.

9. Dianne Costanzo, personal communication.

10. Tim Kelley, *True Purpose* (Transcendent Solutions Press, 2009), 67.

11. Strozzi-Heckler, *The Leadership Dojo*, 112.

12. Rebecca Henderson, *Reimagining Capitalism in a World on Fire* (New York: Public Affairs, 2020), 36.

CHAPTER 9

1. Chris Argyris, "The Executive Mind and Double Loop Learning," *Organizational Dynamics* 11, no 2 (Autumn 1982): 9.

2. Peter Howie, "Working with the Ladder of Inference," *ANZPA*, December 15, 2006, https://psychodramaaustralia.edu.au/sites/default/files/ladder_of_inference_article_peter_howie.pdf.

3. Renee Gregorio, "The Writer Who Inhabits Your Body" (unpublished manuscript), 13.

4. Peter Drucker, "What Makes an Effective Executive?" *Harvard Business Review*, June 2004, https://hbr.org/2004/06/what-makes-an-effective-executive.

5. Blake, *Your Body Is Your Brain*, 174.

6. Fernando Flores, *Surfing Towards the Future*, 27–41, https://nps.edu/documents/103400120/0/Chile+Report+-+3/182b105b-9edc-4b94-b18c-7bf5b888b64f.

7. Glenna Gerard and Linda Teurfs, *A Dialogue Reader*, 2–3, http://www.rylee.de/A-Dialogue-Reader-Dialogue-and-Community-Building.pdf.

8. William Isaacs, "Dialogic Leadership," *The Systems Thinker* 10, no. 1 (February 1999): https://www.csuchico.edu/futurepossibilities/_assets/documents/dialogic-leadership.pdf.

9. Fernando Flores, *Conversations for Action and Collected Essays* (North Charleston: CreateSpace, 2012), 120.

10. Warren Berger, "5 Common Questions Leaders Should Never Ask," *Harvard Business Review*, July 2, 2004, https://hbr.org/2014/07/5-common-questions-leaders-should-never-ask.

11. Gregorio, "The Writer Who Inhabits Your Body," 76.

12. Deborah Richardson, Laura Green, and Tania Lago, "The Relationship Between Perspective-Taking and Nonaggressive Responding in the Face of an Attack," *Journal of Personality* 66, no. 2 (1998): 235–256.

13. Strozzi-Heckler, *Anatomy of Change*, 17.

14. Hunter Gehlbach, "Learning to Walk in Another's Shoes," *Phi Delta Kappan* 98, no. 6 (March 1, 2017): 11.

15. N. H. Longmire and D. A. Harrison, "Seeing Their Side Versus Feeling Their Pain," *Journal of Applied Psychology* 103, no. 8 (April 16, 2018): 894.

CHAPTER 10

1. Strozzi-Heckler, *Leadership Dojo*, 25.

2. James Clear, *Atomic Habits* (New York: Avery, 2018), 36.

3. K. Anders Ericsson, Michael J. Prietula, and Edward T. Cokely, "Making of an Expert," *Harvard Business Review*, July–August 2007, 116, https://hbr.org/2007/07/the-making-of-an-expert.

4. Joan Anderman, "Yo-Yo Ma and the Mind Game of Music," *New York Times*, October 10, 2013, https://www.nytimes.com/2013/10/10/booming/yo-yo-ma-and-the-mind-game-of-music.html.

5. Ericsson, Prietula, and Cokely, "Making of an Expert," 118.

6. Cal Newport, *Deep Work* (New York: Grand Central, 2016), 3.

7. Newport, *Deep Work*, 36.

8. "As Much Truth as One Can Bear," *New York Times Book Review*, January 14, 1962, Section, page BR11.

9. Wendy Palmer, *The Practice of Freedom* (Berkeley, CA: Romdell Press, 2002), 76.

Index

A

abstraction, leaps of, 232
Ace Metal Crafts, 248, 268
acquired learning, 107
adaptive learning, 108
addictions, comfort, 32
adrenaline, 124
advocacy, and getting off Ladder of
    Inference, 233
The Age of Spiritual Machines (Kurzweil), 70
aikido
    catching yourself being yourself
      in, 101–102
    energy of, 176–178
    foundational principles, 125–127
    irimi move, 263
    learning rhythms in, 111–113
    movement and *mushin*, 167–168
    1 is 1 in, 114–115
    shugyo, 270–271
    tenkan, 235–236
    thirty-one-count jo kata practice, 215
    value of pause in, 11
ambiguity, in current state of world, 33. *See
    also* VUCA world
American Psychological Association
    (APA), 86–87
The Anatomy of Change
    (Strozzi-Heckler), 250
Anderson, Ray, 38–39, 41, 106, 190, 219
Angelou, Maya, 207

Argyris, Chris, 231
Aristotle, 258
assumptions, exploring and checking, 246
athletes, importance of practice for, 262
attachment, 100, 163
attention. *See also* mindfulness;
    pause/pausing
    continuous partial, 29–31
    directing, 55–56
    focusing where needed, 37
    as gate, 257–260
    importance to leadership, 7
    and intuition, 110
    multitasking, 24–26
    pausing and attending practice, 63–64
    Pomodoro Technique to increase, 27
    in presence, 145
    split, 30–31
    technology and interruptions, 22–24
attitudes. *See* mindset
automaticity, pausing as stepping out
    of, 63, 65–66
avoidance, 100, 163
Avoider signature stress style, 98, 117
awareness. *See also* self-awareness
    building, 91–93
    of busyness, 28–29
    and getting off Ladder of Inference, 233
    of responses to pressure, 129–131
    of signature stress styles, 95–99
    simultaneous, in presence, 145–146

B

bad, erroneous belief that stress is, 84–86, 88–89, 124, 133–136
Baldwin, James, 266
Barker, Eric, 257
Barrett, Lisa Feldman, 182
beach ball exercise building awareness, 91–92
beginner, being, 267–268
being-in-the-world, 16. *See also* pause/pausing
beliefs
    about leadership, holding lightly, 84
    Ladder of Inference, 231–234
belly breaths practice, 72
belly knowing, 236
Bennis, Warren, 36, 106, 143, 168, 212
best self, triggers and, 151–152
biological response to stress. *See* physical responses to stress
biological shaping, 159–162
black belts, in aikido, 167, 271–272
Blackman, Marc, 147–149
Blake, Amanda, 108, 160
body. *See also* aikido; physical responses to stress
    centering in, 157–159
    deliberate practice and, 262
    energy bodies, 173–175
    movement and *mushin*, 167–168
    pausing into stillness, 166–167
    in Ron's journey toward purpose, 215–216
    shaping and strategies, 159–164
    tension to release practice, 251–252
    triggers in domain of, 153
body-based movement practice, 236–237
Bohm, David, 243
brain
    attention as gate, 257–259
    cell metabolism, 25–26
    effect of deliberate practice on, 265
    effects of multitasking, 24–25
    responses to stress, 116
breaks, planning, 27. *See also* pause/pausing
breath practice, 53–54
Brown, Brené, 28, 192
Browning, L. M., 29
burnout, 82
business, value of pause in, 10–11

Business Roundtable, 5
busyness, 27–29

C

calendaring
    pause practice, 79
    space and time for self, 74
capitalism, conscious, 220–221
care, as key leadership quality, 37
Cashman, Kevin, 105, 169
catching yourself being yourself
    in aikido practice, 101–102
    dose of daily stress practice, 94
    formation and transformation, 99–101
    mindset, 140–142
    1 is 1, 113–115
    overview, 92–93
    signature stress styles, 95–99
    stress responses, 120–122
    triggers, 75–76
Center for Creative Leadership (CCL), 33
centering
    in aikido, 236
    pausing to center, 74–75, 103
    into presence, 157–159
    in Ron's journey toward purpose, 215
    two-stepping, 236–237
CEOs, number one concern of, 33. *See also* leadership
certainty, attraction to, 240
Challenger response to stress, 99, 117–120
change
    and attention as gate, 258–260
    systemic, 32–33
chaos
    in Law of Time and Chaos, 70–71
    seizing, 125–127
Chödrön, Pema, 46, 55
choice, perspective-taking and life of, 252–253
choosing to pause practice, 83
chronic stress, physical effects of, 89–90
Citrix Systems, 222
clarity breaks, 268
climate, need for leadership related to, 3–4
cognition, benefits of pausing for, 61
Comaford, Christine, 179
comfort addictions, 32

comfort seeking, 31–32
communication, power of pause in, 48
compassion, 37
competence, distinctions as driving, 238–239
complexities. *See also* current state of
    world; VUCA world
    in current state of world, 33
    and identity as leader, 154–156
    leaders and, 83–84
confirmation bias, 92–93
Connect reaction to stress, 117
connection
    and Challenger response to
        stress, 119–120
    as key leadership quality, 37
    through dialogue, 244
Connection component, SCOPE
    and energy, 197
    and mindset, 142
    overview, 74–75, 78
    and perspective, 254
    and practice, 273
    and presence, 171
    and purpose, 225
    and stress, 104, 128
Conscious Capitalism movement, 220–221
conscious leadership. *See* leadership
contact dermatitis, 89–90
Continental Sales "Lots 4 Less", 212, 217
continuous partial attention, 29–31
conversation. *See also* dialogue
    continuum of, 243–244
    engaging in, as vital leadership skill, 38
Cooperrider, David, 246
core beliefs. *See* mindset
Core Presence
    defined, 7
    in leaders, 45
    pausing as portal to accessing, 8–10
    pausing into stillness, 166–167
    as primary source of power, 164–166
    and purpose, 207
    working with power, 168–170
core values, 209–211
cortisol, 134–135
courage, oxytocin and, 119–120
Covey, Stephen, 7
COVID-19, 2, 6
Craig, Nick, 208

cram-it-all-in strategy, 113–115
Crum, Alia, 133, 134–136
Csikszentmihalyi, Mihaly, 264
curiosity, 37
current state of world
    broader picture, 32–33
    busyness, 27–29
    choosing full engagement, 266–267
    effect on leadership, 6, 17
    example of skillful navigation of, 46–48
    and identity as leader, 154–156
    leader requirements to deal with, 83–84
    leadership gaps, 3–6
    leadership identity and oppor-
        tunity, 34–36
    leadership pause, 45–46
    leadership qualities and skills, 36–38
    lessons from whitewater rafting, 43–45
    multitasking, 24–26
    opiate of comfort, 31–32
    overview, 1–3, 15, 21–22, 48
    Pomodoro Technique, 27
    role of leadership in sustainability, 38–40
    split attention, 30–31
    technology and continuous partial
        attention, 29–31
    technology and interruptions, 22–27
    through line of fear, 34
    twenty-first-century leaders, 40–43
Curry, Steph, 262
cynicism, 82

D

Dabbler learning rhythm, 111
daily pauses, 59
daily practices, deliberate, 268–270
daily stress, 94
Damasio, Antonio, 54, 57
Davenport, Tom, 30
debate, 243
debilitating consequences of stress, 133–136
decading, 130
deep listening, 109–111
Deep Work (Newport), 265
default mode network (experiencing
    self), 66–67
Defender signature stress style, 97, 117
dehydroepiandrosterone (DHEA), 134–135

deliberate conscious leadership, 263–264
deliberate practices
    choosing, 260–262
    daily, 268–270
    full engagement, choosing, 266–267
    and love of the game, 264–265
developing people, 38
DHEA (dehydroepiandrosterone), 134–135
dialogue
    blocks to, 247
    elements of, 246
    letting go, 247–248
    perspective potluck, 245–246
    questions, 247
    as ultimate interpersonal pause, 243–245
difference, making, 41, 43
different selves, 66–67
direct triggers, 152
discovery
    of perspective, 240–241
    of purpose, 207–209
discussion, 243–244
dismissing, as block to dialogue, 247
distinctions
    crafting new story, 241–243
    listening through, 239–241
    when seeking perspective, 238–239
distraction(s)
    staying busy as, 28
    and technology, 22–24
dose of daily stress practice, 94
Drucker, Peter, 186, 206, 238
Dubliners (Joyce), 184
Dweck, Carol, 131, 132

E

early life
    in Paul's story, 192–193
    and purpose, 203–204
    role in storying a life, 205–206
    in Ron's journey toward pur-
        pose, 213–214
    and signature stress styles, 99–100
Earth Day, 200–201
The Ecology of Commerce (Hawken), 39
Einstein, Albert, 175
embodied approach to learning, 108–111
embodied identity, 162–164

embodied leaders, 36. *See also* leadership
embodied presence, 167–168
embodied stand, 219
emotional fortitude, 178–181
emotional intelligence (EQ), 61, 187–188
emotions
    and energy, 179
    minding emotional reactions, 194–196
    and moods, 182
    revelations of pause, 193–194
    triggers in domain of, 153
empathic concern, 249–251
empathy, 120, 145, 180, 234–235
energy
    of aikido, 176–178
    in Challenger response to stress, 118–119
    effect of constant stress on, 81–83
    emotional revelations of pause, 193–194
    feeling and emotional fortitude, 178–181
    getting from stress, 123–124
    language of sensation, 182–183
    leaders as stewards of, 49
    leadership responsibility related to, 257
    minding emotional reactions, 194–196
    moods, 181–182
    overview, 173–175, 197
    Paul's story, 192–193
    pausing to self-correct, 191
    relevance for leaders, 183–184
    self-awareness, 187–191
    skillful leadership, 186–187
    sweet spot, 175–176
    tracking sensations, 185
    triggers in domain of, 153
    tuning in to, 121
    working with, as vital leadership skill, 37
Energy component, SCOPE
    and mindset, 142
    overview, 77, 79
    and perspective, 254
    and practice, 273
    and presence, 171
    and purpose, 225
    and stress, 104, 128
engagement, choosing full, 266–267
engaging in conversations, 38
enhancing consequences of stress,
        133–136, 138
environmental sustainability, 38–40

Envision IT, 219, 221–223
EQ (emotional intelligence), 61, 187–188
Ericsson, K. Anders, 132, 260, 261, 265, 266
essence. *See* Core Presence
Eurich, Tasha, 188
excite and delight aspect of Challenger stress, 118
executive leadership coaching, value of pause for, 11
exhaustion, when multitasking, 25
expectations. *See* mindset
experiencing self (default mode network), 66–67
experiential learning, 91–92
expertise, developing, 261, 265
explicit memory, 160
external triggers, 152
exteroception, 175

F

fatigue, when multitasking, 25
fear, in current state of world, 34
feelings
    and emotional fortitude, 178–181
    and moods, 182
Felix-Reese, Amy, 269
fight, flight, freeze response, 89–91, 117, 118–119
fight-flight-freeze-appease reaction, 87–88
Firms of Endearment (Sisodia), 220–221
fixed mindset, 131–132
flipping the script, 233
Flores, Fernando, 105, 168, 239, 245
flow
    and Challenger view of stress, 119
    as function of presence, 149
    love of the game, 264–265
    movement and *mushin*, 167–168
Floyd, George, 5
forward focus, cost of, 165–166
frames of reference. *See* mindset
Frankl, Viktor, 7, 207
freaking out, 15, 45
freeze signature stress style, 99, 117
Full Catastrophe Living (Kabat-Zinn), 56, 90
full engagement, choosing, 266–267

G

Gallagher, Winifred, 264
Gandhi, Indira, 241
Gandhi, Mahatma, 227
gate, attention as, 257–260
Gates, Bill, 60
generative leaders, 36
generative practices, 256–257
Gini coefficient, 4
global warming, 3–4
Gold Eagle, 147–149
goldfish, attention span of, 55
Goldilocks Effect, 29
Goleman, Daniel, 52, 56, 187
Gottschall, Jonathon, 206
Gould, Jay, 40
grace, spot of. *See* Core Presence
Grecian Delight, 252–253
Greene, Robert, 266
growing Window of Tolerance, 139–140
growth index of stress response, 134–135
growth mindset, 132, 137
gun violence, 6
gut feelings, 54, 109–110, 120–121

H

habits
    and attention as gate, 258–259
    versus practices, 256–257
    taking honest look at, 83
Hackers learning rhythm, 111, 112
hardiness, stress, 137–139
Hawken, Paul, 39
health, benefits of pausing for, 61
heart beating, noticing, 54
Heidegger, Martin, 16, 30
Helgesen, Sally, 143–144, 145
Henderson, Rebecca, 221
Hendricks, Gay, 164
Hershey, Terry, 165
Hollis, James, 151, 155
horizontal type of learning, 107
hormones
    in Challenger response to stress, 119–120
    stress, 134–135
humility, and presence, 146

I

IBM, 33
identity
    and attention as gate, 259–260
    as embodied phenomenon, 159–164
    formation and transformation, 99–101
    as leader, when triggered, 154–156
    leadership, 34–36
    narrative self, 66–67
    stories, role in, 65–66
    in twenty-first-century leaders, 41
Immobilize reaction to stress, 117
implicit memory, 160
inclusive signature stress style. *See* Challenger
    response to stress
income inequality, 4–5
indirect triggers, 152
Inference, Ladder of, 231–234
information overload, 22–24
inner focus, 56
inquiry, to get off Ladder of Infer-
    ence, 233, 234
insula, 54, 110, 116
intentionality, role in mastery, 113
Interface, 38–39
internal neural guidance system, 36
internal triggers, 152
interoception, 54, 158
interoceptive learning, 183, 185
interruptions
    Pomodoro Technique to decrease, 27
    and technology, 22–24, 25–26
intuition
    and embodied learning, 109–110
    in leaders, 36
    tracking sensations, 185
    tuning in to, 120–121
irimi move in aikido, 263
Issacs, William, 244
"it's all in your head", 133

J

James, William, 46, 161
jo kata, 114–115, 215
Johnson, Chris L., 88–91, 101–102,
    112–115, 126–127, 200–203,
    205, 227–230
Johnson, Roger, 50–52
Joyce, James, 184
judgment, suspending, 246

K

Kabat-Zinn, Jon, 44, 56, 70, 90, 263
Katatekosatori Kotegaeshi, 102
Keating, Thomas, 167
Keller, Helen, 32
Kelley, Tim, 218
kindness, effects of expressing, 141–142
kokoro, 175
Kolb, David, 106
Korn Ferry Hay Group, 188
Kornfield, Jack, 233, 273
Krishnamurti, 204
Kurzweil, Ray, 70

L

Ladder of Inference, 231–234
Laing, R. D., 92
language of sensation, 182–183
Lao-Tzu, 21, 162, 218
Law of Time and Chaos, 70–71
leadership. *See also* pause/pausing; stress
    attention and, 7, 257–260
    awareness and, 91–92, 129–131
    beginner, being, 267–268
    benefits of pause for, 8–10, 45–46, 61
    black belts, 271–272
    book overview, 15–19
    centering as practice in, 158–159
    current gaps in, 3–6
    deliberate conscious, 263–264
    deliberate daily practices, 268–270
    deliberate practices, choosing, 260–262
    embodied learning and deep listen-
        ing, 109–111
    emotional intelligence and, 188
    energy and, 49, 183–187
    example of shift in, 38–40
    example of skillful navigation, 46–48
    full engagement, choosing, 266–267
    identity and opportunity, 34–36
    leaders with presence, 147–149
    learning, role in, 106–108
    learning rhythms, 111–113
    lessons from whitewater rafting, 43–45
    long game, 10–11
    love of the game, 264–265
    magic of the pause, 11–12
    mindset, relevance for, 137–138
    1 is 1, 113–115
    overview, 2–3, 105–106, 272–273

perspective, letting go of, 247–248
perspective-taking and, 235–237
power stress, 50
practices, 255–257
purpose and, 208, 218–223
qualities and skills, 36–38
reasons to focus on, 12–14
responsibilities of, 257
Sacrifice Syndrome, 50
shugyo, 270–271
stories, relevance to, 67–68
and today's complexities, 83–84
training to respond to stress, 124–127
in twenty-first-century, 40–43
The Leadership Dojo (Strozzi-Heckler), 215
leadership presence. *See* presence
leaps of abstraction, 232
learning
acquired, 107
adaptive, 108
embodied approach to, 108–111
experiential, 91–92
interoceptive, 183, 185
to pause, 50–52
rhythms of, 111–113
role in leadership, 106–108
from stressful events, 120
learning mindset, 37. *See also* mindset
Leonard, George, 111, 112, 113, 263
letting go, power of, 247–248
Levitin, Daniel, 25
life energy. *See* energy
life of choice, and perspective, 252–253
limbic resonance, 240
listening
deep, embodied learning and, 109–111
pausing for, 69–70
and presence, 145
through distinctions, 239–241
as vital leadership skill, 38
location, tuning in to, 121
Loehr, Jim, 176
love of the game, 264–265
low-stakes training, 259–260

M

Ma, Yo-Yo, 262
magic of the pause, 11–12

"The Making of an Expert" (Ericsson), 261, 265
Man's Search for Meaning (Frankl), 207
Marjory Stoneman Douglas High School, 6
Mark, Gloria, 23–24, 25–26
Markova, Dawna, 9
martial arts. *See* aikido
mastery
learning for, 112–113
shugyo, 270–271
through consistent practice over time, 260
Mastery (Leonard), 111, 112
Maturana, Humberto, 88
McGonigal, Kelly, 81, 118, 119, 124
McKee, Annie, 50
McLaren, Brian, 206
meaning
and dialogue, 244
and purpose, 206–207
Melson, Mark, 180
memory, implicit versus explicit, 160
mental domain, triggers in, 153
Merton, Thomas, 28
metabolism, brain cell, 25–26
Meyer, David E., 26
micropauses, 59
milestones, in Law of Time and Chaos, 70–71
Millman, Dan, 129
Milstein, Nathan, 265
mind, power of wandering, 54–55
mindfulness. *See also* pause/pausing; presence
crafting new story, 242–243
defined, 56
as force multiplier, 12
in leaders, 36
Paul's story, 192–193
value of pause for, 10
mindset
fixed, 131–132
getting good at stress, 137–139
growing Window of Tolerance, 139–140
growth, 132, 137
noticing ordinary moments, 140–142
overview, 129–131, 142
pausing to reflect on, 136
power of, 131–132
relevance for leaders, 137–138
stress, 133–136

triggers as reflecting, 151–152, 153–154
Mission Zero (Interface), 40
Mobilize reaction to stress, 117
momentary pauses, 59
moods, 181–182
move toward signature stress style, 98, 117
movement
    presence and, 166–168
    tuning in to, 121
    two-stepping, 236–237
multitasking, 24–25
mushin, 167–168
myelin, 265

N

Nadella, Satya, 55
narrative self, 66–67
negativity, 82
neural guidance system, 36
neuroception, 116
neuroplasticity, 174
A New Earth (Tolle), 207
new story, crafting, 224–225, 241–243
Newport, Cal, 265
Nin, Anaïs, 11
nocebo effect, 133
nondoing, 71–72
notifications, turning off, 27

O

O Sensei (Morihei Ueshiba), 125–126,
    149, 177, 270
Obsessive learning rhythm, 111, 112
1 is 1, practicing, 113–115
on-the-spot pause practice, 74
open signature stress style. *See* Challenger
    response to stress
openness component, SCOPE
    and energy, 197
    and mindset, 142
    overview, 75–76, 78–79
    and perspective, 254
    and practice, 273
    and presence, 171
    and purpose, 225
    and stress, 104, 128
opiate of comfort, 31–32
ordinary moments, noticing, 140–142

Ortega y Gasset, Jose, 49
other focus, 56
outer focus, 56
outsourcing, 180
overdetailing, as block to dialogue, 247
oxytocin, 119–120

P

pace
    playing with to recognize trig-
        gers, 156–157
    sustainability of current, 81–83
Pace component, SCOPE
    and energy, 197
    and mindset, 142
    overview, 76, 78
    and perspective, 254
    and practice, 273
    and presence, 171
    and purpose, 225
    and stress, 104, 128
Packer, Toni, 164
Palmer, Wendy, 219, 270
Paralyzed signature stress style, 99, 117
Parthenis, Peter, 252–253, 269
passion
    and practice, 264–265
    and purpose, 203–204
passivity, as block to dialogue, 247
patterns, signature stress. *See* signature
    stress styles
patterns of thinking. *See* mindset
pause/pausing
    and acceptance of complexities, 84
    and attention, 7, 55–56, 63–64
    belly breaths practice, 72
    benefits of, 8–10, 60–61
    book overview, 15–19
    breath practice, 53–54
    calendaring practice, 79
    catching yourself being yourself,
        92–94, 100–101
    centering, 103, 158–159
    choosing to, 83
    for core values, 211
    crafting new story, 242–243
    to cultivate self-awareness, 188–191
    defined, 57–58

deliberately practicing, 262, 263–264, 268–270
different selves, 66–67
dose of daily stress practice, 94
emotional revelations of, 193–194
example of skillful use, 47–48
to explore purpose, 217–218
feeling and emotional fortitude, 180
to get off Ladder of Inference, 233
growing Window of Tolerance, 139–140
and growth mindset, 132
and identity as leader, 155–156
interpersonal, dialogue as, 243–247
and intuition, 110
invoking relaxation response, 88
in journey toward purpose, 216–217
and leadership, 12–14, 45–46
leadership identity and opportunity related to, 34–36
learning to pause, 50–52
long game, 10–11
magic of, 11–12
many faces of, 58–60
minding emotional reactions, 196
overview, 49, 80, 272–273
for perspective, 230, 253
into present-moment sensation, 54–55
progressive muscle practice, 122–123
on purpose, 52–54, 222–223
push pause practice, 68
reasons avoided, 62–63
recognizing Type A thinking, 151
to reflect on mindset, 136
reflections on presence, 147
relevance for leaders, 67–68
Sacrifice Syndrome, 50
SCOPE signposts, 72–79
to self-correct, 191
for sensory self-awareness, 120–122
standing pause practice, 69–70
into stillness, 166–167
into story, 65–68
tension to release practice, 251–252
for time and space, 70–72
tracking sensations, 185
triggers opening door to mindset, 153–154
tuning in to triggers, 156–157
two-stepping, 236–237

when working with stress, 90
working with power, 169–170
Pautsch, Nancy, 219–223, 269
pendulum toggling practice, 251–252
people, developing, 38
perception, biology as, 88, 116, 134
performance
and Challenger response to stress, 118–119
importance of practice for, 262
perpetual whitewater, 33, 43–45
personality
as embodied phenomenon, 159–164
formation and transformation, 99–101
perspective
dialogue, 243–247
discovery of, 240–241
distinctions, 238–243
and empathy, 234–235
getting, 250–251
Ladder of Inference, 231–234
letting go, 247–248
and life of choice, 252–253
new story, crafting, 241–243
overview, 227–230, 254
pause practices for, 230
relevance for leaders, 247–250
tenkan, 235–236
tension to release practice, 251–252
two-stepping, 236–237
perspective-getting, 250–251
perspective-taking, 234–235
pessimism, 82
physical responses to stress
Challenger response, 117–120
effects of chronic stress, 89–90
overview, 87–91, 115–118
progressive muscle practice, 122–123
relevance to leaders, 123–124
stress mindset and, 134–135
training to respond to, 124–127
transforming, 115–118
tuning in to, 115–118, 120–122
Pitzo, Jean, 59, 248–250, 268
placebo effect, 133
planned pauses, 60
planning too much, 113–115
Pleaser signature stress style, 98, 117
polite discussion, 243

Pomodoro Technique, 27
post-traumatic stress disorder, 192–193
potluck, perspective, 245–246
power, 143, 157, 164, 168–170
The Power of Full Engagement (Loehr &
    Schwartz), 176
power stress, 50
Poynton, Robert, 30, 84
The Practice of Freedom (Palmer), 270
practice(s)
    attention as gate, 257–260
    beginner, being, 267–268
    black belts, 271–272
    deliberate, choosing, 260–262
    deliberate conscious leadership, 263–264
    deliberate daily, 268–270
    full engagement, choosing, 266–267
    versus habits, 256–257
    love of the game, 264–265
    mastery and, 112
    overview, 15, 255–256, 272–273
    shugyo, 270–271
presence. *See also* Core Presence
    centering into, 157–159
    full, 3
    and identity as leader, 154–156
    as key leadership quality, 37
    and language of sensation, 183
    leadership, growing, 147–149
    movement and *mushin*, 167–168
    overview, 143–144, 171
    pausing into stillness, 166–167
    pushing pause at work, 156–157
    reflections on, 147
    self-awareness and, 188, 189
    shaping and strategies, 159–164
    simultaneous attention, 145–146
    in skillful leadership, 186–187
    triggers, 149–154
    working with power, 168–170
Presence-Based Coaching (Silsbee), 181
present-moment sensations, pausing
    into, 54–55
pressure, tuning in to, 121. *See also* stress
pretense, 240
progressive muscle practice, 122–123
proprioception, 121
Prosort Services, 46
psychological stress survey, 86–87
psychology, value of pause in, 10

pull back signature stress style, 98, 117
purpose
    core values, 209–211
    discovering unique, 207–209
    journey toward, 212–217
    leadership, extending, 218–223
    meaning, 206–207
    new story, crafting, 224–225
    overview, 200–203, 225
    passion and, 203–204
    pausing on, 52–54, 222–223
    pausing to explore, 217–218
    shugyo, 272
    storying a life, 205–206
purposeful practice, 15
push against signature stress style, 97, 117
pushing pause
    dose of daily stress practice, 94
    to invoke relaxation response, 88
    practice, 68
    tuning in to triggers, 156–157

Q

qualities, leadership, 36–37, 266–267
questions, in dialogue, 247

R

racial inequities, 5
random reinforcement, 25–26
randori, 125–127
recognize-renew-reflect-return-rewire pro-
    cess, 138–139
redefining, as block to dialogue, 247
reflection
    and getting off Ladder of Infer-
        ence, 233, 234
    on presence, 147
Reimagining Capitalism in a World on Fire
    (Henderson), 221
reinforcement, random, 25–26
relaxation response, invoking, 88
resilience
    cultivating, 137–140
    emotional fortitude, 179–180
    energetic, 175–176
response system, stress
    Challenger response, 117–120
    effects of chronic stress, 89–90

overview, 87–91
progressive muscle practice, 122–123
relevance to leaders, 123–124
stress mindset and, 134–135
training to respond to, 124–127
transforming, 115–118
tuning in to, 115–118, 120–122
responsive signature stress style. *See* Challenger response to stress
Rilke, Rainer Maria, 1
Rim, J. R., 57
Robèrt, Karl-Henrik, 38
Rojas, Ron, 212–217, 269
Rumi, 199
running, incorporating pause into, 74, 269

S

Sacrifice Syndrome, 50
Sakyong Mipham, 214
Sarillo, Nick, 270
Scharmer, Otto, 166
scheduling
    pause practice, 79
    space and time for self, 74
Schwartz, Tony, 176
SCOPE signposts
    connection, 74–75
    energy, 77, 197
    and mindset, 142
    openness, 75–76
    overview, 72–73, 78–79
    pace, 76
    and perspective, 254
    and practice, 273
    and presence, 171
    and purpose, 225
    space, 73–74
    and stress, 104, 128
Seale, Alan, 173
Seigel, Dan, 145
seizing chaos, 125–127
self-acceptance, 189–190
self-awareness
    beach ball exercise building, 91–93
    best practices to cultivate, 188–191
    and getting off Ladder of Inference, 233
    as key to emotional intelligence, 187–188
    measuring, 54
    and presence, 149

sensory, 120–122
    signature stress styles, 95–99
self-correction, 190, 191
self-generation, 190
self-observation, 189
self-organization, 174–175
self-talk, importance of, 94
selves, different, 66–67
Selye, Hans, 85–86
Senge, Peter, 144
Senn Delaney, 132
sensations
    feeling and emotional fortitude, 178–181
    language of, 182–183
    and moods, 182
    tracking, 185
sensory self-awareness, 120–122
Seuss, Dr., 209
Seven Habits of Highly Effective People (Covey), 7
shaping, biological, 159–162
shared purpose, 218, 221
shareholder value, 5, 220
sharing, and getting off Ladder of Inference, 233
Sheng-Yen, 255
short, daily pauses, 59
shugyo, 270–271
Siegel, Dan, 137, 159, 175, 192
signature stress styles
    formation and transformation of, 99–101
    overview, 95–99, 115–118
    tuning in to, 120–122
Silsbee, Doug, 146, 181
Simon, Herbert, 22
simultaneous attention, in presence, 145–146
Sinek, Simon, 207
Sisodia, Raj, 220–221
skillful discussion, 243–244
skillful leadership, energy in, 186–187
skills, leadership, 37–38
skydiving, 118
Smithback, Beau, 221
Snead, Sam, 265
Snook, Scott, 208
"So what?," asking, 93
social intelligence, benefits of pausing for, 61
somatic intelligence, 108, 260
somatic markers, 54

soul. *See* Core Presence
space, pausing for, 70–72
Space component, SCOPE
    and energy, 197
    and mindset, 142
    overview, 73–74, 78
    and perspective, 254
    and practice, 273
    and presence, 171
    and purpose, 225
    and stress, 104, 128
spindle neurons, 110
spirit. *See* Core Presence
split attention, 30–31
spot of grace. *See* Core Presence
Stafford, William, 201
Stagen, Rand, 129–130, 169–170, 193–194
Stagen Leadership Academy, 129–
    130, 169–170
stakeholder value, 5, 220
stand, embodied, 219
standing pause practice, 69–70
Start with Why (Sinek), 207
Statement on the Purpose of a Corporation
    (Business Roundtable), 5
still, small voice, 10
"Stillness" (Keating), 167
stillness, pausing into, 166–167
Stone, Linda, 29, 30
stories
    Ladder of Inference, 231–234
    new, crafting, 224–225, 241–243
    pausing into, 65–68
    storying a life, 205–206
strategies
    and attention as gate, 258–259
    embodied, 159–160, 161, 162–164
    in journey toward purpose, 213–214, 215
    Ladder of Inference, 231–234
    in skillful leadership, 186
stress. *See also* physical responses to stress
    as bad, erroneous belief about, 84–86,
        88–89, 124, 133–136
    beach ball exercise building
        awareness, 91–92
    catching yourself being yourself,
        92–94, 101–102
    Challenger response to, 117–120
    choosing to pause, 83
    current levels of, 21–22

dose of daily stress practice, 94
effect on leadership, 17
formation and transformation of
    responses, 99–101
getting good at, 137–139
leaders and today's complexities, 83–84
leadership pause and, 45–46
minding emotional reactions to, 194–196
overview, 81–83, 104, 127–128
pausing to center, 103
power, 50
progressive muscle practice, 122–123
psychological stress survey, 86–87
recovery from, 120
relevance to leaders, 123–124
signature stress styles, 95–99
training to respond to, 124–127
triggers, 149–154
tuning in to responses, 120–122
stress hardiness, 137–139
Stress in America survey (APA), 86–87
stress mindset, 133–136
stress response system. *See* physical
    responses to stress
stress-is-debilitating mindset, 133–136
stress-is-enhancing mindset, 133–136, 138
Strozzi-Heckler, Richard, 109, 113, 157, 178,
    187, 215, 219, 250, 257
survival system, biological. *See* physical
    responses to stress
sustainability
    of current pace of life, 81–83
    role of leadership in achieving, 38–40
sweet spot, energetic, 175–176
switch costs, when multitasking, 24–25
systemic racism, 5
systemic shifts in world, 32–33

T

Taking the Leap (Chödrön), 46
Tao Te Ching (Lao-Tzu), 162
task-switch costs, 24–25
technology
    and continuous partial attention, 29–31
    and interruptions, 22–24
    multitasking related to, 25–26
    ubiquitous and insidious nature of, 8
temperature, tuning in to, 121
tend-and-befriend response, 119–120

tenkan, 235–236
tension to release practice, 251–252
Think Week, 60
thinking, benefits of pausing for, 61
thinking patterns. *See* mindset
thirty-one-count jo kata practice, 215
threat, response system to. *See* physical
    responses to stress
through line of fear, 34
Thunberg, Greta, 4
Thurman, Howard, 203
time, pausing for, 70–72
tipping points, 33
tiredness, when multitasking, 25
Tolle, Eckhart, 152, 207
touch and go practice, 191
tracking sensations, 185
training
    and attention as gate, 259–260
    leadership, problems with, 107, 108
    to respond to stress, 124–127
    shugyo, 270–271
The Tree of Knowledge (Maturana &
    Varela), 88
triggers
    and embodied strategies, 163–164
    and identity as leader, 154–156
    overview, 149–150
    pause practice for, 153–154
    pausing to self-correct, 191
    pushing pause to tune in to, 156–157
    types of, 152
    understanding influence of, 152–153
    and your best self, 151–152
trust, perspective-taking and, 235
Turkle, Sherry, 29, 30
Turning the Mind into an Ally (Sakyong
    Mipham), 214
twenty-first-century leaders, 40–43
two-stepping, 236–237
Type A thinking, 150, 151

U

Ueshiba, Morihei (O Sensei), 125–126,
    149, 177, 270
uncertainty. *See also* VUCA world
    in current state of world, 33
    fear of, 34

unconscious mindsets. *See* mindset
unique purpose, discovering, 207–209
United States
    gun violence in, 6
    income inequality in, 4–5
    racial inequities in, 5
U.S. Army War College, 33

V

vacations, 60
values, core, 209–211
Varela, Francisco, 88
ventral prefrontal cortex (vpfc), 54
vertical type of learning, 108
VUCA (volatile, uncertain, complex, and
    ambiguous) world. *See also* current
    state of world
    choosing full engagement, 266–267
    experience with, reflecting on, 41, 43
    leader requirements to deal with, 83–84
    overview, 33

W

Wallace, Lacey, 6
wandering mind, power of, 54–55
"The Way it Is" (Stafford), 201
weekly pauses, 59–60
wellness, benefits of pausing for, 61
"What now?," asking, 93
"what's so," observing, 93
white belts, in aikido, 167
Whitelaw, Ginny, 176, 183
whitewater, perpetual, 33
whitewater rafting, lessons from, 43–45
Window of Tolerance
    growing, 139–140
    overview, 137–138
word-out-of-mouth ratio, 195, 196
world, current state of. *See* current state of
    world; VUCA world

Y

yourself, catching. *See* catching yourself
    being yourself

● ● ●

About the Author

CHRIS L. JOHNSON is the founder of Q4 Consulting Inc. and passionately committed to creating feedback-rich environments that result in transformational change. Chris integrates teachings on the neurobiology of experiential learning with mindful awareness and embodied practices to offer programs that train attention—*The Leadership Pause*—and tap the body as a rich source of intelligence, wisdom, and action.

Chris holds a PsyD from the Chicago School of Professional Psychology where she's taught in the Business Psychology and the Executive and Professional Development Programs. Trained in Mindfulness-Based Stress Reduction (MBSR) from the Center for Mindfulness and certified as both an Integral Coach (New Ventures West) and a Master Somatic Leadership Coach (Strozzi Institute), Chris's unique training serves her deeper commitment: to extend embodied leadership to innovators who are creating the future—exemplary leaders, collaborative teams and workplaces, and engaged, thriving communities.

To that end, she's been involved in the Chicago Chapter of Conscious Capitalism for over a decade, an organization committed to "elevating humanity through business," currently serving as chair.

When Chris is not working, she's likely gardening or hiking, reading a great book or making art, or at the aikido dojo where she practices the art of peace.

Learn more at Q4-Consulting.com.